QUEERING KINSHIP

Gender, Sexuality and Global Politics

Series Editors: **Ali Bilgic**, Loughborough University, UK, **Synne L. Dyvik**, University of Sussex, UK, **Gunhild Hoogensen Gjørv**, UiT The Arctic University of Norway, Norway, **Thomas Gregory**, The University of Auckland, New Zealand and **Swati Parashar**, University of Gothenburg, Sweden

---

Expanding the boundaries of International Relations, this series reflects on politics globally with innovative and transdisciplinary perspectives. With a focus on feminist, lesbian, gay, bisexual, trans and queer activism, the series examines existing hierarchies, practices and power relations, investigating the often violent effects of these on different peoples, geographies and histories.

Scan the code below to discover new and forthcoming titles in the series, or visit:

bristoluniversitypress.co.uk/
gender-sexuality-and-global-politics

QUEERING KINSHIP

Non-heterosexual Couples, Parents, and Families in Guangdong, China

Han Tao

First published in Great Britain in 2024 by

Bristol University Press
University of Bristol
1–9 Old Park Hill
Bristol
BS2 8BB
UK
t: +44 (0)117 374 6645
e: bup-info@bristol.ac.uk

Details of international sales and distribution partners are available at bristoluniversitypress.co.uk

© Bristol University Press 2024

British Library Cataloguing in Publication Data
A catalogue record for this book is available from the British Library

ISBN 978-1-5292-3327-8 hardcover
ISBN 978-1-5292-3328-5 ePub
ISBN 978-1-5292-3329-2 ePdf

The right of Han Tao to be identified as author of this work has been asserted by her in accordance with the Copyright, Designs and Patents Act 1988.

All rights reserved: no part of this publication may be reproduced, stored in a retrieval system, or transmitted in any form or by any means, electronic, mechanical, photocopying, recording, or otherwise without the prior permission of Bristol University Press.

Every reasonable effort has been made to obtain permission to reproduce copyrighted material. If, however, anyone knows of an oversight, please contact the publisher.

The statements and opinions contained within this publication are solely those of the author and not of the University of Bristol or Bristol University Press. The University of Bristol and Bristol University Press disclaim responsibility for any injury to persons or property resulting from any material published in this publication.

Bristol University Press works to counter discrimination on grounds of gender, race, disability, age and sexuality.

Cover design: Blu inc
Front cover image: Unsplash/sharonmccutcheon
Bristol University Press uses environmentally responsible print partners.
Printed and bound in Great Britain by CPI Group (UK) Ltd, Croydon, CR0 4YY

Contents

About the Author vi
Acknowledgements vii

Introduction: Have 'Families of Choice' Arrived in China? 1

1   Queering Research: Ethnography, Positionality, and Ordinary 'Queer' 26
2   Queering Intimacy: 'Just-as-Married' Same-Sex Relationships 41
3   Queering Reproduction: Changing Moral Dilemmas for Chinese Non-heterosexual People 62
4   Queering Technology: Becoming Queer Parents through Assisted Reproductive Technologies 87
5   Queering Parenting: Raising 'Our Children' 111
6   Queering Family: Modern Rainbow Families 134

Conclusion: Queering Chinese Kinship and Futures 154

Appendix I: Key Research Participants 162
Appendix II: Roman (Pinyin) to Simplified Chinese 164
Notes 167
References 170
Index 188

About the Author

Han Tao is Postdoctoral Researcher at the IT University of Copenhagen. She received her PhD in Social Anthropology from the University of Sussex. Her doctoral research examined the practices of queer intimacies, queer parenting, and family making in urban China. Han's research interests centre around kinship, sexuality, migration, data, and technology.

Acknowledgements

I began this book project during my PhD journey at the University of Sussex in September 2017. Along the way, I have been fortunate to receive an outpouring of support and encouragement from various individuals within and outside of academia. I am sincerely grateful to my PhD supervisors, Filippo Osella and Paul Boyce, for their unwavering guidance and warm support throughout my PhD expedition. Their patience and understanding, especially during the times of the pandemic, have been instrumental in my progress. I extend my gratitude to my amazing fellow scholars in the Anthropology department who read and commented on my draft chapters. Thank you to the online writing group who made the writing process less stressful during my lockdown life in China. I am also thankful to my viva examiners, Elisabeth Lund Engebretsen and Elizabeth Mills, for their valuable comments and encouragement.

My research in the field would not have been possible without the kindness and openness of the queer friends and PFLAG China volunteers I had the privilege to meet in Shenzhen, Guangzhou, Chengdu, and various other parts of China. They welcomed me into their lives and shared their time, experiences, and insights. I am particularly indebted to my key friend informants who believed in the significance of my research and allowed me to delve into their worlds. Many individuals approached me at the outset of my fieldwork, introducing me to their friends, and I am sincerely thankful for their trust and assistance.

I would also like to express my sincere appreciation to Zoe Forbes, Stephen Wenham, and the series editors at Bristol University Press for their contributions to this project. I am grateful to Rachel Douglas-Jones, Jesper Willaing Zeuthen, Ane Bislev, Hailing Zhao, and the anonymous reviewers for their helpful feedback and suggestions, which significantly contributed to the improvement of the initial manuscript.

I owe a great debt of gratitude to my friends who have provided unwavering support, helping to ground me on this journey. A heartfelt thank you to Kirsty, Naoms, Ash, Shan, Yunyi, Cong, Hanjie, Jie, and JY, who have become my friends and my chosen family. I also thank my cat, Maoqiu, whose comforting presence and peaceful naps beside my desk provided solace during long hours of writing and research. Lastly, I owe my deepest gratitude to my grandparents for their unconditional trust and support.

Parts of Chapter 2 appeared in Tao (2022) and parts of Chapter 4 appeared in Tao (2023).

Introduction: Have 'Families of Choice' Arrived in China?

From 2018 to 2021, I spent a lot of time with the lesbian couple Xie and Hong and their baby son Doudou in Shenzhen, China. Many non-heterosexual friends praised them as a model lesbian family as they have been together for nearly ten years and had children together. Xie was in her early 40s with short hair, calling herself a typical T (short for 'tomboy') who has often been mistaken for a man. Hong described herself as a P (short for '*po*', or 'femme') and was in her early 30s. Xie and Hong's romantic relationship started in 2009 when they met through their lesbian friends. They were both from Hunan Province and later settled in Shenzhen. Xie worked as a self-employed medical device sales agent and Hong joined her in 2015. They joked that they stayed together 24/7 as same-sex partners and work partners. We became familiar with each other as *laoxiang* (people from the same town). Assuming I was a junior still 'studying' for my PhD, Xie would always pay for dinner.

After having two dinners together, I learned about Xie's previous heterosexual marriage with a straight man and her older son who was already an adult. Xie was pressured by her father to get married and gave birth to a son in her early 20s. After that, she came out to her parents and divorced her former husband. Xie let her former husband take custody, which further irritated her father. Disappointed by her family of origin, Xie left home and started her business step by step. Like some other middle-aged non-heterosexual people I have met, Xie had a 'normative past' in her hometown and a 'queer present' in Shenzhen. Xie, Hong, and their son are one of the emerging 'rainbow'/ 'chosen' families in urban China. Through the technique of artificial insemination, Hong gave birth to Doudou in 2018 using her egg and Xie's brother's sperm. During our dinners, Hong and Xie always took turns to hold Doudou and walk around in the restaurant. They took Doudou to weekly baby swim lessons, where the teachers were aware of their lesbian family model and addressed them as 'Mama' and 'Mommy'.

Like other middle-aged friend informants in this ethnography, Hong and Xie found it strange and even uncomfortable to articulate their kinship practices and life choices in terms of sexual identity. When I first introduced my research project to them, they looked bewildered and asked, "Why bother researching us? We are all the same". Xie and Hong's words resonated with most non-heterosexual individuals in China, who did not think of their sexual practice as a determining factor in constructing their identity and thus making them different. Rather, they saw themselves as ordinary and hard-working Chinese citizens who earned their decent family life in a metropolitan city. Hong did not feel she was different from most Chinese people and, more crucially, she desired the same socio-economic capital and a middle-class[1] lifestyle as many other Chinese citizen subjects. As this book will illustrate, Chinese non-heterosexual subjects' strategies in forming and sustaining long-lasting queer relationships are marked by their complex understanding of love, care, family, risk, and moral selfhood. Non-heterosexual people can simultaneously refer to a son/daughter, a partner, a parent, a husband/wife, and so on in different given social relations. Each kinship role involves discursive moral expectations that intersect with kinship norms, state policy, capitalism, and homonormative politics.

I first came back to Guangdong, China to do fieldwork in 2018, expecting to hear a lot of queer people's coming-out (*chugui*) stories and family pressure to enter heterosexual marriage. Nevertheless, as I got to meet queer individuals from different generations and backgrounds, I found my friend informants talked about their strategies to sustain their loving relationships, their journeys to create their own queer families, and how they take care of their parents, partners, and children. What does it mean for Chinese non-heterosexual people to form a desirable and legible queer family which seems to go against existing state regulations and kinship norms? How do Chinese non-heterosexual individuals envision their futures and potential risks from being in queer relationships? By exploring their dynamic understandings and practices of love, care, parenting, and family making, this book unpacks the intricate link between cultural imaginations produced by Euro-American-originated queer politics, social transformations in Chinese society, and personal choices in queer daily lives.

It is essential to clarify my use of the term 'queer' at the very beginning of the book. Originally meaning 'strange' or 'unusual', 'queer' came to be used as an umbrella term for sexual and gender minorities and as a theoretical critique in and beyond academia. In ethnographic research, media studies, and activist literature on Chinese sexual minorities, scholars have made various choices in terminology. For instance, 'gay' and 'lesbian' (see Sang, 2003; Rofel, 2007; Kong, 2010); '*tongzhi*' (which literally means 'comrades', roughly referring to lesbian, gay, bisexual, and transgender (LGBT) people) (see Chou, 2001; Zheng, 2015; Bao, 2018); '*lala*' (roughly referring to queer women) (see Engebretsen, 2008, 2009, 2014; Kam, 2013); 'queer' or its Chinese translation '*ku'er*' (Engebretsen and Schroeder, 2015; Bao, 2018;

Wei, 2020). These terms were also used interchangeably, demonstrating fluidity in meanings. It is worth noting that the word 'queer'/'ku'er' is neither the common vernacular nor an identity label widely recognized among ordinary Chinese people (Wei, 2020, p 19). In everyday use, each of these terms may be perceived differently. My friend informants have used innumerable terms such as gay, bisexual, les, *lala*, *tongzhi*, and *zhiren* (straight person) to refer to themselves or their same-sex partners at certain life moments. In other words, not all perceive Chinese terms like *lala* and *tongzhi* as essentially culturally unique and appropriate. Some of my friend informants have experienced changes in gender or sexual identity. Some of my friend informants were not certain about labelling themselves with any term. Some of my friend informants used these terms interchangeably. As I shall discuss later in this book, I do not perceive these terms as fixed identity categories for certain 'types of people'; neither should these terms be put into an alleged Western–Oriental comparison. Even the concept of being Chinese no longer involves commonly accepted cultural standards (Cohen, 2005, p 59; see also Liu and Rofel, 2010). Therefore, using any of these idioms as if they were self-evident signifiers would be problematic. In short, my friend informants were far from a homogenous group, but, for the sake of simplicity, I choose 'queer' as the key word to distinguish their lives and relationships from heterosexual intimate and familial relations and heteronormative social spaces in urban China.

In this book, I use 'queer' as both a fluid descriptive term and an analytic perspective, verb, and method. Firstly, I do not intend to use 'queer' as a categorical or politicized identity but rather to understand queerness strategically as an umbrella term to refer to various forms of non-heteronormative genders and sexual experiences. This means I will not use 'queer' as a noun to refer to human subjects. Instead, I use it as a loose adjective interchangeably with 'non-heterosexual' to refer to my friend informants. In this way, I view 'queer' as disrupting the essentialist categorization of sexuality and centrality of identity. Secondly, I use 'queer' as a verb with relation to the ongoing and transforming forms of conjugal love, parenthood, and family relations in urban Guangdong, China. My focus on 'queering' kinship involves not only non-heterosexual people and sexualities *per se* but also the practices of kinship that destabilize normative kinship norms and provide us with new perspectives on reproduction, family, futurity, and relatedness. Queer theory, as a scholarly field, has expanded beyond issues of sexuality and identity politics (Boyce et al, 2019; Moore, 2019), and 'queer' itself might act less like a noun/adjective and more like a verb, 'a "queer studying" even of things not self-evidently queer' (Boellstorff, 2010, p 215). By bringing the term 'queer' into Chinese kinship studies, I perceive it as beyond sexuality and identity, using it as 'a critique, an analytic' (Weiss, 2016, p 628). The 'queering' of kinship is not perceived merely within the scope of (queer) sexual desires but exists in every aspect of society at large.

The theme of this book has arisen as a result of my ongoing academic interests and close involvement in Chinese queer communities. The ideas of family and marriage in Chinese societies have changed enormously in recent decades as the younger generation enjoys more individual autonomy and privacy, and is subject to less parental authority when it comes to love and marriage (Riley, 1994; Yan, 2003). Still, being in a hetero-reproductive family remains the dominant social norm. Chinese non-heterosexual people are often seen through the lens of non-normative sexuality and gender rather than the lens of care and durable relationships. Chinese non-heterosexual subjects are rarely imagined as being able to form families, and hence non-heterosexual families and queer parents remain invisible to the public. The number of queer Chinese studies has been growing but is still small compared to Euro-American regions and even other Asian regions. Over the past decades, ethnographic studies on contemporary Chinese queer life have emerged concerning a wide range of topics, including but not limited to queer subjectivities, coming-out/coming-home strategies, cultural citizenship, neoliberalism, and homonormativity (Li and Wang, 1992; Li, 1998; Chou, 2001; Wei, 2007; Engebretsen, 2008, 2009, 2014; Ho, 2010; Kong, 2010, 2019; Yau, 2010; Engebretsen and Schroeder, 2015; Zheng, 2015; Bao, 2018; Wei, 2020). Some of these monographs use family of origin as the key site for examining queer kinship, and these are equally important. Still, there are many important stories that have not yet been told.

In this book, I present a critical ethnographic exploration of non-heterosexual intimate and family lives in Shenzhen and its neighbouring urban areas of Guangdong Province, China. This ethnography is theoretically grounded in kinship and queer scholarship that denaturalizes the notion of biology and the centrality of hetero-reproductive relationships (for example, Collier and Yanagisako, 1987; Butler, 1990; Strathern, 1992a; Hayden, 1995) with the purpose of furthering our understanding of kinship, queer life aspirations, and Chinese social change. My analysis is rooted in my ethnographic fieldwork in Shenzhen, Guangzhou, and Dongguan in Guangdong, China from 2018 to 2021. By focusing on the practices of same-sex intimate relationships, gay–lesbian *xinghun* (contract) marriage, and queer parenting, I investigate shifting kinship values in relation to sexuality, the state, moral landscapes, and the market. Through the lens of queer personal lives, I also explore socio-economic transformations in Chinese society and queer futurity more generally. This ethnography includes how queer co-parenthood is constructed and strengthened through the language of bodily experience and affective recognition. I will argue that, although the idea of blood ties and patrilineal continuity still holds centrality in Chinese family life, the various arrangements of parenting and family-forming practices in queer lifeworlds demonstrate the mobilizing possibilities beyond the singular definition of 'blood and biology'. This study has found that the emerging queer kin-making practices in urban Guangdong have created innovative and diverse forms of belonging, family, and relatedness beyond blood ties and the heterosexual nuclear family; at the same time, class stratification and inequalities are often reproduced in these processes. In the context of socio-economic transformations and the technologization of biological reproduction, this book demonstrates how queer future imaginaries in urban China are made vivid and normalized by state-constructed modernity and glocal market actions.

In short, kinship in China is transforming, and queer relationships should not be defined as imitative or alternative to blood ties. Through an in-depth exploration of how queer individuals engage in acts of care and cultivate *jiban*/mutuality within an environment marked by uncertainty, I propose a re-evaluation of the conventional division between transgressive and assimilative approaches in the construction of 'chosen' families and queerness. This book hopes to expand meanings of family and parenting and queer futures. Furthermore, it invites us to employ a standpoint derived from Chinese queer life to decentralize the dominant framework of sexuality in social and queer studies. Drawing on new kinship and queer theories and building upon previous queer ethnographic studies, this book offers fresh insights into Chinese queer life, assisted reproduction, and kinship. Through its analysis, the book also offers a new ethnographic perspective for queer studies and the anthropology of kinship.

In the remainder of this chapter, I will first contextualize queer intimate relationships and families in Chinese society, followed by the theoretical concerns that inform the main themes of this book. I then go on to provide a brief note on local history of my field sites in Guangdong, China and, lastly, outline the structure of this book.

Chinese same-sex sexualities and intimate relationships

The historical documents of same-sex desire and romance in China are as ancient as China itself.[2] Although male homoerotic behaviours were believed to be tolerated in ancient China, it is crucial to note two facts: one is the coexistence of homosexual erotic relations and heterosexual marriage; the other is the absence of female homosexuality in ancient Chinese literature (Hinsch, 1990; Sang, 2003; Ho, 2010). Despite any belief that it was tolerated, homosexuality was in a marginalized position in ancient Chinese culture, 'existing as peripheral to the gendered hierarchies of the Confucian family and marriage institutions' (Kong, 2010, p 151). Traditional Confucian[3] values place little weight on conjugal relations and pay no attention to love among women. The youth had little autonomy, especially young women.

In traditional China (pre-19th century), marriage was arranged by family elders and was viewed as a corporate relationship between two families rather than an individual matter.

Throughout the last century, discourses of sexuality in China became 'the site of cultural production in discrepant dialogue with Western power' (Rofel, 2007, p 95). It is widely believed that the penetration of Western imperialism in the late Qing Dynasty (1840–1911) imported a scientific discourse of gender and Western homophobia into China (Ho, 2010). During the Republican period (1912–1949), especially the May Fourth decade (1915–1927), China experienced a notable change in gender and sexual knowledge that associated same-sex intimacy with psychobiological abnormality (Sang, 2003). Male homosexual relationships, in the form of sodomy (*jijian*),[4] became legal and moral concerns. Little scholarly attention has been paid to sex, sexuality, and intimacy during the Maoist era and their impact on contemporary Chinese queer identities; this gap is mainly due to the scarcity of historical material on sex and sexuality from that time (Bao, 2018, p 10). During the Maoist era (1949–1976), China was highly unified and centralized; the Communist Party of China monopolized all kinds of resources, including material resources like land, property, and income, political resources of power, and cultural resources like education (He, 2000, p 69). It should also be noted that, during the Maoist era, not only sexual desires but individual desires in general could not be openly celebrated in public. Public discourse of homosexuality and sexuality remained silenced until the late 1970s. Sexual activities were strictly regulated to be within marriage.

Following Mao Zedong's death in 1976 and a short Maoist transitional period, Deng Xiaoping (paramount leader from 1978 to 1989) proclaimed that the contradiction was no longer between classes but between 'the backward and the advanced forces of production' (Osburg, 2013, p 4). Reform and opening policy was passed in 1978, marked as the beginning of market reforms. Since then, collective interest has been de-emphasized and individual mobility has increased. In the early 1980s, independent household businesses began to emerge as small shops, restaurants, and similar ventures. China's economic reforms have led to a shift in social stratification, giving rise to new ideologies and altering dynamics in terms of gender, sexuality, personhood, and family relationships. The development of the private sector leads to the rise of the 'enterprising self' or 'desiring self', which is expressed and maintained mostly in terms of individual desires and self-interests and, at the same time, under the restraining power of the Chinese state through the language of neoliberalism (Kleinman et al, 2011, p 4; see also Rofel, 2007). Gay and lesbian identities in China emerged in coexistence with its 'opening-up' commitment. The appearance of terms such as '*tongxinglian*' (homosexual), '*tongzhi*', 'gay', and 'lesbian' in public media and on the internet has helped non-heterosexual people from urban and rural areas to express their sexualities. Urbanization and increased geographical mobility have led to the emergence of same-sex communities in major Chinese cities. As Tze-lan Sang (2003) suggests, modern lesbian identities in China are not merely a Western import or a local representation; the production of these identities is multifaceted. Wei Wei's (2007) research focuses on the formation and transformation of local homosexual identities in Chengdu; his argument that the tropes of 'coming out' and 'the closet' are problematic in the Chinese context resonates with Lucetta Kam's study (2013) on queer women (*lala*) in Shanghai. Loretta Ho's study (2010) on same-sex communities in Beijing suggests the articulation of gay and lesbian identities in China is tied to the history of colonialism and modernity. As Ho points out, it is 'the state discourse of "opening up", propelled by mass globalization, that has facilitated the development of a paradoxical Chinese identity, along with a paradoxical Chinese same-sex identity' (2010, p 4). Hongwei Bao (2018) traces the construction of *tongzhi* identity during and after the Maoist era and uses this particular term as an angle to articulate Chinese queer experience. In this sense, *tongzhi* and queer are not merely indigenous or global, socialist or neoliberal conceptions.

In 1997, homosexuality was excluded from legal prosecution through the abolishment of the category of hooliganism (*liumang xingwei*) under the old criminal law, which had previously included male homosexual activities. In 2001, the Chinese Psychiatry Association removed homosexuality (*tongxinglian*) from the medical category of 'perversions'. Although these two changes are often regarded as signifying the decriminalization and de-pathologization of (male) homosexual behaviours, Chinese non-heterosexual people face continual stigmatization. To date, many Chinese universities still use textbooks that define homosexuality as 'abnormal' or as a 'mental illness', and the publishers of these textbooks refuse to make any change. No domestic law protects gender and sexual minorities. In Chinese public discourse, male homosexuality is almost always linked to the high risk of HIV in public discourse, while female homosexuality is often ignored or not acknowledged (Sang, 2003; Kam, 2013).

Despite the fact that online surveys often show increasing awareness and acceptance towards homosexuality, a survey conducted by the United Nations Development Programme (UNDP) in 2016 suggests that, although the public attitude towards same-sex relationships has been changing for the good, especially among the younger generation,[5] non-heterosexual people remain invisible and vulnerable within society, with only 5 per cent of them willing to live openly. For most non-heterosexual people, no matter what gender and sexual desires they have, there is still a strong injunction for them to be in a heterosexual marriage and have children. According to the UNDP's (2016) report, non-heterosexual people generally marry less than straight people of the same age, but the pressure to get married and the marriage rate increases as non-heterosexual people grow older. Among the respondents, 84.1 per cent of married LGBT respondents are married to heterosexual people, 13.2 per cent are in a 'marriage of convenience', and 2.6 per cent are in same-sex marriages registered in foreign countries. *Xinghun* marriage, or 'marriage of convenience' between a gay man and a lesbian, is one of the popular strategies discussed in Chinese same-sex communities. In the case of *xinghun*, the husband (who usually identifies as a gay man) and the wife (who usually identifies as a lesbian) do not marry for romantic love but mainly for the purpose of releasing tensions between individual freedom and familial duty (Engebretsen, 2014, 2017; Choi and Luo, 2016; Wang, 2019; Lo, 2020). Some non-heterosexual people simultaneously co-parent with their opposite-sex *xinghun* partners, show filial piety to their *xinghun* parents-in-law, and date same-sex partners. The relationships they have with their same-sex partners, their *xinghun* partners, and extended families both complicate and destabilize the concept of the conventional Chinese family. In this sense, the boundary between 'conventional/normative' and 'alternative/queer' forms of family and kinship seems to be vague as the practice of *xinghun* marriage creates not singular but multiple truths and perspectives. In this book, I explore non-heterosexual people's practice of *xinghun* marriage beyond the lens of marriage pressure, as *xinghun* marriage is often linked with parenting arrangements. As this book will detail, non-heterosexual people in *xinghun* marriages struggle to walk the blurred line between the concepts of a 'nominal' and a 'real' family.

Marriage and family transformations

To understand the pressure to marry that Chinese non-heterosexual people face, we need to first unpack what marriage, family, and childrearing mean in their lifeworlds. Chinese kinship values are rooted in the traditions of patrilineal continuity and Confucian philosophy (Yang, 1957; Walker, 1996). Traditional Chinese families consist of a line of male ancestors and descendants, while daughters and wives are not considered insiders. The ritual practices of ancestor worship and filial piety emphasize the continuation of patrilineal lineage rather than intimate relationships when it comes to marriage. Five kinds of relations were put in descending order: ruler–minister, father–son, elder brother–younger brother, husband–wife, and friend–friend. Since 1949, parental authority has weakened and arranged marriage has become rare in rural and urban China. The shift in control over the decision to marry from parents to young people was promoted by the Communist Party of China, both explicitly through the introduction of the Marriage Act of 1950 (and 1980) and indirectly through encouraging women into the job market (Pimentel, 2000). Women's social and economic status has improved since 1949.[6] The average age of a first marriage and the divorce rate have risen since then.[7] The younger generation in mainland China enjoys more autonomy and values romantic love and freedom of marriage. The notion of 'romantic love' in China is constituted through the rejection of arranged marriage and is linked to a sense of modernity (Yan, 2003; Pan, 2015). On the other hand, what Chinese couples have said about 'love' can be viewed as 'unromantic' in Westerners' eyes and is more similar to the Western conception of 'companionship' (Pimentel, 2000, p 44). The China Family Panel Study has shown a dramatic rise in premarital cohabitation rates from nearly absent before the 1980s to one third in 2010–2012 (Yu and Xie, 2015). One reason for this is the change in the Marriage Law that decriminalized the practice of cohabitation.[8] Urbanization and migrational experience are also important factors. The relationship between sex, romantic love, and companionate love is constantly being negotiated by young urbanites, and they marry for various reasons (Jankowiak and Li, 2017). The one-child policy introduced in 1979 has also played a critical role in improving the status of urban daughters (Fong, 2007). In the traditional patrilineal kinship system, parents tended to invest in sons rather than daughters. Being the one and only child who is expected to support her parents in the future, an urban daughter has access to more emotional and material support than a daughter with siblings. Briefly speaking, the traditional disadvantaged identity categories of women and young people have gained increased individual freedom. Nevertheless, parents are still involved in spouse choice and married lives (Pimentel, 2000; Li, 2011; Davis, 2021). Furthermore, singlehood remains rare.[9] Heterosexual marriage is still the dominant preference in Chinese society. Consequently, youths may have increased freedom to choose whom to marry, but they may not have such freedom to choose not to marry at all.

Childbirth and parenting in China are tightly associated with its sociocultural emphasis on reproduction and unique birth-planning policies (Handwerker, 2002; Klein, 2017). Filial duty (*xiao*), as the moral standard in Confucian China, focuses on the continuation of the family line (Ikels, 2004). In this sense, reproduction is a family duty bonded with marriage. In 1979, the state introduced the one-child policy to restrict births per household, and it was replaced by the two-child policy in 2015. The Population and Family Planning Law became effective on 1 September 2002. Many other administrative issues are directly related to the state's strict birth-planning project (Jiang and Liu, 2016). For instance, in 2002, the State Council promulgated the measures for the administration of the collection of social maintenance fees, a euphemism for fines as a punishment for excess/unplanned births,[10] and it remained in effect until 2021. In 2001, the Ministry of Health issued two orders to regulate the use of assisted reproductive technologies (ARTs) and sperm banks. They came in line with the Population and Family Planning Law, meaning that ARTs, including IUI (intrauterine insemination, also known as artificial insemination) and IVF (in-vitro fertilization), were only available to married infertile couples. Recent national surveys indicate that out-of-wedlock childbirths remain almost non-existent partly because of the governmental control over the household registration (*hukou*) system (Xie, 2013). The *hukou* system is based on families, where individuals who are living together in the same dwelling are established as one household. Each household is registered under a specific household register book (*hukou ben*).[11] A household is generally headed by the owner of the property rights of the house or the lead tenant of a state-owned house. Without two parents who are legally married and complying with the family-planning policy, the newborn risks becoming a legal non-person (*heihu*) (Greenhalgh, 2003). Until the 2020s, unmarried parents often had to pay a high social maintenance fee to get *hukou* for out-of-wedlock children. Although there is a trend towards the nuclear family in urban China, strong parent–child bonds and the high percentage of elders co-residing with/living close to their children are still remarkable.[12] Family care remains the main model for elderly support. A significant number of elderly people still count on their children for support due to the patrilocal tradition and the lack of public support. Recent studies have demonstrated continuing sturdy intergenerational bonds in urban China (Xu and Xia, 2014). Since elderly care is strongly dependent on kinship norms under the current welfare system, not having children can be a profound concern when considering the future and old age.

Several paradoxes in the kinship values and practices arise in transforming Chinese societies. On the one hand, there is a growing pursuit of individual freedoms when it comes to love, intimacy, and marriage. On the other hand, entering heterosexual marriage remains a dominant life choice tightly associated with parenting (Xie, 2013; Santos and Harrell, 2017). Long-term cohabitating relationships and non-marital childbirths remain extremely rare for cultural and legal reasons (Yu and Xie, 2015; Yeung and Hu, 2016). Old-age support is still expected to be provided primarily by one's offspring (Tang and Chen, 2012; Xie, 2013). Living a 'stable' (*wending*) and 'harmonious' (*hexie*) life is tied to heterosexual marriage and expressed through the language of belonging and cultural citizenship (Engebretsen, 2008). These paradoxes imply a difficult situation for alternative life choices, including queer relationships and family formation. It is also crucial to investigate the actual practices behind the official statistics. Again, research findings situate contemporary Chinese marriage and family values in tensions between the traditional and the modern. Drawing from manifold inconsistencies, scholars thus argue that Chinese marriages and families still hold some distinctive characteristics that are different from the Western pattern, and the Chinese kinship experience has remained recognizably 'similar to itself' despite ongoing social transformations (Brandtstädter and Santos, 2008, p 2; see also Pimentel, 2000).

Overall, queer personal lives in contemporary China reveal discursive and affective tensions between individual desires and state discourse, blood ties and chosen families, free love and moral duties, and cultural conventions and queer global politics. The following sections go on to outline the key sources and scholarly works that underpin this book.

Global sexualities, transnationalism, and queer modernity

The theoretical concepts of gender, sexuality, and heteronormativity form a crucial foundation for queer theory and this ethnography. During the last century, the essentialist view of sex, gender, and sexuality as binary distinctions and natural facts has been challenged by feminism and lesbian and gay studies. Simone de Beauvoir (1953) distinguishes gender from sex as she points out that one's body is sexed, yet sex does not cause gender, and gender cannot be used to express sex. In discussing the construction of knowledge of sexuality within institutions, Michel Foucault (1984) points out that the body gains meaning only in the context of discursive power relations both produced and undermined by discourse. In *Gender Trouble*, Judith Butler further elaborates that while sex might exhibit apparent biological constants, gender is 'culturally constructed; hence, gender is neither the casual result of sex nor as seemingly fixed as sex' (1990, p 9). Gayle Rubin (1984) points out that sexuality, like gender, is political. Following Rubin's critique that to be a sex implies having sex in a given way that reflects a heterosexist cultural assumption that 'sexuality is reducible to sexual intercourse and that it is a function of the relations between women and men' (1984, p 169), Judith Butler makes it clear that sexual relations cannot be reduced to gender positions. Butler's (1990) theory of performativity shattered the binary constructs of masculinity and femininity, suggesting that gender identity evolves through repeated acts constructed within societal norms.

Nowadays, many scholars would agree that sexuality and gender are historically and socially constructed (Sullivan, 2003). Butler (1990) argues that heterosexuality is a complex matrix of discourse that requires something to negate and sublate. Hence, in order for heterosexuality to remain integral as a distinct social norm, the very notion of homosexuality needs to be constructed to remain repressed as a taboo. In this sense, heterosexuality always presupposes homosexuality to ensure its normativity, as they are constructed in a reciprocal but hierarchical relationship (Jackson, 2005). Intrinsic is the relationship between sexual subjectivities, discourse, and power. In *Touching Feeling*, Eve Kosofsky Sedgwick illuminates the importance of repressive hypothesis in Foucault's analysis of sexuality, prompting a reconsideration of understanding human desire as structured quite differently from 'the heroic, "liberatory," inescapably dualistic righteousness of hunting down and attacking prohibition/repression in all its chameleonic guises' (2003, p 10). Stevi Jackson describes heteronormativity as a changing set of discourses that 'is mobilized and reproduced in everyday life not only through talk, but also through routine activities in which gender, sexuality and heterosexuality interconnect' (2006, p 114). Moreover, heteronormativity extends beyond discussions of sexual behaviour; it also encompasses the framing of a 'normal way of life' (Jackson, 2006, p 107). As a construct developed in contrast to non-normative sexualities, heteronormativity constantly faces challenges from queer theories and practices. Valerie Traub notes the 'tendency to use the term "heteronormativity" to describe an earlier system of sexuality and gender', which seems to make heterosexuality and heteronormativity ahistorical and universal (2008, p 23). In light of such concerns, I pay attention to the processes through which the social ordering of gender, sexuality, and heterosexuality are produced and probably transformed in the Chinese context.

The emergence of queer theory in the 1990s has indeed contributed to the denaturalization of the masculinity–femininity divide and the destabilization of the notions of the normal and the normative. As scholarship on sexuality is globalized, Elizabeth A. Povinelli and George Chauncey highlight the need for scholars in lesbian, gay, and queer studies to 'think sexuality globally and transnationally' (1999, p 446). Moreover, growing ethnographic research conducted in various non-Euro-American contexts has challenged both the universalist view of gay and lesbian identities and the essentialist view of 'Oriental/Asian cultures' (for example, Manalansan, 2003; Sinnott, 2004; Blackwood, 2005; Boellstorff, 2007a; Bose and Bhattacharyya, 2007; Boyce, 2008; Osella, 2012). Tom Boellstorff discusses how nation-states 'make underwriting normative heterosexuality central to their practices of governance and ideologies of belonging and how in the process they inadvertently help people conjure "alternative" sexualities and desires' (2007b, p 22). Naisargi Dave points out the two social facts: 'the Western imperative to make of queerness a political identity' and 'the local reality of the incommensurability of queerness with religion or nation' (2012, p 15). Queer politics is tangled with post(colonial) politics (Liu and Rofel, 2010; Chiang, 2014; Hunt and Holmes, 2015). Scholars concerning cultural universalism or queer Western hegemony argue that the universal imagination of being queer tends to place non-normative gender and sexual minorities from the non-West in a forever late arrived and less modern position. In this sense of Western–Oriental/global–local binaries, the East either rejects or takes up Western (queer) theories. Yet, as Petrus Liu suggests, the language of West–East difference 'may naturalize and justify the "West" as an indispensable and normative point of comparison' (2010, p 314).

In other words, rejecting queer identities and theories originated from Euro-American contexts and emphasizing cultural specificity could also risk essentializing both the 'East' and the 'West' (Chiang, 2014; Tan, 2017). Rather than perceiving queer identities and cultures in sets of global–local and tradition–modernity divides, Inderpal Grewal and Caren Kaplan propose a mode of study that adopts a more nuanced framework of transnational relations in which 'power structures, asymmetries, and inequalities become the conditions of possibility of new subjects' (2001, p 671). Similarly, in recognizing the problem of queer Western centrism, Ara Wilson (2006) emphasizes an emerging transnational, post-Orientalist approach that acknowledges the power-laden complexity of social life within Asia while also revising Eurocentric notions of sexual modernity. After all, the purpose is 'to relativise "Western" paradigmatic knowledge in the study of gender and sexual diversity' (Boyce et al, 2018, p 847). Given these theoretical insights, in this study, I do not conceptualize 'gay and lesbian' as a globalised modern culture; nor do I conceptualize '*tongzhi* and *lala*' as representing an 'authentic' Chinese culture. Following the transnational approach, I see China as a site to actively produce, problematize, and decolonize queer studies.

Furthermore, sexuality, as Akshay Khanna (2017) suggests, emerges as an aspect of personhood, a 'modern' phenomenon, a political object, and a context of queer movement. I concur with Khanna (2017) that the sense of sexuality as an aspect of personhood and the epistemology of homosexuality are partial and ultimately unhelpful frames for understanding sexual possibilities in non-Euro-American contexts. Rather, we shall develop an understanding towards 'sexualness' that unsettles the overarching framework of sexuality types. The meanings of the categories of gender and sexuality 'shift according to historical, cultural and social context' and the question is 'ultimately ethnographic and historic rather than purely theoretical' (Bose and Bhattacharyya, 2007, p xxiv). Similar to Khanna's theorization of 'sexualness' in Indian culture, I offer up thoughts for the politics of ambiguity in the realm of visibility. In this book, I employ a standpoint derived from Chinese queer life to unsettle the heteronormative approach to anthropology as well as to decolonize/decentralize the dominant framework of sexuality in queer studies (Khanna, 2017; Hendriks, 2018).

'New' kinship studies and uncertain queer kinship

This book is grounded in theoretical principles drawn from the field of the anthropology of kinship. Traditionally, anthropologists and other social scientists have tended to focus on the discourse of 'natural facts' such as lineage systems (biological) and marriage (affinal), which were seen as the roots of kinship. Kinship was the study of reproduction rather than connection in the early-twentieth-century anthropology (Strathern, 1992a, p 119). David

Murray Schneider's (1980) critique challenges the Euro-American tendency to equate kinship exclusively with blood relations, as he highlights that the concept of kinship is culturally variable and not universally based on so-called natural facts. Since the 1990s, kinship has lost its ground most obviously to gender as the naturalization of gender difference has been challenged (Collier and Yanagisako, 1987; Yanagisako and Delaney, 1995; Butler, 1993; Carsten, 2000). The biological facts, as many have discovered, do not form the ground of social relations in every society. It has firstly become clear that kinship is not reducible to biology. Nature, which has been viewed as pre-existing biological facts 'discovered' by people, seems to be separated from culture, which has been viewed as social knowledge 'constructed' by people. Yet, nature is constructed, though it is claimed to be discovered (Latour, 1993, p 31). As Marilyn Strathern (1992a) puts it in *After Nature*, kinship is the place of overlap, the meeting place of nature and culture. By exploring the use of new reproductive technologies in the Thatcher political era, which were seen as both enabling nature and interfering with nature, Strathern (1992a) analytically blurs the boundaries of nature and technology and makes it clear that the facts of kinship are simultaneously facts of nature and facts of culture and society. The very ground for nature to be seen as a distinct domain from culture has become questionable as nature needs to be protected by technology. In this sense, kinship is no longer a biological fact in varying social forms but a 'complex, hybrid process of establishing relations of proximity not separable from the most general phenomenon of intimacy and relatedness' (Brandtstädter and Santos, 2008, p 9). Ultimately, 'there is no truly authentic anthropological modelling of local cultures and relatedness' (Carsten, 2000, p 34). Sarah Franklin's *Biological Relatives* (2013) provides a comprehensive historical and ethnographic exploration of contemporary reproductive technologies, notably, IVF. Franklin introduces the model of 'biological relativity', through which 'biology now exists as a more explicitly contingent, or relative, condition' (2013, p 16; see also Hayden, 1995). In *What Kinship Is–and Is Not*, Marshall Sahlins proposes the idea of the 'mutuality of being', that is, 'kinfolk are persons who participate intrinsically in each other's existence; they are members of one another' (2013, p ix). Inspired by Sahlins, this book further introduces the concept of mutuality as being within queer studies, illustrating how different forms of *jiban*/mutuality are constructed.

Social changes worldwide have shaped the contemporary landscape of kinship studies and queer family making. The rapid development of ARTs, the emerging emphasis on intimate recognition, and the increasing visibility of non-normative families have undoubtedly redefined and expanded the sphere of gender, sexualness, kinship, parenthood, and family. Possibilities of parenting are increasingly becoming imaginable for queer relationships. Non-heterosexual people are building families, though their choices are limited, and their situations vary. In contrast to biological kin, the term 'chosen/fictive' kin is often used by the media to describe kin relations that are not based on biology. Public discourses on queer kinship have tended to define same-sex couples as 'pretended family relations' and 'so-called family', implying their 'fictive' and 'imitative' non-original status (Weston, 1991). In this sense, queer intimacy is figured as against 'family', and queer love and queer parenthood are figured as against 'nature' (Folger, 2008). Elizabeth Povinelli (2006) explores intimacies in Australian indigenous community and radical faeries in *The Empire of Love*, suggesting the immanent dependencies of the two seemingly non-common-sense and incommensurate groups are challenging the liberal and binary conception of individual freedom and social constraints. Povinelli finds that the saying that 'love makes a family' in contemporary mainstream America emphasizes the value of intimate recognition, while the genealogical imaginary has not died; nor has it been replaced by intimacy. In *Families We Choose*, Kath Weston (1991) has challenged the kinship discourse that traditionally defined gay and lesbian families as 'fictive', substitute, and derivatives of the 'real', 'authentic', 'blood and biological' kinship. She suggests that gay and lesbian families in the Bay area emphasize 'choice and creativity' in opposition to 'blood and biology'. In this context, 'choice' is understood as an individualistic notion that centres around self, and 'creativity' denotes a utopian vision often expressed as 'I create my own tradition'. For Weston, chosen families are neither substitutes for blood ties nor pretended family relations. I share Weston's perspective in treating queer kinship ideologies 'as historical transformations rather than derivatives of other sorts of kinship relations' (1991, p 106).

The uncertainty between state legislation and queer kinship revealed in various studies (Borneman, 1997; Mamo, 2007; Goodfellow, 2015; Sorainen, 2015; Patton-Imani, 2020) leads us to critically think about the relation between state and culture. Although gay marriage is not the same as gay kinship, they are often conflated in the debates that are turned into sites of displacement for other political fears about technology, unity of nation, and ultimately the openness of kinship (Butler, 2002, p 21). Moreover, arguments against same-sex marriage and queer parenting reveal a discourse about what the state should do and which relationships should be recognized by the state. Research on queer kinship exposes intricate links between 'biological facts', culture, and legal recognition (Butler, 2002, p 21). In short, research on (queer) kinship exposes intricate connections among 'biological facts', culture, and state legislation. Critiques of romantic love and individuality further situate queer kinship as in tension between personal choices and social constraint. Since the kinship theories have been constantly destabilized and renewed, we should be careful not to make presuppositions about what constitutes 'authentic' forms of kinship. Rather, in this research, I explore why queer people want to have children (as a conjugal technique), how the other socio-legal factors shape queer (co-)parenthood, and, ultimately, 'what exactly, if anything, makes a same-sex family *queer?*' (Dahl and Gabb, 2019, p 226). *Queering Kinship* exemplifies and advances the perspective on the uncertainty/ambivalence and fluidity/malleability that characterizes sexuality, kinship, modernity, and technology (Haraway, 1991; Beck, 1992; Franklin, 2013; Murphy, 2013; Goodfellow, 2015; Khanna, 2017). The diverse parenting and co-parenting practices among queer individuals illustrate the potential for forging connections beyond biological ties, as (co-)parenthood is formed and reinforced through bodily experience (such as pregnancy) and affective recognition (conjugal/parental love). This book contributes to this discourse by engaging in an exploration of the intersections between biological relative, queer kinship, and reproductive technologies.

Doing Chinese kinship and moral personhood

It has been widely argued that traditional Chinese society is 'patriarchal, patrimonial, patrilineal, and patrilocal' (Xie, 2013, p 3). Confucian ideologies have shaped every part of Chinese society, from ruling principles to family values. Prior to the 1970s, only a limited number of Western social researchers were allowed to conduct ethnographic research within mainland China. Instead, they often focused on fieldwork in Taiwan, Hong Kong, and other overseas Chinese communities, revealing unique regional attributes (Cohen, 2005). Charles Stafford (2000) notes that traditional portrayals of Chinese kinship have prioritized regional and historical assessments and overlooked the significance of participant observation; by doing so, scholars partly missed the fluid nature of Chinese kinship (p 49). Similarly, Janet Carsten (2000) underscores the emphasis on everyday practices of constructing relatedness. James L. Watson (1982) thus suggests a reconsideration of the 'closeness' of Chinese kinship groups. With the turn of 'new' kinship studies, anthropologists have played important roles studying broader forms of relationships and the fluid nature of Chinese kinship (Szonyi, 2002; Brandtstädter and Santos, 2008; Santos and Harrell, 2017). For example, Charles Stafford (2000) suggests that the cycles of *Yang* (parent–child relationships) and *Laiwang* (relationships between friends, neighbours, and acquaintances) are equally important. Sara Friedman (2008) suggests that women's practice of *dui pnua* in eastern Hui'an and similar forms of homosociality outside patrilineal familism can expand the scope of intimacy. Looking into children raised by grandparents in urban cities, William Jankowiak (2008) emphasizes the emotional bonds in families. Through exploring the diverse forms of queer families in Guangdong, this book joins other emerging anthropological studies that provide a meaningful way to understand the malleability and variations in the making of Chinese kinship and human kinship in general, for kinship is subject to cross-cultural historical transformations (Brandtstädter and Santos, 2008, p 2; see also Weston, 1991).

Moreover, the recent discussion about romantic love and Chinese kinship identifies selfhood as an important yet contested imaginary. In *Deep China*, Kleinman et al (2011) find that the Chinese 'self' today can be 'divided by a number of "dividers," such as past versus present, public versus private, moral versus immoral, and so on' (p 5). The divided selfhood of being a Chinese individual who is encouraged to pursue freedom, desires, and self-interests yet also accepts that part of their identity is defined by 'their loyalty to the party and the state' (p 9). The complex situation places Chinese people, particularly non-heterosexual people, on the edge of conflicting ethical values and practices. Yunxiang Yan (2017) has furthered the discussion on this divided selfhood and suggests a tripartite approach to understanding Chinese personhood. He argues that, in the process of 'doing personhood' (*zuoren*), the moralist self is employed to control the desiring individual for the purpose of making oneself the proper relational person (p 3). Kleinman and Yan's arguments regarding Chinese moral personhood take us back to the discussion of sexuality and sexualness, as they powerfully stress the manifold and dynamic process of constructing one's sense of 'self'. The dividual, relational, and social articulations of selfhood in Chinese and various other contexts need to be considered when it comes to understanding sexual experiences and subjectivities (Khanna, 2017; see also Yan, 2017). This research adopts this fruitful approach to explore Chinese non-heterosexual subjects' personal desires, social relations, and inner struggles as all indispensable features of the self. I am interested in how the complexity of personhood is associated with the emerging and morally controversial lifestyles and practices in queer lifeworlds. In *Queering Kinship*, I offer a perspective from queer everyday lives to understand transformations in Chinese kinship and further unsettle the 'blood and biology' patrilineal kinship. I also link Chinese queer people's family and reproductive choices to their understanding of the moral self, echoing the call to understand sexual desires as flowing through a subject but not necessarily informing them (Khanna, 2017).

Queer Chinese citizenship and the queer 'nuclear' family

Many scholars have argued that citizenship rights are multidimensional and 'citizen' is more than a legal or political category; it is a sociological and an economic category (for example, Bell and Binnie, 2000). According to John D'Emilio (2007), it is the free labour system under the historical development of capitalism that allows gay and lesbian identities and communities to emerge and, at the same time, reproduce heterosexism and homophobia. Studying sexualities through the lens of citizenship can be complicated in non-Euro-American societies, given their distinctive political landscapes, the notions of rights and citizenships, and the varying taxonomies of sex, gender, and sexualities (Mackie, 2017, p 146). What does sexual citizenship mean in transforming China? As a double-edged sword, China's economic reforms have contributed to the growth of individual mobility and simultaneously formed unequal social stratums (Anagnost, 2008; Zhang, 2011; Osburg, 2013). Lisa Rofel (2007) links the production of desires in China to neoliberalism and transnational queer studies, revealing how the emergence of Chinese gay identities is intertwined with aspirations for cultural citizenship and new modes of inclusion and exclusion (p 95). Following this idea, Travis Kong (2010, 2019) examines the making of sexual citizenship and masculinities among Chinese gay men in Hong Kong, London, and mainland China. For Kong, being gay in mainland China has shifted from 'the medical and deviant discourse of homosexuality' to a new type of cultural and urban citizenship emphasizing 'quality (*suzhi*), individuality, difference and modernity' (2010, p 12). Tiantian Zheng (2015) offers an ethnographic analysis of male same-sex relations and the intersectionality of sexuality and social class in Dalian. Bao (2018) suggests that *tongzhi* subjectivity and queer politics in contemporary China are both produced by and, at the same time, resist the state and capitalism. John Wei (2020) finds that queer non-governmental organizations (NGOs) and film clubs encourage their participants to live an honest and ethical lifestyle, which again enforces the notion of being a good sexual citizen in post-2008 Chinese cities. All of these scholars point out the continued impact of the *suzhi* (quality) discourse on social stratification within and outside queer communities. The word *suzhi* first appeared in the 1980s, linking one's all-encompassing types of capital closely to the state governance and the neoliberal economy (Anagnost, 2004; Kipnis, 2007; Wei, 2020). As this book will unfold, the discourse on cultural citizenship and *suzhi* is important for understanding queer family-making processes: they are people who include themselves in and who are excluded from them.

Emerging research has also focused on queer Chinese citizens' negotiation with heteronormative norms and explored their strategies of navigating their queer desires with their families of origin (Engebretsen, 2014; Choi and Luo, 2016; Wang, 2019; Liu and Tan, 2020; Lo, 2020). Elisabeth Engebretsen (2008, 2014) investigates *lalas*' developing subjectivities, everyday practices, and strategies in contemporary Beijing with a nuanced analysis of their desire of 'being normal'. The 'normal' life within Chinese society is tied to heterosexual marriage and expressed through the language of belonging and cultural citizenship (Engebretsen, 2008, 2014). Engebretsen links the concept of 'chosen kinship' and the filial family system by describing the *lala* couple who take the role of second daughter to 'normalize' into their partners' families. John Wei (2020) discusses how internal/international migration has diluted queer migrants' physical and emotional connections with their families of origin, making queer kinship negotiation stretched and stressful. *Queering Kinship* builds on recent queer Chinese studies to develop a grounded analysis of the study of non-heterosexual intimate and family lives from an anthropological perspective.

Despite the absence of legal recognition for same-sex marriage and stringent limitations on childbirth outside wedlock in mainland China, the visibility of non-heterosexual individuals with children has been increasing within queer communities and professional ART agencies. Under existing legal policies, one of the gay co-parents would be neither biologically related to the child nor married to his partner. Also, the ART business sectors that assist non-heterosexual clients in having children reveal complex links between sexualness, kinship, citizenship, and the transnational market, as the high costs and duration needed for IVF and surrogacy automatically make economic capital a prerequisite for intended clients.

Since Chinese non-heterosexual people are scarcely imagined as being able to form enduring relationships that can reproduce and establish families, queer parents remain invisible to the public, and social research into Chinese queer people's participation in assisted reproduction remains marginal (Lo et al, 2016; Lo, 2020; Tao, 2021; Wei, 2022). The diverse modalities of non-heterosexual families and their practice of establishing enduring relationships and parenting have yet to been thoroughly researched. The main areas of kinship studies within mainland China have focused on heterosexual relationships and natal families.[13] The fact that Chinese domestic quantitative studies frequently reduce family and kinship to blood ties (sometimes excluding marital relations) seems to highlight the very primacy of parent–child relations and the privileged position of blood ties. Yet, kinship is not reducible to biology, and it is not reducible to 'family' (Butler, 2002; see also Halberstam, 2011). Such a deficiency in research into Chinese queer parenting and family making in the social sciences is connected to the lack of these relationships' wider representation in Chinese society and the heteronormative perspective that dominates mainstream social studies.

In retrospect, this chapter engages with the ongoing discussions on the relationships between the global and the local, the modern and the traditional, the biological and the social, the normative and the queer. It is against this backdrop that I locate my research in the landscape of queer conjugal relationships, parenting, and family making in urban China. In *Queering Kinship*, I explore broadened forms of relatedness without making presuppositions about what constitutes a family and what defines a modern queer lifestyle. The book identifies queer intimate love, queer reproduction and parenting, queer family, and queer futurity as its ethnographic and analytical focuses. By examining how the notions and practices of establishing mutuality/*jiban* among queer subjects in urban China simultaneously perpetuate and challenge the dominant paradigm of 'blood and biology' patrilineal kinship, this book expands the meanings of family and parenthood in the transforming Chinese society. Moreover, it encourages the adoption of a perspective rooted in Chinese queer relationships to dismantle and shift away from the prevailing sexuality framework in both anthropology and queer studies. In doing so, it introduces innovative avenues for approaching queer relationships and envisioning queer futures.

Urban Guangdong: cities of migrants and queer utopian futures

The major part of my fieldwork was conducted in Shenzhen, the well-known city of migrants in Guangdong Province, China. Located on the southeast coast, Shenzhen is the city that links Hong Kong and mainland China. Within an hour's train ride from Shenzhen, Guangzhou is the capital city of Guangdong Province. Dongguan is located in between Shenzhen and Guangzhou. Shenzhen, Guangzhou, and Dongguan belong to the Pearl River Delta Metropolitan Region, the largest economic hub in China (see Figure I.1).

The emergence of market economy and the relaxation of the household registration (*hukou*) system since the 1980s have contributed to a rural-to-urban migration surge. China's *hukou* system was formally set up in the 1950s. Until the early 1980s, internal migration was tightly controlled under the *hukou* system. Each citizen is required to register in one and only one place of permanent residence (*hukou suozaidi*) (Chan and Zhang, 1999). The *hukou* residence links one's accessibility to a wide range of state-provided benefits and opportunities such as public schooling, healthcare, housing, and eligibility to work in state sectors. Changing *hukou* residence and status was extremely difficult (Bao et al, 2011). From the late 1980s, Chinese cities began to issue temporary resident permits to migrants and gradually eased the restrictions on the in-migration of rural workers. The economic and *hukou* reforms considerably encouraged labour mobility. The temporary (or 'floating') population away from their *hukou* residence had increased from 6.1 million in 1982 to 149.4 million in 2005 (Shen, 2013). The four first-tier cities – Beijing, Shanghai, Guangzhou, and Shenzhen – are the most popular for migrants in China.

Here, I emphasize the internal regional variation within China in understanding and comparing queer Chinese studies. Other than Hong Kong, Taiwan, and overseas Chinese communities (Kong, 2010; Tang, 2011; Brainer, 2019), each region inside mainland China has distinct cultural and historical contexts that shape personal lives. Shenzhen is the youngest and smallest city among the four first-tier Chinese cities, being as it was merely

Figure I.1: Guangdong Province, from Google Maps (2021)

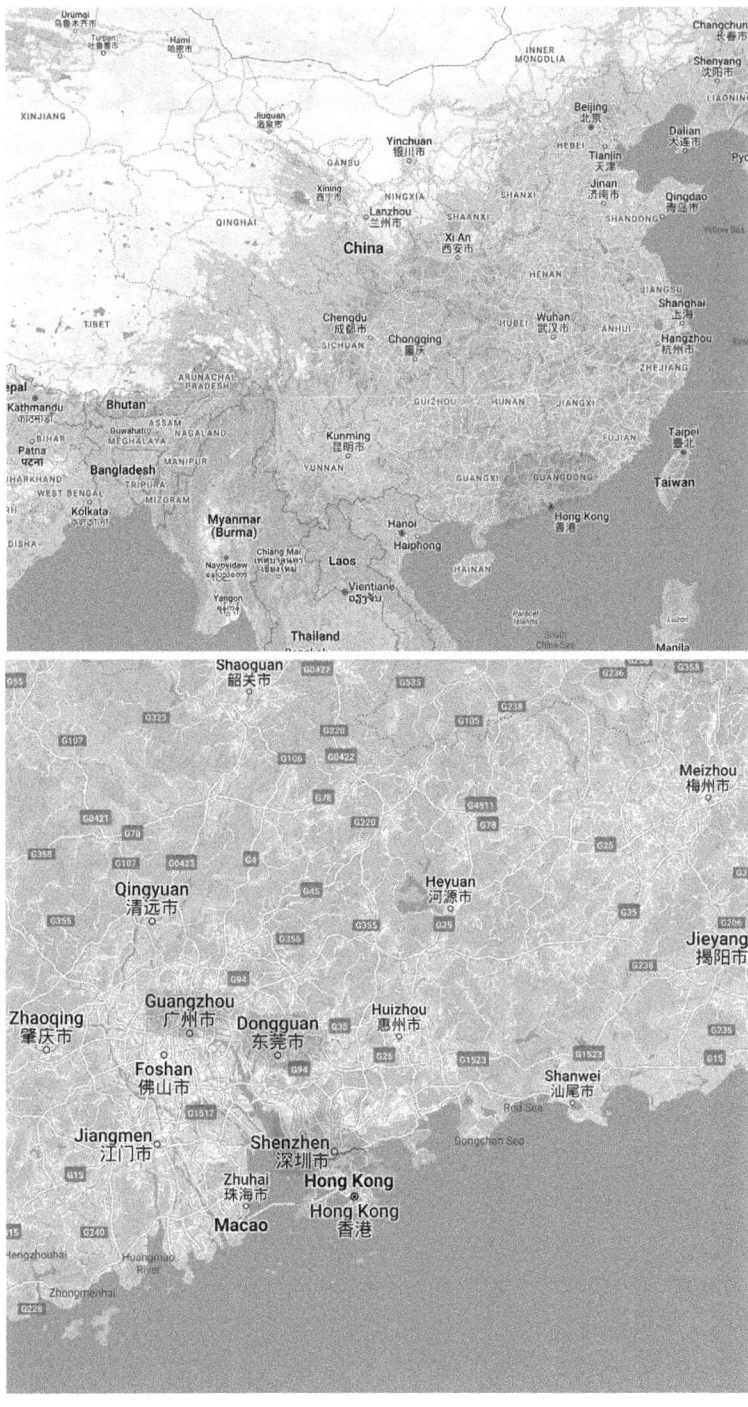

Source: Google

an 'uncultured' fishing village of 30,000 people three decades ago. As part of its reform and opening-up plan, China established special economic zones, including Shenzhen. The increased social mobility and the growing number of migrants have contributed to the rapid industrialization and urbanization in Shenzhen. By 2017, Shenzhen had 4.3 million permanent registered citizens, while the total permanent population, including migrants without local *hukou*, was 12.5 million (Shenzhen Municipal Bureau of Statistics, 2018). Shenzhen released its famous slogan in 2012: '*laile jiushi shenzhenren*' (once you come here, you are a Shenzhener). Growing vigorously, Shenzhen has many nicknames: 'mushroom/instant city' for its rapid growth, 'Chinese Silicon Valley' for its renowned high-tech industry, and 'cultural desert' for its lack of cultural history. It attracts the greatest number of young university graduates in China.[14] As the capital city of Guangdong Province, Guangzhou also attracts thousands of migrants each year.

The prominent urban areas in southeast coast China became my chosen sites for exploring the interplay of urban utopian imaginaries and queer kinship. Indeed, first-tier cities like Shenzhen have become a destination for young non-heterosexual people who are attracted by the promise of better opportunities, metropolitan anonymity, and sexual freedom (Luo, 2020). Yet, such queer utopian imaginaries of cosmopolitan life have been questioned in recent queer anthropological literature (Sorainen, 2015; Boyce and Dasgupta, 2017). In an endeavour to bring together queer kinship and queer futurity, this ethnography demonstrates that the rising living expenses and the constricting possibilities for upward mobility have shaped young queer subjects' material desires, relationships with their parents, careers, marriage and parenting choices, and future aspirations.

Outline of chapters

The main body of this book consists of six intersecting chapters. The following chapter explains the rationale of the research design and traces the progress throughout my ethnographic fieldworks in urban Guangdong, China from 2018 to 2021. I detail the methodological and ethical challenges I have faced and how I dealt with them, from recruiting research participants to negotiating the power dynamics between the researcher and the 'researched'. I view participant observation and semi-structured interviews as interconnective research methods to depict the everyday practice of queer relationships. I also discuss how my biography connects with my multiple roles and queer reflectivity in my home field. Lastly, I make it clear that I research with ethics of ethnographic research as well as ethics of friendship. This chapter offers a timely 'recipe' for doing fieldwork in a sensitive setting and contributes to the small but growing discussion on 'queering' the methodology in social research.

In Chapter 2, I discuss queer intimate relationships within the shifting landscapes of role terms, love, dating culture, and modernity. I explore non-heterosexual people's changing attitudes towards same-sex relationships, as the seemingly gendered relationship modes have been mobilized in various ways. I explore queer couples' strategies to sustain their romantic cohabitating relationships when same-sex marriage is not in China yet. The key to a 'just-as-married' same-sex relationship is creating unbreakable *jiban*/mutuality, a concept I will develop throughout the book. This chapter demonstrates how queer subjects' understanding and practice of intimate love is conditioned by their economic capital and legal context in urban China. As two of the most prominent economic hubs and migrant-attracting cities, Shenzhen and Guangzhou are relevant scenes to discuss ideas around career and romantic opportunities. Drawing from detailed life histories, the chapter opens up the material underpinning of loving relationships in Chinese queer lives.

Chapter 3 deals with queer reproductive choices in relation to changing kinship conventions and moral personhood in urban China. I begin by asking when and why non-heterosexual people of different age groups and backgrounds want to have children or remain childless in urban China. I suggest that we reconsider the symbolic importance of the child when studying reproduction. Following this, I document the existing practices for Chinese non-heterosexual individuals and couples around having children and the moral implications raised by them. Queer parents frequently have children through their previous *zhihun*/heterosexual marriages, *xinghun*/contract marriages, *guoji*/relative adoptions, or the employment of ARTs. I also discuss the tendency in online and offline queer communities to evaluate non-heterosexual people's pathways to parenthood through changing moral discourses. I suggest we take all three components – the moralist self, the desiring individual, and the relational person – to understand Chinese queer (intended) parents' selfhood and moral practices in a spatial, temporal, and relational context.

As Chapter 3 suggests that ART has emerged as an ideal way for queer subjects and especially queer couples in urban China to have children, Chapter 4 moves to explore the interplay of queer reproductive justice and the emerging (underground) ART market in China. As data collected from legal documents, online discussions, and my field observation indicate, the legal and moral debates brought by queer parents' participation in assisted reproduction are perceived differently among diverse gender and sexual groups in Chinese society. This chapter illustrates how the ART companies and queer organizations sponsored by them come together to shape the understanding and consumption of ART in queer lifeworlds. Through detailed narratives regarding how queer subjects make reproductive and consumer decisions as clients of high-tech medical services, I show that the marketization and consumption of ART in Guangdong have both 'queered' reproduction and enacted stratified reproduction that is only available to middle-upper-class queer citizens in big cities like Shenzhen.

In Chapter 5, I delineate how queer parents in Guangdong use their understanding and language of blood kin, biology, and parental love to distinguish between 'my children', 'my partner's children', and 'our children'. By examining how they integrate such distinctions into their social worlds, I reveal the complexity of defining the boundaries between blood relative and queer kin. The cases of single queer parents and queer couples having children together amplify their understanding of blood ties and children's position in sustaining conjugal love and a protected future. I also explore how demonstrations of parental love for their children closely link to their socio-economic capabilities. I argue that the idea of blood and biology still holds its centrality in Chinese family life, while it is also proved to have elastic potentialities for queer couples who desire joint parenthood. The notions of biology and patrilineal continuity alone did not work to achieve or demolish the co-parenting relationship; rather, it was the queer subject's capacity to eliminate the involvement of a third biological or legal parent outside their intimate relationship, to negotiate with the uncertainties caused by state law, to secure financial resources in big cities, and to gain parental acceptance.

Developed from previous ethnographic chapters, Chapter 6 focuses on the changing understanding of family in urban China in the context of social changes, migration, and queer politics. I investigate the concept of '*jia*' (family/home) for Chinese non-heterosexual people through its cultural meanings and socio-legal meanings. This chapter unfolds the various modalities of the non-heterosexual family. By capturing the emerging family-forming practices and the image of the role-model rainbow family promoted in queer communities, I stress the dynamic interplay of socio-economic class, state law, and moral values that come to articulate queer families and relatedness in today's queer everyday lives. Moreover, I explore how these forms of queer families become visible or vague in different times and spaces and therefore complicate the assimilative–radical, visible–invisible, and modernity–traditional dualities in everyday life. I therefore suggest an approach to understanding the queer family that unsettles the hegemonic discourse on queer modernity.

Throughout this book, the two major types of moral discourse playing out in Chinese queer daily life cannot be discounted. The first discourse is arguably constructed by state policies and Confucian familism and is often referred to as the 'traditional' ideology. It suggests that one has no choice but to fulfil family duties through entering a heterosexual marriage, having biological offspring, and cultivating harmonious relationships with family elders. The second discourse is arguably constructed by Chinese LGBT/ *tongzhi* organizations and Western-originated coming-out politics and is often regarded as the 'modern' ideology. It asks that one firmly embraces a progressive queer lifestyle while being a responsible and good citizen. These two discourses seem to be in radical conflict with each other at first glance; however, the ethnographic chapters combined demonstrate how Chinese citizen subjects in queer relationships seek to navigate these moral dilemmas and ultimately unsettle dominant Chinese kinship norms. The various kin-making practices documented in this ethnography both reproduce and transgress the assumptions about biological parenthood and its centrality in family-forming processes.

1

Queering Research: Ethnography, Positionality, and Ordinary 'Queer'

I conducted my ethnographic research mainly in Shenzhen, Guangdong Province, China from June 2018 to July 2019. Additionally, I returned to Guangdong for a series of month-long follow-up fieldwork sessions and friend gatherings in 2020 and 2021. Doing ethnographic fieldwork allows me to depict the ongoing transformations in queer relationships. In this chapter, I delve into the intricate web of methodological and ethical challenges that arose during my research journey, detailing the various strategies and methodologies I employed to navigate these complexities in each stage. This chapter aims to offer a timely 'recipe' for conducting research in a sensitive setting, while realizing fieldwork as a partial, liminal experience.

I have used my queer networks, various Chinese social media platforms, and queer non-profit organizations as the main sources for recruiting research participants. My primary research methods encompassed participant observation and semi-structured interviews. I consider these methods to be interconnected, and I perceive the research 'field' as an expansive and unbounded space. Research data was also collected from legal documents, mass media, and online discussion on various social media platforms to help me locate my observations within the wider social and political context. My life experience as a Chinese and queer woman also complements this research. I use the term 'friend informants' throughout this book, meaning that I conduct research that is guided by the ethics of both ethnographic research and friendship. In this sense, I propose that we view friendship as a queer methodology. Finally, this chapter engages with the small but growing discussion on 'queering' social research and queer scholarships. Halberstam (1998) describes a queer methodology as a scavenger approach that employs diverse methods to gather and produce information on subjects 'who have been deliberately or accidentally excluded from traditional studies of human behavior' that seek to blend methods 'that are often cast as being at odds with each other, and it refuses the academic compulsion toward disciplinary coherence' (p 13). Thus, *Queer Kinship* endeavours to integrate methods that may or may not conform to conventional social research, offering insights into queer everyday practices that extend the realm beyond radical lifestyles and activism.

Locating participants

In correspondence with the focus on queer kinship practices, I came to Shenzhen to look for same-sex couples, gay and lesbian people in *xinghun* marriages, and queer parents. There were participants who met more than one criterion; for example, some were co-parenting with their opposite-sex *xinghun* partners (in a *xinghun* marriage) and dating same-sex partners simultaneously. As stated earlier, it is not helpful to ascribe the diverse forms of genders and sexualness to 'types of person' since sexual desire does not always inform interiority or the 'truth' about someone (Khanna, 2017). The idea of a mature, stable, and bounded knowledge of selfhood is problematic, for identities are 'multiple, ambiguous, shifting locations in matrices of power' (Kondo, 1990, p 26). Taking such fluidity and intangibility into account, I address individual friend informants with the term of their choice without assuming it is a universal identity category with clear boundaries. In this way, I do not propose to disavow sexual categories for all but rather to revalue the prevalence of sexuality-as-personhood in queer studies. Also, my research includes a diverse group of queer parents, including but not limited to same-sex couples who use assisted reproductive technologies (ARTs) to have children, gay–lesbian *xinghun* co-parents, and single and divorced queer parents.

At the beginning of the fieldwork, I posted a recruitment article on my WeChat[1] public account, explaining the aim and methods of my research and introducing myself as a queer researcher who aimed to make positive changes for Chinese gender and sexual minorities.[2] My friends and peers, including those who identify as straight, forwarded this article to their friends and chat groups. At the same time, I have been meeting regularly with my queer friends in Shenzhen and discussing my research with them. Although many of them joked that they were single and childless and not qualified to participate in my research, they introduced me to their friends. Thanks to my friends' referrals, I have had little problem with gaining trust and building rapport with participants whom I came to know in this way.

Although I had been socializing with queer women both online and offline in Shenzhen for years, I knew few who had children when I started this research. Few middle-aged queer couples and parents responded to my recruitment article. One reason for this was that most of my queer friends are in their 20s; to find queer parents, I had to reach out to non-heterosexual people older than me. Moreover, queer parents in China were widely believed to live in a relatively invisible status and were cautious about revealing their private lives to unrelated others. Many online queer parent chat groups are exclusively for non-heterosexual people who are either in the process of becoming parents or already have children, and the group chat administrators verify each member's parental status before letting them in. During the first phase of the fieldwork, I reached several micro-celebrity gay fathers and lesbian mothers who had been actively sharing their personal lives with followers on social media. Through their queer networks, I got to know more queer parents who were not 'out in public'. I also attended ten lesbian, gay, bisexual, and transgender (LGBT) social events to learn about queer parents and in-vitro fertilization (IVF)/surrogacy companies. Many of these events were held by PFLAG (Parents, Families, and Friends of Lesbians and Gays) China.[3] In addition, I paid regular visits to ART companies and had casual chats with employees during their free time. Eventually, not only queer employees but also the heterosexual-identified employees became acquainted with me.

Chinese mainstream social media platforms and same-sex socializing apps including *Sina Weibo*, *Douban*, *Lesdo*, *Rela*, and *BlueD*[4] also became sites to recruit potential participants. The pattern was repeated during the fieldwork: firstly, I joined a WeChat group and attended their group dinners or nights out; then, I introduced my research project and asked for their consent to participate in my research individually. Most people became warmer with me after knowing that I was not a journalist, and I was not writing headline stories using their actual names. Through repetitions of this pattern, I have found myself entering diverse queer social circles and meeting new friend informants from diverse backgrounds and age groups that I would never have met if I had not done this research. By the end of the fieldwork, the number of non-heterosexual people in my WeChat contact list expanded to 250, aged from 18 to 50 years old.

The major group of my research participants were non-heterosexual individuals who had migrated to major cities in Guangdong Province from other parts of mainland China. The fact that they left their hometown is a crucial social variable. Their experience migrating to a big city indeed interacted with their intimate and familial experiences. Many middle-aged participants in this research had achieved a higher social position and settled in Shenzhen or Guangzhou. Many of them saw themselves as middle class (*zhongchan jieceng*), an emerging and heterogeneous stratum in China made possible by privatization since the economic reform (for example, see Zhang, 2010). Drawing from a study on queer parents from middle-class and working-class backgrounds, Taylor (2010) reminds us of the persistent methodological challenge regarding the interconnection between sexuality and class when researching queer subjects. To understand ethnographically queer culture 'requires a willingness to de-naturalize the primacy of sexuality as a basis of individual identity – both desired and practiced versions'

(Engebretsen, 2008, p 89). Queer lives are not only sexualized and gendered but also classed; thus, we must not take queer subjects' social privileges or disadvantages for granted.

Overall, my queer network, which I have had for years, and the various social media platforms have been my major resources for finding research participants. In most circumstances, my role as a queer researcher was quickly acknowledged by potential participants, which smoothed the progress of introducing my research and asking for consent.

As a 'native' and as queer

As a queer female researcher who was born and raised in mainland China, this research is rooted in my life experience. I am a native ethnographer, an insider, and an outsider from many perspectives. Such positions are simultaneously beneficial and problematic. Anthropology began as the study of 'others'. The purpose of ethnography, to 'grasp the native's point of view, his relation to life, to realize his version of his world' (Malinowski, 1922, p 25), is often challenging to non-native anthropologies as they run the risk of never developing an intimate and inside understanding of the society. Yet, the easy assumption that native anthropologists' insider status is unproblematic has been overturned (Altorki and El-Solh, 1988; Fitzgerald, 1999; Davies, 2008). Narayan calls for work that melts down the insider–outsider divides and 'acknowledges the hybrid and positioned nature of our identities' (1993, p 682). Also, the emic and etic viewpoints are not necessarily conditioned by one's native identity and insider role; rather, they are dynamically shifting in the fieldwork's subject experience and consequently in the forms of knowledge that ethnographers produce. The underlying concept raised by Narayan is that the identity of an anthropologist – like any other – is 'shifting, multiplex, and situated in specific sociological and historical context' (Lewin and Leap, 1996, p 7).

My experience of 'being Chinese' and 'being queer' undoubtedly shapes my role, my motivation, and my subjectivity in my research. Growing up in China, the social norms were 'natural' to me. Such certainty was destabilized after I went overseas to obtain my bachelor's degree. Having experienced being a foreigner for years in Euro-American societies, the sense of otherness came to my understanding. Due to an increasing interest in the concept of 'culture' and the complexities it opens, I went to study social anthropology for a master's degree and continued to pursue doctoral studies. Those years of studying and working abroad have genuinely changed my understanding of 'nativeness' and 'foreignness', as I moved back and forth between China and other countries. I am aware that familiarity with a society is neither a privilege nor an obstacle to a native researcher. Ultimately, 'what is "home" and what is "abroad" is no longer always clear' (Eriksen, 2010, p 29).

Despite being in lesbian communities for years, I had struggled with 'picking' my role. I cannot count how many times people have tried to put me in a category such as a P ('*po*', or 'femme'), bisexual, or lesbian, so they might figure out how to talk with me in an appropriate manner. Yet, I recognize that these categories, such as tomboy (T)/P roles, are not seamlessly stable and often cause confusion. I will unpack this matter when I explore queer intimate relationships in the following chapter. Over the last years, meeting gender and sexual minorities in different cultural spaces and reading queer theory have constantly shaped my subject position within queer communities. Noticing how people around me understood and used these seemingly categorical terms differently also became my motivation to complete this research. That is why I use 'queer' to unsettle the over-categorization or false binaries. Instead of answering theoretically what these role categories in queer communities are, I am interested in exploring ethnographically what work these roles do in their everyday practices.

My personal experience indeed intersects with my development as a researcher and my objectives for fieldwork. I hope my research will contribute to academia as well as to my community, and this continues to be my aspiration. On the other hand, the risk of over-rapport needs to be carefully avoided, and the interconnections between gender, sexualness, and class in the field should be made visible. Ever since I started fieldwork, I have realized that sharing a similar cultural identity does not necessarily mean sharing similar experiences and values. Thus, I constantly felt partially an insider and partially an outsider. The purpose of including my autobiography is not to strengthen my authorship but to inform how my friend informants and I related to each other as both individuals and cultural categories in the field. Drawing from gay and lesbian anthropologists' experiences, Lewin and Leap suggest that 'in many contexts it is being an anthropologist that defines experience and identity even more than particular characteristics such as race, gender, or for that matter, sexual orientation' (1996, p 15). Therefore, my multiple cultural identities and the intersubjective relationship between me and my friend informants were taken into account at every research stage. I do not intend to conceal my subjectivity and involvement in fieldwork. To cite Callaway, 'her own life was her fieldwork' (1992, p 42). By allowing the ethnographer's self to investigate my life, I take a position as neither an authentic representative of my culture nor a detached observer.

Interviews and participant observation as interconnected methods

During my stay in Guangdong, I conducted 30 semi-structured, in-depth interviews. Interviews took place in cafes, restaurants, participants' offices, and apartments at their convenience. All interviews lasted for more than three hours as all friend informants came prepared to tell their life stories. I usually let the conversation unfold as open-endedly as possible. The flexible approach prioritized interviewees' interests and allowed me to notice emerging issues raised by them without losing the key research questions. People treated my research in different ways, and their motivations for participating varied. Some interviewees working in the ART industry invited me to their offices and, at least in my perception, our interviews were shaped by their desire to improve their moral image. Three interviewees encouraged me to use a voice recorder, and one of them hired cameramen and recorded the whole interview to put on his online portfolio. I did not use an audio recorder for most interviews and only had a notebook to write down shorthand notes. Since the interviews were conducted in Mandarin, I wrote down respondents' exact words in Chinese and translated them into English afterwards. For each interview, I wrote a diary as soon as I went back home. I sought to not only gather detailed lived experiences but also to reflect on the engaged interactions with friend informants (Hockey and Forsey, 2012, p 75). How did they choose to present their intimate and familial lives in an interview and what kinds of topics remained potentially challenging or unspoken? It became crucial to recognize the topics they liked to talk about and the topics they avoided in different circumstances and with different people. The interview has become a 'rehearsal of processes of covering and uncovering', and the work for the researcher has only just begun at the end of the interview (Strathern, 2012, p 266).

Moreover, recording narratives of interviewees' life histories was not only an essential part of this research but also represented a breakthrough in fostering closeness between myself and them. These in-depth interviews often worked unexpectedly as an entry point for a growing friendship. During each interview, I exchanged a great amount of my life history with interviewees, which allowed us to develop a rapport in a profoundly short period. There were moments when we found we shared similar struggles and exchanged useful information on various topics. Some friend informants joked, "now you know more about me than my family/friends!" and I often replied, "you too" with laughter. I was not a mere listener. Since many of them were older than me, they often treated me to a drink or a meal after the interview. This gave me an excuse to ask them out the next time to return the hospitality. The follow-up meetings allowed me to learn more details about their lives. By this means, they gradually became my long-term friend informants rather than one-time interviewees. Two interviewees agreed to do only a one-off interview, while we had each other's social media accounts and occasionally had small talks online. In other words, I did not stop gathering data right after an interview was completed; rather, the interview was a part of an ongoing participant observation for me, which continued to yield ethnographic knowledge (Skinner, 2012). For instance,

I have heard one of my friend informants, Tian, talking about his son on multiple occasions, including our first interview, an LGBT event, and casual get-togethers with his gay friends. On each occasion, Tian presented his familial life differently. The data I gathered in semi-structured interviews are therefore not set apart from data collected from other approaches.

During fieldwork, I participated in a wide range of formal and casual activities, including LGBT talkfests, group dinners, get-togethers, and karaoke nights. Participant observation represents the heart of anthropology and the defining tool for ethnographic fieldwork (Spradley, 1980; Schensul et al, 1999). This open-ended, reciprocal, and reflective method was the core of my research, as my goal was to explore my participants' everyday practices and their knowledge worlds in a coherent context rather than conducting selective learning. Specifically, the goal was to observe the ways they address their relatives, reflect on past events, employ kin terms, express affection and care for others, have children (or not), make living arrangements and spend holidays with their families of origin and chosen ties, invest in their future lives, and negotiate their practices with different moral values and state law.

To address my research goals and questions, I made weekly plans to spend time with friend informants closely by asking if they were interested in any leisure activities in their free time. Sometimes, it was the other way around when they asked me to join them or help them with their minor tasks. I made myself very flexible during my time in Shenzhen, so many friend informants were aware that I could show up and join them anytime. Having such time flexibility was indeed impressive to others in a booming city, where people are often too busy to make time for others. I accompanied them to their offices and shops, went shopping with them, and played with their kids. Moreover, regular online chats with key friend informants were had via WeChat as we gossiped and exchanged complaints about ex-partners, relatives, and house prices.

Before starting my fieldwork, I never thought that being in a relationship was going to be my entry ticket in numerous circumstances. The fact that I was not single implied a 'safe signal' that I would not go beyond the friend zone, becoming a potential threat to couples. I would not have been able to ask many of my female informants out individually without mentioning my girlfriend. It also occurred to me that since I 'looked like a *zhinv* (straight woman)' to some friend informants, my partner Jin's presence somehow assured my queerness to them. It also became evident that most queer couples would prefer to go out with other couples. I was told repeatedly that once a gay/lesbian found a partner, they would both disappear in the same-sex social worlds until they broke up. Quite a few queer couples affirmed with me that they only hung out with other queer couples because only these couples shared mutual topics with them. Thus, Jin always accompanied me when I went to meet a couple. At some point, she became as familiar with them as me, and we went on a few trips with queer couples. In the later phase of the fieldwork, I was in more frequent contact with five same-sex couples and four single queer parents.

Key themes and short notes were recorded on my mobile phone or in my notebook when I was with friend informants. I wrote diaries along with field notes to allow myself to reflect on my subjective experience and embodied knowledge. Reflexivity 'implied a conscious reflection on the interpretative nature of fieldwork, the construction of ethnographic authority, the interdependence of ethnographer and informant, and the involvement of the ethnographer's self in fieldwork' (Robben and Sluka, 2006, p 443). This means to be sensible about the tensions created by multiple taken-for-granted binaries that are not limited to everyday practice–theory, researcher–researched, insider–outsider, assimilative–resistant. Inspired by the Women's Liberation Movement in the 1970s, Okely contends that 'in an academic context the personal is theoretical' (1992, p 9). Fieldwork is undeniably an emotional and (inter)personal experience for the researcher and the researched. The lived interactions, participatory experience, and embodied knowledge that take place in fieldwork are both personal and theoretical. My field experience indicates that the relations between me and my friend informants were not constantly equal but rather shifting; so was my positionality. It is illusionary to think of the fieldworker's position as neutral, stable, detached, and out of cultural categories (Cohen, 1992; Okely and Callaway, 1992; Altork, 1995; Gearing, 1995). I came to understand that if I conducted fieldwork as a senior foreign researcher or as a man who identified as straight, I would still have done the research but it would have been different. My ethnicity, gender, age, class, and even relationship status affected the very way I viewed my research participants and the way they viewed me. The next section goes on to illustrate the interplay of queer methodologies and friendship, reflecting on my role as a friend researcher.

Queer friendship as (queer) methodology

Being treated as an ordinary queer woman and being included in my friend informants' social worlds was part of my fieldwork. In the last week of my fieldwork, Jin, myself, and two other *lala* women were invited to Joey's flat for a house-warming dinner. The five of us each brought some snacks and drinks. Just turned 30, Joey was in a *xinghun* marriage with a gay man. Joey and her *xinghun* husband agreed to live separately. Joey and the other two friends learned about and agreed to participate in my research after our first group meet-up. The second time I chatted with Joey, I asked her if she would like to participate in my research. Joey gave me her consent but not her full legal name. Just like my many other friends, Joey asked, "When will you be back in China? We will miss you terribly". After I said that I was going back to China in a few months for the winter vacation, Joey seemed relieved and reminded me to message her when I got back to China. During dinner, we gossiped about her new girlfriend, discussed recent news, and talked about the housing prices in the neighbourhood. Our conversation was like any conversation normally occurring among queer friends. There seemed to be no real boundary between social life and fieldwork, the researcher and the 'researched'.

Friendship and fieldwork are similar in many ways as we must gain entry, negotiate our roles and behaviours, participate, observe our involvement, and build reciprocal bonds in the world with others (Tillmann-Healy, 2003, p 732). As our connections grow stronger, we encounter challenges, conflicts, and moments of loss. We navigate through relational dialectics, balancing our level of privacy and openness, our individuality and togetherness, and our stability and change. Eventually, research projects and lives come to an end, requiring us to 'leave the field' (Tillmann-Healy, 2003, p 732; see also Rawlins, 1992).

Building on feminist and queer perspectives, Tillmann-Healy (2003) calls for 'friendship as method' that involves 'the practices, the pace, the contexts, and the ethics of friendship' (p 734). Owton and Allen-Collinson (2014) further suggest that 'friendship as method' is a methodological approach underpinned by the philosophy of friendship. In this book, I use the term 'friend informants' to describe my research approach, which integrates the ethics of ethnographic research with the ethics of queer friendship. First of all, my research is guided by the 2012 Ethics Statement of the American Anthropological Association.[5] I brought a consent form to every interview, detailing my research project and methods. Although many said that they trusted me and did not need the form, I sent a digital copy to everyone via email or WeChat. I explained the purpose of my research in detail to every potential participant and obtained their consent before moving to the next stage, letting them know that they could refuse to answer any question and quit at any time. I informed the administrator of each online chat group I joined about my research and let them decide on whether to grant me access. Research participants' personal information was securely protected and made anonymous in all documents. Three friend informants were queer-identified micro-celebrities themselves and acknowledged the use of their actual web names. Confidentiality and the informed consent process was ongoing; I mentioned my research whenever I hung out with friend informants, asking explicitly if I could write about specific conversations or events.

Moreover, I want to clarify that by moving towards friendship as methodology, I did not mean to foster a close relationship with every friend informant or get to know their inner secrets (Ellis, 2007) but to treat my friend informants as I would treat a queer friend – whom I share trust, a sense of alliance and vulnerability, respect, empathy, and support with. Friendship is indeed a vital, yet underexplored, element in queer ethnographic work. Building on Tillmann-Healy's (2003) and Owton and Allen-Collinson's (2014) works, I further propose that we conceptualize queer friendship as a methodological approach that we use to form queer sensibilities (Boyce et al, 2018), to reflect on our constant negotiation on roles and power dynamics, and to use our friend informants' stories for humane and just purposes (Tillmann-Healy, 2003).

Given that I had been making queer friends long before I decided to do this research, I understood why Chinese queer individuals could be more sensitive about revealing personal detail. In a get-together, one friend informant said she and her girlfriend never saw each other's IDs until they were together for a year. At that time, we were all using nicknames, and I was the only one who disclosed my job position and affiliated institute. Trust relationships among queer friends can be different from those among straight people, especially concerning issues around one's coming-out status (Tao, 2022). I had queer friends whose legal names I knew, visited their apartments and workplaces, and met their colleagues; establishing such rapport from online relationships often took months or even years. Thus, I never requested complete names from friend informants just as I would not anticipate such information from a queer friend. In other words, not knowing/asking each other's names did not prevent us from building trusting relationships; in some contexts, it worked the opposite way. It was having many local queer friends that raised issues of trust, as some potential participants no longer perceived me as a detached researcher who would safeguard their confidentiality. Instead, they viewed me as a friend who might share their secrets with mutual acquaintances. To address this, I expanded my social network as widely as possible and avoided confining myself to a single social circle.

While the friendship as method approach has proved to encourage dialogical relationships between the researcher and participants, I must also acknowledge the challenges it generates (Owton and Allen-Collinson, 2014). Fieldwork is a form of emotional labour, and so is friendship. In most meet-ups, people generally showed much more interest in my story with Jin than abstract research topics. I needed to be mentally prepared to hear any comment or advice on my relationships with Jin and our future plans. Many of my friend informants were older than me and had a considerable income, which positioned them in a relatively high social position. For non-heterosexual people in *xinghun* marriages and those with children, Jin and I were a younger queer couple who would sooner or later be in a similar situation. I frequently received advice on how to maintain a long-lasting relationship and how to raise children together. Although I could tell that they felt relatively relaxed and talkative, some of their advice was hard for me to cope with. For example, a friend informant tried to persuade me to find a gay man for a *xinghun* marriage after I said I would not marry a gay man. In another case, a queer couple tried to encourage me to have children as soon as possible because my uterus "couldn't wait" and "I would regret not having offspring". In such circumstances, I chose to express myself instead of being an acquiescent junior note taker. In this way, we could enter into a dialogue (Gusterson, 1997). Through my effort to negotiate my role as a queer fieldworker and a queer friend, my relationships with them were also shifting, and we gradually learned much more from each other outside the scope of this research.

After making a considerable number of new queer friend informants in Shenzhen and the surrounding areas, I inevitably acquired more roles. For single, non-heterosexual people, I was a reliable matchmaker. I also became a matchmaker for queer friendship in the way I organized gatherings where queer intended parents and co-parents could come together and connect over shared experiences. "So, what do they (other non-heterosexual people) do?" was frequently asked in casual conversations. Some friend informants asked me to use my research findings to persuade their same-sex partners to come out to their parents. Negotiation of roles became particularly difficult when some friend informants working in the ART industry tried to encourage me to recommend their IVF/surrogacy service to potential clients. When two queer intended parents did ask me if I knew local ART agencies, I said yes but warned them about the legal risks of using these agencies. As a friend researcher, I am aware that negotiating with these emotional, ethical, and even legal complexities requires honesty, empathy, and sensibilities.

After my fieldwork for this research project came to an end, I remained in touch with most of my friend informants and continue to learn about the major events in their lives. In April 2023, one lesbian friend who became a mother in 2022 started a conversation by saying, "I encountered a problem – do you need my case of same-sex co-parenting, or just gossip/chat about it?" I replied, "I am doing fieldwork on other topics now, but yes, I am concerned and would like to know if I can help. Let's chat about it!"

'Partial' data; 'partial' field

As mentioned previously, my research data consist of field notes and diaries, interview transcripts, government publications, media reports, personal blogs, online posts, and photos. The fieldwork data are partial and unruly and should not be interpreted as social truths (Tyler, 1986; Strathern, 2004; Davies, 2008). The question to address, then, is how I make sense of the incompleteness of data I collected and make visible my theoretical pathway through the data.

Fieldwork is a liminal experience, and it is of crucial importance to make sense of liminality (Johnson, 1984). This involves acknowledging the major barriers to reflective subjectivity such as age, gender, and professional status (Fitzgerald, 1999). Although I conducted as many interviews with queer men as with queer women, most of my key friend informants were women. I spent a lot more leisure time with queer women than men as it was easier for me to build rapport with women and join their daily social activities. Besides, I was aware that the fact I did not have children restricted my access to the social groups of queer parents. Such othering was especially obvious when participants put, "you will understand me when you have children". Most of the queer parents willing to participate in this research were middle-class individuals known for being 'successful' queer parents, and queer parents from the working class remained under-researched in this book. These limitations are critically examined along with the data. After all, valid ethnographic accounts can be produced 'without complete participation and total acquisition of local knowledge by ethnographers so long as they honestly examine, and make visible in their analysis, the basis of their knowledge claims in reflexive experience' (Davies, 2008, p 104).

Furthermore, the data I collected are not interpreted as if they are from a self-contained field site. For me, the idea of a physically and temporally bounded field was especially problematic. Did I leave my field site when I finished dinner with my queer friends? Did my fieldwork simply exclude the moments when I went out with my straight friends in Shenzhen? This confusion arose once when one of my straight friends mentioned her interest in the American TV show *Queer Eye* and played a short video clip while we were in a foot spa room; the masseurs stared at our screen for a while and abruptly asked, "are these sissy (*niang*) guys *tongxinglian* (homosexual)? Are *tongxinglian* all like that?" Realizing the masseurs were making fun of the queer hosts in the show, my friend and I stopped watching it, and we both felt uncomfortable. After we walked out of the spa centre, my friend said, "you were too nice trying to explain to them; you knew what these kinds of guys were gonna say". Like my other queer friends, she further linked homophobic attitudes to class position. We knew that *tongxinglian* was still stigmatized as a mental disorder in school textbooks and linked with HIV on media platforms. I could not help relating this to my friend informants' endorsement of public tolerance towards homosexuality in big cities. When my friend informants contended that urban China is tolerant towards homosexuality, what space and people did they really refer to? Our everyday interactions with all other individuals (besides queer participants) imply multiple lived realities that cannot be neglected as irrelevant to research. Taking an intersectional approach, I examine Chinese social policies, media reports, and online posts to situate queer personal life within the wider social-economic and political context (Hildebrandt, 2018; Mills, 2018).

Queer as 'ordinary' folks

Queer theory emerges as a critique that resists not only the normativity of heterosexuality but also a wider field including research methodology. The 'studies' of 'queer studies' itself might act less like a noun/adjective and more like a verb (Boellstorff, 2010, p 215). To what extent can we say a methodology is queered? In discussing the writing of ethnography, Hastrup (1992) reveals the inherently hierarchical relationship between the researcher and the researched. No matter how equal and intimate we are in the field, it is me, the anthropologist, who reframes informants' stories into text with my choice of fieldwork materials. On the one hand, we are encouraged to study queer theory as radical, transgressive, resistant, and anti-normative. On the other hand, what counts as normative and what counts as transgressive in the production of queer scholarship might already be normalized (Wilson, 2006; Lewin, 2016; Weiss, 2016). So are the questions of who the queer people worth studying are and what the queer practices worth documenting, theorizing, praising, or criticizing are.

It should be reiterated that I deliberately chose not to use Chinese LGBT organizations and activists as the entry point for my field research since I was aware of the visible disparity between queer activists' social networks and non-heterosexual people's everyday 'ordinary' social circles in mainland China. As mentioned earlier, it is vital to avoid seeing research participants as belonging to a static social category. The multilayered interplay of social status, gender norms, and sexualness are taken into consideration, as my friend informants' experiences of queer relationships intersect with their experiences of being in diverse dynamic social groups. It is rooted in my tacit knowledge not to view them as generalizable. Although this research benefited from my attendance at LGBT events and my connection with employees and volunteers in LGBT organizations, the everyday kinship practice which formed a major part of my observation was rarely considered activism-related; neither were my friend informants' practices always encouraged in queer activist communities.

As a researcher who decided to study non-heterosexual intimate and familial life in urban China, I quickly found my friend informants to be different from the queer activists depicted in most queer scholarship, perhaps in an unexciting way. For example, few of my friend informants showed interest in the annual LGBT pride parade in Hong Kong despite Shenzhen being less than an hour's train trip from Hong Kong. In November 2016, I went to the Hong Kong pride parade with four university students majoring in humanities and social sciences. In November 2018, I travelled to Hong Kong with Jin and a curious lesbian couple, Alice and Fiona. The young couple lost patience before the pride parade officially began and left to go shopping. When we reunited in a bar at night, Fiona said, "we thought it would be joyful, but it felt serious; also, the speech is boring". I asked if they would like to participate in a pride parade again, and they shook their heads. The pride simply does not make sense to them. Jin agreed with them, and they concluded that "such events are for activists and researchers like you, not for us".

When I talked to queer individuals who actively participated in queer public events and those who did not, I often noticed antagonistic sentiments as if the two groups viewed themselves as coming from very different worlds. Queer couples and parents I met during the fieldwork often claimed that they were 'ordinary people' (*putong ren*) and wanted to "focus on practical things rather than political things". Many of them might have watched *The L Word* and *Call Me by Your Name*, but few knew (or cared about) the Chinese queer filmmakers and activists who frequently appeared in English media. They showed up at LGBT events for pragmatic reasons such as finding dates and seeking advice for coming out to parents and sustaining same-sex relationships. I often felt that a discussion of LGBT rights (and civil rights in general) was unwelcome in an online same-sex chat group because such topics were considered 'sensitive' (*mingan*), 'boring', or 'radical'. When queer activists quickly responded and took action in most oppressive events during my fieldwork, my friend informants seemed silent and indifferent. Even when the 'les' and relevant topics were being removed from major Chinese social media platforms in April 2019, many of my friend informants did not demonstrate any anger or concern. They showed little interest in LGBT rights and online protests. Yet, it did not mean that queer ordinary people believed social and political factors had less influence on their intimate and familial lives. In today's China, politics is indeed a sensitive topic, and people only felt comfortable talking about it with their most familiar ones. For most Chinese people, social and political factors would not change for them, but they could change themselves to secure better living arrangements. Non-heterosexual people's ambivalent responses to sexual rights reveal the 'complex relationships between sexual subjectivity, economy, law, the state, and people's most intimate aspirations' (Boyce, 2014, p 1201).

Unlike the 'ordinary' non-heterosexual folks, many queer activists and queer organization volunteers despised the practice of *xinghun* marriage and blamed non-heterosexual people who entered heterosexual marriages as damaging the overall moral image of Chinese sexual minorities. Some queer women further condemned the use of surrogacy. A feminist scholar friend once suggested that I reframe some narratives to avoid making non-heterosexual people look worse than heterosexual people. Occasionally, one of my friend informants would find out that I interviewed another queer person they knew and say, "You should not be studying them!" However, neither the most transgressive queer activist networks nor the everyday 'ordinary' in China should be depicted as representative of Chinese

LGBT/queer experience. The point of anthropological discourse is not 'how to make a better representation, but how to avoid representation' (Tyler, 1986, p 128). Also, there should not be a representative Chinese heterosexual experience.

Rather than ranking the moral worth of each and excluding the 'not queer enough' people out of the scope of queerness or queer studies, I seek to understand how my friend informants know what they know, their needs and struggles, and their key theories of life (Franklin, 2019). We must recognize that to be transgressive or to be assimilative within society is not an available choice and is 'not easily practiced and achieved; rather they are complexly inhabited and refused, structured and reproduced' (Taylor, 2010, p 75). When we deem one group more 'radical/resistant/transgressive' and the other more 'conservative/assimilative/normative', we erase the possibilities of exploring the complexity of their lived realities. Following Lewin's and other queer anthropologists' reminder to 'base our conclusions on what our informants say and do, rather than using what our informants say and do to sustain already formulated ideas' (2016, p 604), this book aims to avoid universalizing queerness solely as an overt resistance to dominant institutions and norms. If I limited my participants to people who engaged with queer movements and LGBT rights, or those who were wealthy and successful, I would not be able to realize the everyday practices of queer subjects that unintentionally mobilized and queered the dominant kinship knowledge in their society. What shall be reconsidered in queer lifeworlds and research is the seemingly bounded ordinary–queer or transgression–assimilation dichotomies. By exploring how Chinese non-heterosexual individuals make and reflect on their life choices and relationships in different times and moral landscapes, the following chapters articulate a dynamic understanding of queer kinship in contemporary Chinese societies.

2

Queering Intimacy: 'Just-as-Married' Same-Sex Relationships

When I first posted a recruitment article saying I was looking for queer couples to participate in my research, my friends and a lot of other people who read my post asked, "I have a girlfriend/boyfriend now, but our relationship is not stable (*wending*) yet. Do we qualify to participate in your research if we are not yet like a married couple?" Some of them did not live with their partners, some had not come out to their parents, and some did not think they had the financial independence to make their own decisions without parental interference. Many of them would message me whenever they met a same-sex couple whom they thought were stable (*wending*).

The first time I met Mo and Lin, they introduced themselves as "a *lala* couple in a stable relationship". This statement gave me many assumptions about them that were toppled later. I was surprised when I soon learned that Lin was in a marriage with a straight man and had an 8-year-old son in her hometown. On the other hand, Lin had arranged to disconnect herself from her legal 'husband' physically and financially. Lin's account, which will be detailed in this chapter, proves that even the living arrangements of heterosexual married couples might vary. What, then, is a 'just-as-married' same-sex couple like? As I learned more and more details about their life experiences, I noticed the concept of a 'stable relationship' could be elastic and consolidated among my friend informants' minds. Intimacy has indeed become a crucial yet ambivalent practice in modern life. As Berlant (1998) points out, stories of the intimate are inseparable from stories about citizenship, capitalism, aesthetics, political violence, and historical narratives (p 288). Lee (2014) further suggests that the notion of romantic love in today's Chinese society may be the 'most privileged trope of modern stranger sociality' linked with the sense of modernity (p 274). In this regard, the everyday serves as a site for critically reading and interpreting not just love but also modernity (Boym, 1994, p 21; see also Manalansan, 2003).

This chapter explores the practices of same-sex intimacy in relation to the shifting understandings of role terms, love, online sociality, modernity, and mutuality/*jiban*. It firstly articulates non-heterosexual people's changing attitudes towards same-sex relationship modes and the seemingly gendered role terms. Then, it goes on to document queer couples' existing strategies for seeking, negotiating, and sustaining their loving relationships when same-sex marriage is not in China yet. The key to a 'just-as-married' same-sex relationship is creating unbreakable *jiban* (mutual burden, mutuality), which will be discussed throughout the book. In a manner akin to Patel's (2007) exploration of insurance as a 'technology of risk', my intention is to closely examine 'a series of financial practices that tie people to the ways in which it is possible for them to visualize and fantasize a life future' (p 100), one that is shared by queer couples. It should not be discounted that queer couples in this ethnography were heterogeneous in terms of their age, educational background, and social status, and therefore their attitudes and practices need to be apprehended within their social context. Belonging to the most prominent economic hubs and migrant-attracting cities, Shenzhen and Guangzhou were desirable sites to explore non-heterosexual people's migration experiences and urban utopian imaginaries.

Beyond categorial roles: a partner in life rather than a partner in bed

It was difficult to neglect the frequent use of role terms '1/0/0.5/T/P/H' in Chinese queer social spaces. The term 'T' stands for 'tomboy', and 'P' is short for '*Po*' (female), or 'pretty girl'. In this sense, 'T' and 'P' appear to be two role terms complementary to each other. Likewise, 1/0 jargons were widely used in gay communities. The term '1' graphically indicates an inserter, and the term '0' graphically indicates a circle inserted in bed. '1' is equivalent to '*gong*' (top, literally meaning 'attack'), and '0' is equivalent to '*shou*' (bottom, literally meaning 'receive'). The 1–0 model thus reflects a sense of binary opposition of sexual roles, both graphically and linguistically. The T–P relationship model and the 1–0 relationship model in same-sex communities arose in mainland China years later than the butch–femme structure in the United States and the tomboy–femme structure in Southeast Asia. They first emerged as popular subcultures in Taiwan and then rapidly prevailed in the queer communities in mainland China through the internet. They became jargons, sex roles, subcultures, and performative styles (Chao, 1999; Engebretsen, 2008; Ho, 2010; Kong, 2010; Kam, 2013; Wang, 2020). The 1/0 roles and the T/P roles have been studied by numerous researchers from both inside and outside China. These terms might be used to indicate one's (stereotypically gendered) dressing style, sexual preference, temperament, and dependency in a same-sex relationship. Some found the T/P and 1/0 roles reflected stereotypically gendered personalities as informed by heterosexuality or Chinese patriarchy (Chen, and Chen, 2007; Li, 2007; Zheng, 2015). Yet, such discourses risk neglecting some foundational discourses on the production of gender norms and heteronormativity. Kennedy and Davis (1992) point out that while butch–femme relations shared resonances with heterosexual relations, they challenged heterosexuality and heteronormativity. Butler (1990, 1993) points out that the idea of imitation suggests that heterosexual is the 'origin' that is copied by the homosexual, whereas the originality of heterosexuality is in doubt. If the seeming distinction between masculinity and femininity is constituted to limit the performative possibilities outside the restricted frame of gender identities, it is oversimplifying to describe the T's masculine dressing style as an imitation of men or the 0's stereotypically feminine behaviours as an imitation of women. Furthermore, the role categories change over time, with new trends constantly emerging in the queer community. For instance, the 'H/0.5/*bufen*' (versatile, not classified) role has become popular in recent years within Chinese queer communities, while 1–0 and T–P relationship models have been losing their predominance among urban queer youth.

It is worth noting that people who employed '1/0/0.5/T/P/H' included not only self-identified gays and lesbians but multiple forms of non-normative genders and sexualness. For example, Feng told me that when he learned the definition of 'transgender' at a lesbian, gay, bisexual, and transgender (LGBT) salon, he realized that he fitted into the category of a transgender man after presenting himself as a *ye* (manly) T-lesbian for 30 years. Feng explained that he never felt comfortable with his female body, and he desired to be seen as a man. In the meantime, he did not completely stop using *ye* T to describe himself and still blended in well in lesbian social circles. According to Feng, this change did not have any effect on his life, including his work and romantic relationship. His peers and his girlfriend, who had lived with him for 12 years, had always called him 'Uncle Feng' (*Feng Shu*), and that would not change no matter what his gender and sexual identity were. His girlfriend, who used to think of herself as totally straight (*zhi*), started to introduce herself to others as bisexual/*ku'er* (queer) after falling in love with him. Feng and his girlfriend's account was just one example where the boundary sense of gender and sexual identification was deconstructed. Until the end of my fieldwork, most transgender people remained invisible in China. The public frequently misconceived transgender people as homosexuals, and transgender individuals would often have to seek intimate relations in the alleged lesbian and gay communities. Huang (2015) complicates the T and transgender identity in Chinese lesbian culture and suggests that we understand T beyond the lesbian–transgender binary. Also, bisexual and sexually fluid people often employed 1/0/0.5/T/P/H to introduce themselves when seeking partners, thus expanding the role terms beyond the domain of gay and lesbian subcultures in China.

Against this backdrop, I conceptualize these terms as flexible epistemologies and social practices that encompass a diverse range of sexual and gender practices. Borrowing from Povinelli's analysis of radical fairies, it is not desirable to define these seemingly categorical and gendered terms and then find those who fit the definition. Instead, we need to understand the modes of life across which these categories are 'dispersed, contested, and made sensible' (Povinelli, 2006, p 109). This book focuses on kinship practices and does not intend to delve deeper into the discussion on role terms and gender performativity (which has been extensively studied); rather, it is concerned with what they do within queer dating and socializing cultures and wider kinship practices.

For those who recognized the proliferating T/P/H/1/0/0.5 roles and their mouldability in same-sex relationships, interactions with people who still understood T/P and 1/0 roles in a binary and stereotypically gendered logic became problematic. People who employed 'H', '0.5', and *'bufen'* were relatively younger and saw themselves as embracing global same-sex dating cultures. Moreover, shifting attitudes towards female masculinity and male femininity in recent years are observable. *Tie* (literally meaning iron, referring to queer women who do not like to be touched erotically) T and *mu* (literally meaning mother, effeminate) 0 were not only regarded as unpopular in the dating pool but obvious female masculinity and male femininity were further stigmatized as lowbrow, linked to the Chinese discourse of low quality (*suzhi*). By contrast, lesbian femininity and gay masculinity occupied a more accepted and favourable position (Wang, 2020; Kong; 2021). Yina, a lesbian friend informant, claimed, "How can I be with a woman who looks and behaves like a man? We should date each other as lesbians, not as heterosexual people". In her words, female masculinity, similar to male effeminacy, was described as gender unconformity and therefore degraded to lesbian inauthenticity. The argument that the rigid T–P relationship was just the same-sex version of the traditional heterosexual relationship was used by many young queer women who spoke against the T–P model. The trend for seeing T/P roles as more traditional and lower class did not just occur in Chinese society but in other Asian societies as well (Blackwood, 2005; Boellstorff, 2007a).

In recent years, an increasing number of gay men and lesbians have viewed the 1–0 and T–P as outdated and undesirable relationship models and tried to abandon them to a certain extent. Eric, a 24-year-old gay man, said:

> 'Though I dislike such simple categorization, I need to use it at some point when I am about to go to bed with someone who only acknowledges the 1–0 logic. If you don't specify your roles in the gay dating app, you simply get filtered by other users. Unless you don't

want a sex life, you cannot avoid using 1–0 terms as gay. However, I try to leave 1–0 roles to sexual life and avoid bringing them to everyday life. You know, even if I were a heterosexual man, I would not want my wife to stay at home without a job.'

Eric's words reflect many young queer individuals' attitudes towards the role terms, as they found them disturbing rather than useful when using same-sex dating apps.

Danny, a 29-year-old T-lesbian woman, mobilized T-ness beyond a visible masculine gender style when interviewed:

'I used to have short hair and an obvious manly T style as I felt I had to be like men to date women. My ex-girlfriend made me realize that she liked me even if I dressed feminine. I have long hair now and still attract Ps. As I grew older and got into a serious relationship, the T–P binary became too *biaomian* (superficial) for me.'

Danny's description of T/P roles as *biaomian* could be interpreted in two ways. *Biaomian* literally means 'surface' or 'superficial', which implies that T/P roles are not linked with one's inner feeling of self. Also, *biaomian* indicates that the T/P roles only seem to be fixed truths, while they can be easily broken or adjusted. Danny used the discourse of *biaomian* to mobilize the T/P roles beyond an observable masculinity–femininity binary as she chose to make her T-ness less obvious without it affecting her lesbianism. Billy and her P girlfriend lived in Billy's apartment with Billy's parents. Billy had her own business and did not require her girlfriend to earn an income. Instead, she was satisfied that her girlfriend was more than willing to cook for her. In other words, for Billy and Danny, the fundamental trait of being a desirable T had shifted away from observable masculine styles to more delicate and flexible practices which could be negotiated in same-sex conjugal relationships. Billy's and Danny's accounts suggest that T/P roles are relationally apprehended and practised in queer relationships.

The innovative use of 1/0/0.5/T/P/H-related slang in queer communities further shows their elasticity. Ben, a self-identified gay man studying sociology at a university in Guangzhou, told me he would rather say he was 0.75. He explained: "Although I like to be 1 (top) in bed, I don't want to miss good guys just because they are not 0. After all, dating is not just about sex". Ben also described his ex-boyfriends as positioned somewhere between 0 and 0.5. In Ben's case, the 1–0 binary was merely an issue in bed, and he needed to mobilize such a binary because he desired a life partner rather than a sex partner.

In short, queer subjects' attitudes towards same-sex relationship modes and their use of role terms were diverse and elastic. As these role terms in queer intimate relationships proliferated from absolute binary to diverse blends, such a trend has also inevitably produced a hierarchy of same-sex relationship models. Younger non-heterosexual people emphasized that same-sex relationships should be equal and interdependent in terms of emotional, sexual, and economic roles. They also showed a tendency to delink their sexual roles from division of labour in their domestic lives. Many criticized the T–P and 1–0 relationships as being informed by traditional Chinese gender culture while celebrating the versatile (*bufen*) couples as being infused with modern gay and lesbian culture. Yet, such arguments also revealed the tendency to perceive heterosexual relationships in a timeless and fixed model in which the man/husband was dominant and caring and the woman/wife was submissive and dependent. In this sense, heterosexual relationships, like T–P and 1–0 relationships, were reduced to abstract discourses similar to what Danny described as *biaomian* (superficial, ostensible). Regardless of roles they identified with, queer couples in this book have demonstrated a capacity to be fluid in practising conjugal relations, *xinghun* marriages, (co-)parenting, and family formation.

Seeking true love, avoiding 'counterfeit' people

It should be unsurprising that among the 20 same-sex couples I interviewed, over half of them found their partners through social media. Meeting new friends and dates within online sociality modes has become increasingly common for non-heterosexual people in first-tier cities like Shenzhen. Nowadays, one could connect with fellow queer people online through either mainstream Chinese social media platforms such as *Weibo*, *Tieba*, or *Douban* or through same-sex exclusive dating/socializing apps such as *BlueD* and *Rela*.

In Shenzhen alone, there were at least five gay bars and four lesbian bars by 2018. However, according to accounts from my friend informants, the prospect of finding true love through chance encounters at bars or nightclubs was considered unreliable (*bu kaopu*). This sentiment was not limited to just Chinese queer communities; it was a prevailing notion in Chinese society at large. Many mentioned that they rarely or never consumed drinks at gay and lesbian bars. Some had visited such venues out of curiosity, only to be disappointed by the tasteless music and performances, as well as an atmosphere they perceived as excessively promiscuous. For most friend informants, bars and nightclubs were primarily seen as spaces for fun nights or casual erotic encounters rather than committed relationships. Some also voiced complaints about the perceived lack of manners exhibited by the gay/lesbian waitstaff, whom they often viewed as lacking in education. This claim echoes the findings of other studies that highlight the complexities of cultural and social hierarchies within queer communities (Rofel, 2007;

Kong, 2010; Bao, 2018; Wei, 2020). Still, neither gay clubs nor queer film clubs can provide a full grasp of queer cultures in contemporary China (Wei, 2020, p 154). This prompts an exploration of how these social sites, especially the digital communities, have shaped the perceptions and experiences of same-sex intimacies.

Before the exploration of same-sex (online) dating practices, a few words must be said of the context of personal interactions and social trust in Chinese society. Traditionally, Chinese society was organized through different types of social circles where the individual's moral duties were specifically identified in accordance with their positionality in each social relation (Fei, 1992). In such a world of acquaintances, people relied on personal trust cultivated from long-term interactions within their social circles. In this sense, one's reputation and moral worth were relationally defined mainly through kin ties and local work networks. The rapid modernization and increased geographical mobility in China resulted in increasing interactions among strangers who shared no past (Yan, 2011; Lee, 2014), thus creating prevalent trust concerns within society. Such rapid changes in Chinese social life are closely associated with the shifting ethical discourse and moral panic about stranger sociality. The rising online dating fraud cases in recent years[1] suggest that online anonymity and stranger sociality have inevitably created trust concerns in the domain of virtual romance. That is to say, individuals are worried about counterfeit goods as well as 'counterfeit people'. As Liu (2016) notes, researching social media through the lens of sexuality could reveal the complex interconnections between political, cultural, economic, and 'private' realms of intimacy.

Real-time, location-based, heterosexual dating apps such as *Momo* are often characterized as hook-up sites which serve the purpose of *yuepao* (getting laid with strangers) in mainstream culture. The reputation of being a *yuepao* app is linked with the low possibility of finding a 'high-quality' (*suzhi*) partner that one may develop a serious relationship with (Liu, 2016; see also Wei, 2020). The hegemonic discourse of *suzhi* is embodied in the figure of the urban middle-class citizen (Anagnost, 2004; Kipnis, 2007). Among queer men in Beijing, the language of 'low quality' is always targeted at money boys who are from rural China and are believed to have no morals (Ho, 2008). For my friend informants, *suzhi* encompasses one's cultural, physical, and moral 'qualities' which one must carefully assess before entering serious relationships. Same-sex apps like *Lesdo* have added 'community' features similar to forums in recent years, as they strived to look less like a hook-up site and more like a virtual cultural space similar to *Douban* and other web forum-based queer spaces. Yet, one may realize that everything online can be falsified, from profile photos and age to education and marital status.

I met Sally in April 2019 only shortly after she ended her three-month relationship with her ex and came back to the lesbian social circles to seek a potential girlfriend. In Shenzhen gay or lesbian-themed chat groups, it is a common practice to organize offline gatherings on a regular basis, allowing members to meet face to face. The main but often unspoken intention behind these offline social events is to potentially find a romantic partner. These meet-ups usually involve casual dinners and may progress to visits to bars or KTV (karaoke) rooms. At a dinner with several other *lala* friends, Sally, a 33-year-old lesbian, shared her experience, mentioning how she was intentionally approached by her ex-girlfriend in one such group due to her respectable job and property ownership in the city centre. Their first in-person encounter ended with a kiss, leading to an intimate relationship where they frequently visited each other's residences. However, Sally soon found out her ex-girlfriend was involved with other lesbians and was using her financially. Reflecting on her dating experience, Sally also recounted her high school crush. Her first girlfriend was a classmate, and their relationship continued for six years until they graduated and went their separate ways for work. Subsequently, Sally's colleague became her second girlfriend, and they lived together for two years. Both Sally's first and second girlfriends were married to heterosexual men in recent years, and Sally called them '*zhinv*' (straight women). Although Sally referred to her earlier relationships with her first and second girlfriends as pure love with a nostalgic undertone, she admitted that she did not want to be hurt by *zhinv* anymore, and her only option was to use online social media platforms to find a lesbian-identified partner. Sally remained critical of meeting same-sex dates online:

> 'I know my first girlfriend so well, but my ex is still like a stranger to me now. I shouldn't trust her so quickly. You thought you knew the person as you talked with each other online, but you might find out she was faking her personal characteristics once you were in a relationship.'

Sally's attitude towards online dating reflects the ambiguous boundary between the traditional kinship networks and the stranger sociality in industrialized societies (Lee, 2014), that is, one could not consult any mutual acquaintance or authority member about another stranger's socio-economic background and moral worth. Although I have heard many touching, successful love stories from my key friend informants, I have to admit that I heard many more bitter stories within queer communities. In some cases, the other one lied about their educational background and job; in other cases, the other one hid their heterosexual marriage.

Another extreme example to illustrate the trust crisis in queer dating culture is *Shazhu Pan* (pig-butchering scam), which refers specifically to an emerging type of online fraud in which swindlers attempt to gain the trust of victims through a romantic relationship before tricking them into financing traps. In their training material, the swindlers used 'pigs' to refer to their targets, which were slaughtered after being fatted. While the official news websites have reported many *Shazhu Pan* frauds since 2019, all reported victims are heterosexual. Online love scams among queer people attract little attention from the public and the police. During my fieldwork in 2019, this was a story spreading in the major online lesbian communities. A woman who claimed to be P and working in Shenzhen met several Ts from a lesbian-themed forum and became girlfriends with them after they met offline. This woman then pretended to suffer serious family crises and borrowed money from these Ts from time to time. A few months later, one of her T girlfriends found out that her job title and family background had been falsified. The T victim immediately exposed this woman to multiple online forums. The story became heated as other T victims of this fraud showed up one by one to expose the P swindler. A T-identified lesbian concluded, "Of course homosexual people like us are the target of love fraud. We are lonely and desperate for love and pretty girls! All swindlers need to do is to post a fake photo and wait for us to swallow the bait!" Other than borrowing money, there were a lot more examples of *Shazhu Pan* frauds. Some online discussants claimed the swindlers persuaded them to invest in their fictitious commodities or play the lottery in made-up websites. The money involved in the online love frauds ranged from several hundred to millions. Hardly any of the victims got their money back due to inadequate evidence and incomplete policies regarding online fraud. When our queer friends heard that Jin and I met each other through *Douban* in 2017, they all said, "You are lucky; *Douban* forum is full of scams now!"

Fu (2015) has explored the gay social sites in Shenyang which changed from urban public spaces in the 1980s to consumer-driven spaces in the 21st century. Same-sex desires in the old days were characterized as 'simple' and 'nice' when one did not have to worry about property safety or health risks. Same-sex desire in the last decade has been regarded as dangerous when male–male sex consumption, swindling activities, and HIV/AIDS risks visibly increased. While Fu's research does not focus on gay and lesbian social media platforms, online and offline interactions are inseparable and equally valid in queer daily life. Similar to Fu's respondents, a few queer individuals in this research blamed the capitalist system as the main reason behind the lowering of the moral bottom line and the loss of trust among strangers. The development of the private sector since the reform era and the emergence of individualization has inevitably created losers and winners; as a result, most Chinese individuals 'had to internalize the negative impacts of individualization by assuming more responsibilities, experiencing greater uncertainty and risk, and working harder' (Kleinman et al, 2011, p 15). Queer people seeking romantic relationships, in this case, had to learn to recognize suspicious behaviour and be vigilant crime fighters themselves since the market economy did not offer any viable solution to the moral crisis. Being involved in fraud or extortion was understood as an example of extreme immoral behaviour by most Chinese people, but, unfortunately, it had a very negative impact on personal trust in their social worlds. As Rege (2009) notes, online love scams disrupt one's sense of trust in themselves, potential online dates, and the overall online networking experience.

In short, the idea of seeking romantic partners from online platforms evoked manifold uncertainties and risks in Chinese society, queer and straight alike. Generationally, the concerns about same-sex dating have increasingly shifted from exposing one's sexuality to public judgement to being taken advantage of emotionally and financially (see also Fu, 2015). Certainly, queer individuals have developed a range of strategies to identify and guard against suspicious behaviour and 'counterfeit' people. For instance, I have noted an increasing presence of matchmakers within same-sex communities, a phenomenon that is only possible in large urban centres. As many of my friend informants stated, they have chosen to move to the big city for both career and romantic opportunities. Contrasted with their hometowns, these cities are home to a larger population of young, well-educated (therefore deemed as high-quality/*suzhi*) queer individuals. Moreover, given that many queer migrants are distanced from their families of origin, there is a reduced likelihood of encountering individuals who present themselves with fake profiles or photos.

Negotiating love: 'normative past', 'queer present'?

Zhao was born in 1980 in Jiujiang, Jiangxi Province. He started teaching at an elementary school after graduating from teacher-training college. He had worked at the school for 13 years. He told me he was working at one of the best elementary schools in the Jiangxi Province. His position at the public school was considered extremely *wending* (stable). However, Zhao felt his work routine in his hometown was getting dull and found "no hope" there. He realized he liked men at a very early age and always desired life in the big city where he could be himself openly. In his 20s, he started using online forums to meet other non-heterosexual men, who were often older than him and married. "I don't judge them, but I don't want to live a counterfeit life like this," Zhao said.

Zhao met his boyfriend Ma in 2004 at an online Euro-American pop music forum (when the online world was arguably "pure" and "uncontaminated"). Ma was born and raised in Guangzhou and was two years younger than Zhao. They soon became web friends with similar music tastes. Subsequently, Zhao went on a business trip to Hong Kong, and they had an opportunity to meet face to face in Guangzhou. Later, they spent a holiday in Zhao's hometown together and expressed their affection for each other: "Ma asked me to be his brother (*xiongdi*) to tighten our relationship. I replied that I didn't want us to be brothers because I liked him; I wanted us to be partners (*ai'ren*)".

After that, they became boyfriends and started a long-distance relationship from 2004 to 2012. Zhao and Ma visited each other and stayed in their apartments for a few days whenever they were free. Zhao had vacations as a schoolteacher, and Ma worked at his family shop. Both of them were living with their parents during these years. After years of a long-distance relationship, Ma's mother sensed the relationship between her son and Zhao. One day in 2012, Zhao received a phone call from Ma's mother, who euphemistically pointed out that Zhao had come to Guangzhou to visit her son too many times. Shortly afterwards, Zhao learned that Ma was on the brink of collapse and came out to his mother. The next day, Zhao took the train to Guangzhou and had a four-hour talk with Ma's mother. At the end of the talk, Ma's mother had nearly accepted their relationship. After Ma came out to his parents, Zhao came out to his parents as well. Zhao's father also came to Guangzhou to visit Zhao and Ma's parents. During their first meeting, Zhao's father said to Ma's mother, "think like we have one more son. As long as they are happy, let them be".

Zhao told me that his resignation from the elementary school was shocking for others:

> 'When I quit my job in 2012, my resignation was the only "naked resignation" (*luoci*, meaning quitting one's job without securing another job) in the school's history! You know my position is quite stable and with all the retirement benefits. People worked hard to get the position and they wouldn't leave it so easily. They couldn't believe that I didn't have a better job lined up! But I didn't think that way. Imagine yourself sitting in an office with the same crew for decades until you retire! Too boring for me. In fact, I was ready to work in McDonald's in Guangzhou when I decided to leave that elementary school and leave Jiangxi.'

Zhao still returned to Jiujiang to visit his parents every year during Spring Festivals, sometimes with Ma. Both being migrants in a first-tier city, we exchanged our views briefly:

Me: How is your hometown right now?
Zhao: No change at all. If you open the *BlueD* app in Jiujiang, you see lots of blank profile pictures or fake photos. Those gay men are scared to show their actual face to others. Here (in Guangzhou), you see real faces when you use the app.
Me: So, does Guangzhou meet your expectation of the big city?

Zhao: It's even better than my imagination! There are many more resources here.

Me: I agree with you, but it has changed. My friends and I are suffering from the dramatic housing prices right now.

Zhao: But I bet you will stay here. You all will. I know you can't go back to your hometown. You simply no longer share the same topic with people in your hometown.

Our conversation reflected many young queer migrants' conflicting attitudes towards living in big cities. It appeared that Zhao disliked the prevailing practices of same-sex erotic relationships in his hometown. His lasting relationship with Ma would not have been possible if he had not moved to Guangzhou. After moving to Guangzhou, Zhao got a position in Parents, Families, and Friends of Lesbians and Gays (PFLAG) China. "I have been together with my partner since 2004" was the unchanged opening sentence every time Zhao introduced himself to other queer people, and it always impressed everyone in the room.

While Zhao's narrative seems to echo the queer utopian imaginaries of cosmopolitan life, it should be noted that Zhao's and Ma's parents are well-off families, and both parents bought a matrimonial home for their only sons. The housing prices were not a vital problem for Zhao, as his partner Ma already owned a flat in Guangzhou. To a certain extent, such prerequisites allowed Zhao to leave his stable career in his hometown for an openly queer life in Guangzhou. For queer individuals relocating to Shenzhen or Guangzhou, their encounters of same-sex intimacies are conditioned by factors such as age, gender, education, and recourses. The next case of the *lala* couple Mo and Lin exemplifies this matter, whereas it also suggests that the demarcation between the 'normative' past and the 'queer present' can be tactically navigated through the process of urban migration.

Mo was born in 1989 in Chengdu. She was living in Shenzhen with her T-identified girlfriend Lin and two cats. They had been living together for two years when I started my fieldwork in 2018. Mo's main job was as a designer, and her girlfriend Lin's main job was in sales. Mo and I had our first interview at her favourite cafe. It was nearly 6 pm, and Mo said, "come to my home for dinner! Lin bought some good shrimps in the local market. I just tell her to cook now".

Mo received her master's degree in graphic design from an Italian university. She came back to China in 2013 and started working in Shenzhen. After a year, she tried to start her own company in Chengdu but failed in the early stages. Mo explained that she could not handle the complex social relationships in Chinese society. She came back to Shenzhen since there were few decent job opportunities for designers in Chengdu. Being the only child in the family, Mo told me her parents almost spoiled her when she grew up. She came out to her parents when she was studying in Italy. Just like other lesbians from middle-class families I met in second-/third-tier cities, Mo's parents had already bought an apartment for their only daughter in Chengdu. Mo's parents also came to Shenzhen occasionally to visit Mo, knowing she was living with her girlfriend.

Mo's girlfriend Lin obtained her education from junior high school. Lin was born in 1986 in a rural town in Anhui Province. She came to Shenzhen when she was 16 years old as a migrant worker. The mobilized economic market in Shenzhen allowed Lin to gradually move from being a factory worker to a salesperson in a beverage company. When I saw Mo and Lin for the first time, Lin introduced herself as a *ye* T, and she had a masculine appearance. Later, I learned that when Lin reached 20, her family arranged a marriage between Lin and a man she had never met. At that time, Lin could not do anything except go back to her hometown and get married. The next year, she gave birth to a son. Lin thought she had fulfilled her duty and "no one can say anything anymore". She left her husband and son in rural Anhui and went back to Shenzhen for work. After that, Lin started dating women. In the last ten years, Lin had only come back to her hometown once a year. She also sent money and toys back to her parents and her son.

Mo's salary was ¥15,000/$2,000, and Lin earned a base salary of ¥2,500/$343 plus sales commission. Mo paid for the rent of their two-bedroom apartment (¥4,000 per month), and Lin regularly bought household goods and food. I asked Mo whether their backgrounds and economic conditions have had any effect on their relationship, and she smiled:

> 'Well, I knew we were different at the very first time we met. We started a chat on *Rela* through its "Searching Other Users in the Vicinity" feature. The app showed our physical distance was just a mile, so we decided to have a casual hang out. It turned out that we certainly lived in the same area, but I was living in an apartment, and she was living in a budget room (*nongmin fang*).[2] It didn't bother me. She was the one dithering over our backgrounds. None of her ex-girlfriends earned more than she. We had been friends for half a year until we confirmed our affection for each other.'

Based on Mo's narrative, Lin had viewed her T role as a financial provider in an intimate relationship. On the other hand, Mo did not see herself as a P nor dependent even though she was attracted to T's gender style. It took Mo and Lin months to mediate their different understandings of their roles in the relationship. For Mo, Lin had the socializing skills she lacked. In 2018, for example, Lin and her colleague had the opportunity to take over an alcohol and tobacco store and secured the prime costs with the mall and supplier. All Mo did was to pay for the major costs, and Lin was responsible for the operation.

Furthermore, Lin gave Mo the feeling of home. Since Lin's working hours were flexible, she cooked for Mo every day. Even after they opened the alcohol and tobacco store, Lin would still prepare bento meals to take to the store during weekends. Ever since Lin had moved to her apartment to live together with Mo, Mo always felt like going back home after work when she knew her girlfriend would welcome her with a warm meal.

Mo did not mind Lin's married status as she said, "anyway, she hasn't slept with that guy for years, and I understand her family background". Mo warned me about using kin terms in front of Lin. Lin was angry at Mo when Mo referred to "that guy" as Lin's "husband". In 2018, Lin wanted to officially end her heterosexual marriage as she had earned her life and romantic relationship in Shenzhen. The man refused to divorce and told Lin that she must take their son with her if they got divorced. Although I never met the man who married Lin, I could tell that he was unpopular from their words. For a middle-aged divorced man staying in a village, it would be difficult to marry again, especially with a child. The man's parents clearly could not afford to arrange another marriage for their son again. Also, Mo refused to live with Lin's son. Eventually, the marriage did not end, and Lin's son stayed in the village in Anhui with the grandparents. Both Lin and the man have their reasons to keep their marriage even though they barely knew each other and had no affective bonds. Such a marriage arrangement was far from rare among heterosexual people in rural areas, according to many. As a solution to this continuing marriage, Lin never kept any property under her name to avoid potential property disputes. During the fieldwork, I met several other middle-aged queer women who had entered into heterosexual marriages when they lacked the negotiating power to refuse. They all emphasized the middle-class lifestyles they had achieved through migrating to urban centres, which subsequently enabled them to leave their 'normative' past to some extent and pursue same-sex relationships.

In 2021, Mo and Lin moved from Shenzhen to Guangzhou due to the Covid-19 pandemic situation. They opened a design studio together, meaning they became even more bonded as business partners. Since Mo owned an apartment in Chengdu, she and Lin planned to go back to Chengdu in a few years and start a company together. Although their same-sex relationship might not be considered as stable for many other non-heterosexual people, Mo and Lin's detailed plan for their future was easily attainable.

Maintaining love: forming *jiban* (mutual burden) without a marriage certificate

The emergence of queer social spaces and communities in urban China as a result of the wide access to the internet and rapid economic reform in recent decades has been recognized in various research (Rofel, 2007; Ho,

2010; Kam, 2013; Engebretsen, 2014; Fu, 2015; Bao, 2018; Song, 2022). Nowadays, one can locate same-sex potential dates online through either mainstream Chinese social media platforms such as *Weibo*, *Tieba*, or *Douban* or same-sex exclusive dating apps such as *BlueD* and *Rela*. What my friend informants desired from romantic relationships in many ways looked like conjugal love, characterized by reliability and companionship.

In our interviews and daily conversations, my friend informants stressed the importance for a loving couple of sharing similar interests, values (*sanguan*), and life objectives. Tommy, who was a 50-year-old gay who had been together with his partner Joe and their son Jack for more than 20 years, told me about the time that transformed their relationship:

> 'I worked so hard and bought an apartment in Guangzhou in December 1990 for us (Tommy, Joe, and Jack) to live together. We have entered the family mode since then. Because Jack was so young, Joe has been staying at home as a "house husband" (*jiatingzhufu*). I look after the outside, and Joe looks after the inside (*wozhuwai, tazhunei*).'

Indeed, living together in an owned apartment symbolized stability and family for Tommy and Joe. Tommy said in our interview that "the key for two people to make a relationship durable is to desire the same lifestyle and life pattern". When he found out that I had been with Jin for one year, he smiled: "You have a long way to go". I was a junior queer woman merely in the early stages of a loving relationship in their eyes. I was still a 'student' who needed support from my parents, did not know where to live in the future, and my girlfriend was the same. In their understanding of it, I was far from in a stable relationship.

Before examining same-sex cohabitating relationships, a few words need to be said to readdress the shifting legal context and understanding of cohabitation as a non-marital intimate relationship in Chinese society in the last decades. During the socialist period, cohabitation outside marriage was regarded as an immoral and illegal practice. The Chinese Marriage Law of 1980 referred to cohabitation as 'illegal cohabitation', while a 2001 amendment to the law changed the wording to 'non-marital cohabitation' (Yu and Xie, 2015). The premarital cohabitation rates had increased dramatically, and a trend in social acceptance towards cohabitation and premarital sex is pronounced (Kleinman et al, 2011; Zhang, 2011). Nevertheless, cohabitation is not legally protected.[3] Also, the tolerant attitude towards cohabitation may still only be within the territory of marriage, as cohabitation is considered a temporal and transitional status before getting married. Long-term cohabitating relationships remain rare (Yeung and Hu, 2016). It remains questionable whether cohabitation is accepted as a form of union among people in contemporary China. The question is pronounced among Chinese non-heterosexual cohabiting couples, for they cannot 'upgrade' their cohabiting relationships to legal marriage. Furthermore, their experiences are different from heterosexual cohabiting couples, for they may not be recognized as cohabiting couples at all within a heteronormative perspective.

Non-heterosexual cohabiting couples, according to the lawyers I talked with, could only be at a disadvantage. We need to acknowledge that family of origin is not always the central heteronormative unit. Butler (2002) makes the connection between state legislation and intimate relations, elucidating how delegitimization of sexual relations can de-realize viable and significant sexual alliances and cause self-doubt. In this context, the Chinese state was 'far from realizing equal citizen's rights on specific issues such as marriage, housing, and so on' (Zhang, 2011, p 123). In a sharing session held by PFLAG China, the lawyer speaker, who introduced herself as a lesbian, concluded: "legally, our (queer couples) cohabiting relationships don't even qualify as *feifa tongju* (illegal cohabitation) even though we have to deal with the issues like joint ownership".

Against this background, the relatively well-off queer couples in my research have employed several major strategies to make their relationships as 'solid as marriage'. Many of the queer couples I met in urban Guangdong never explicitly came out to their parents, or they came out to their parents after they entered 'just-as-married' relationships and had children. According to them, having a stable relationship would increase the probability of success in coming out to parents. I have borrowed the Chinese term *jiban* (mutuality, mutual burden) from many of my friend informants to demonstrate their strategies for forming mutuality in various aspects of their lives. *Jiban* literally means nets/fetters/strings that tie up horses and cattle, to make them become entangled in nets. This word did not have a positive meaning based on the ancient Chinese dictionary. Some argue that it has become influenced by the Japanese word *kizuna*. Nowadays, *jiban* is frequently used to refer to an unbreakable relation that two are entangled in. In this sense, *jiban* is similar to bond, while the former implies restraint if one tries to leave the relationship.

Buying housing property together is frequently mentioned in queer communities as one of the most desired strategies to secure a same-sex relationship since this could enable a couple to cohabitate independently and make them mutual owners of immovable property. The purpose is to obtain mutual ownership or partnership recognized by existing private law. In this sense, queer couples purchase *jiban* as legal and economic protection for their conjugal relationships. Similar strategies for forming mutuality/*jiban* include registering a company jointly, writing a will and getting it notarized, and buying insurance for each other.[4] Since I had started the fieldwork, some young queer couples in first-tier cities had tried registering for voluntary guardianship and succeeded. Adult voluntary guardianship, permitted by

Article 33 in the General Provisions of the Civil Law 2017 version, allows adults with a full capacity for civil conduct to name a trusted person to make decisions for them in case they lose or partially lose the capacity for civil conduct. Initially, this article was not formulated to protect same-sex relationships by any means, although it was quickly circulated in same-sex communities as a practical tactic to tighten conjugal relationships in urban China. It was soon referred to as a low-cost practice in case a queer couple could not afford to buy a house together.

An was born in 1985 in Fuyang, a prefecture-level city in the northwestern Anhui Province. He came to Shenzhen for leisure travel in 2008 and immediately fell in love with the green and humid city. He then moved to Shenzhen, borrowed ¥30,000, and opened a company. Two months after moving to Shenzhen, An met Ye on an online *tongzhi* live chatting room. They met in person a week later and soon lived together. An gave a narrative that demonstrates the complexities of mutual property ownership, love, and a feeling of security in a same-sex relationship:

> 'In 2010, Ye quit his job in a foreign trade company and joined my company. Ye's parents are richer than mine. I am from Fuyang; his family is from Shenzhen. He suffered from depression and didn't enjoy his former job, so I told him that he could quit. I bought apartments in Shenzhen for myself and for Ye as well. Ye felt insecure, so I bought several apartments in Shenzhen under his name. Also, our cooperative relationship is stated in the company policy. If something terrible happened to me, Ye would receive my capital.'

In our interview, An did not explain why Ye would feel insecure because he assumed that I, as a Chinese citizen, did not need such an explanation. Based on An's narrative, Ye's feelings of insecurity towards their relationship was due to his economic dependence and the lack of legal recognition of same-sex relationships, and An solved this by forming a mutual partnership and ownership with Ye. They also have three sons together, which I will detail later.

Xie and Hong, a lesbian couple living in Shenzhen with a son, told me:

> 'We have consulted the lawyer about securing our relationship as a same-sex couple, and the lawyer told us the law has no safeguard for us same-sex couples at all, so we've decided that we would buy properties and put our names on the properties one by one.'

Hong once said that "Xie puts her heart into our relationship". To explain this, Hong told me that after Xie found out she liked the bread from a local bakery, Xie went to buy every kind of bread from the bakery and brought it to her workplace every day. Hong and Xie's friends commented, "Isn't Xie romantic?"

The three same-sex couples mentioned previously were all middle-aged and had few resources when they migrated to Shenzhen/Guangzhou. They, and other friend informants who bought one or more houses in the big city, highly appreciated the potential for upward mobility in this fast-developing city. Some extended their gratitude to the state for the economic opportunities they grasped during market reform. Moreover, An, Tommy, and Xie highlighted their love for their same-sex partners by linking their economic capital together under private law (property, contract, company law). They understood that forming mutual ownership was key to maintaining their loving relationship. For them, *jiban* was both emotional and material. Such narratives arguably embraced consumer culture since buying goods for a loved one was highly encouraged. Many of my friend informants half joked that mutual ownership of immovable property could be more powerful than a marriage certificate. They reasoned that, in the case of divorce, even a wife in a heterosexual marriage could not take a part of a flat that was categorized as her husband's prenuptial property. When a same-sex couple who bought a flat together decided to break up, they had to go through legal processes to split property, which some described as more complicated than divorce. In this sense, mutual ownership takes the form of insurance of a relationship that can be purchased.

Due to the rising real estate prices, younger same-sex couples in Shenzhen and other first-tier cities generally could not afford to buy an apartment unless their parents provided financial support. It is the case that parents in urban China nowadays must pay a lot more to purchase housing property for their children to secure their future. A private house in post-reform China is bonded with notions of marriage, family, and middle-class lifestyle (Zhang, 2010). As I shall discuss in the next chapter, housing ownership not only impacts the intimate practices of queer individuals but also influences their parenting choices. The houses that parents bought for their sons traditionally served the purpose of the matrimonial home, and such a practice was extended to the only daughter after the one-child policy was introduced. Legally speaking, non-heterosexual people could not add the same-sex partner's name to a property certificate already purchased by their parents or themselves.[5] The successful cases of middle-aged same-sex couples who bought houses by themselves might be even rarer among young generations. An increasing number of young same-sex couples showed an interest in learning the process of notarizing their cohabiting relationships and testaments during my fieldwork, as it would not require one to own a house or company to be eligible. Still, many young non-heterosexual people displayed strong desires for "owning an apartment and living with a partner in our little world".

Queer love in a Chinese first-tier city

The term 'intimate relations' signifies social connections that encompass elements of physical and/or emotional closeness, personal attachment, sexual intimacy, privacy, care, and affection (Constable, 2009, p 50). However, it is important to note that these relations extend beyond the boundaries of domestic environments. Intimate relations often involve the practices of intimate labours that embody social orders and, at the same time, enable self-making (Heberer, 2017; Parreñas, 2017). I have discussed the dynamic use of 1/0/0.5/T/P/H-related slang in queer dating practices and how these roles are perceived through comparison with heterosexual relationships and gender norms. Overall, the 1–0/T–P relationship modes have proliferated into a diverse range of relationship modes and role terms, especially among urban, young, queer couples. Younger non-heterosexual people emphasized that same-sex relationships should be equal and interdependent in terms of emotional, sexual, and economic roles. On the other hand, these role terms are rather *biaomian* (superficial) in queer relationships, and they might or might not be understood as gendered personalities. Those who contended that modern same-sex relationships should be different from heterosexual relationships risked understating heterosexual relationships as an eternally static object for comparison. After all, we cannot reduce heterosexual relationships to a fixed model in which the man is dominant and caring and the woman is submissive and dependent. The debate on 'what a modern and authentic same-sex relationship should be' in queer communities is constantly being shaped by notions of modernity, lesbian/gay authenticity, and love.

When we apprehend queer intimate relationships through the very idea of romantic and conjugal love, it is worth noting that the conception of 'love' in Chinese society has never been fixed. Povinelli (2006) discusses the constitution of the discursive divide between the autological subject and genealogical society – which she calls imaginaries involving discourses, practices, and fantasies. As Povinelli describes, 'to assert a bond of love was to assert simultaneously a rejection of social utility' (2002, p 230). The 'intimate event', as she uses it, is the way in which the event of normative love is formed and the intersection and crisis of the autological subject and genealogical society. Borrowing from Povinelli, we shall not read love as a set of universally actual truths but, rather, examine it as a developing discourse. In ancient China, marriage was arranged by family elders primarily for the purpose of having male offspring, exchanging resources, increasing manpower, and forming alliances. Pan suggests that 'while marriage was one of life's central experiences in China, the ideal of the primacy of love never was' (2015, p 280). In other words, the basis of marriage was patrilineal lineage rather than affection or 'love'. The youth, especially young women, had little autonomy. There is a rich collection of poetry and folk songs about 'love' in Imperial China, which is neither related to sexual desire nor freedom in marriage.[6] The ideology of 'romantic love' in China is constituted through the rejection of arranged marriage and is linked to a sense of modernity and individual autonomy (Yan, 2003; Lee, 2006; Pan, 2015). The emerging discourses on 'romantic love', 'true love', and 'free love' in 20th-century China symbolize the contradictions between tradition and modernity. How queer people in today's Chinese societies understand and maintain loving relationships outside the doctrine of marriage further contributes to the denaturalization of love.

The emerging digital platforms have become a seemingly cultural space for young queer people to locate potential friends and dates who share similar cultural tastes, backgrounds, and social status (see also Wei, 2020). Online queer spaces have therefore allowed the construction of newer kinds of queer affective bonds (Dasgupta and Dasgupta, 2018). Meanwhile, the vague path from an unrelated intimate stranger to a real-life partner in same-sex online dating practices complicates the modern aspiration that romantic love can bring two strangers together and turn them into intimate kins. When queer people develop an intimate relationship with an individual completed outside their established social webs, their sentiments, health, and money are all at potential risk that they must internalize by themselves. Such a shift in same-sex relationships in recent decades needs to be understood within both the context of queer cultures and ethical shifts in urban China. Through the process of seeking reliable dates, queer individuals come to recognize their own position in the hierarchy of *suzhi* as well as the need to match with a high-*suzhi* partner. Among Chinese queer individuals, the most highly valued 'quality' is the very ability to maintain a long-lasting same-sex relationship and queer life (Wei, 2020, p 104). Overall, what my friend respondents desired from same-sex romantic relationships in many ways looks like conjugal relations, characterized by reliability and companionship.

Mo and Zhao's narratives of their love stories cannot be articulated alone without acknowledging their family backgrounds, career paths, and migrating experiences to the big cities in Guangdong, China. Mo and Zhao emphasized their similar cultural tastes and complementary personal characteristics as the main factors explaining why they fell for their same-sex partners. In other words, they perceive and describe their relationships as soulmates instead of erotic lovers or a couple 'matched for marriage' (*mendanghudui*). When Zhao compared lives in his hometown and Guangzhou, his description of same-sex dating practices in the two places resonated with queer urban utopian imaginaries countering normative lifestyles (Huang, 2017). Zhao could not stand life in his hometown, especially after realizing the gay men in his hometown were likely to enter heterosexual marriage and heteronormative lifestyles. The urban atmosphere of Guangzhou allowed Zhao to grasp his queer affective needs and pursue romantic relationships.

Mo envisions a *wending* (stable) relationship with Lin and made detailed plans for their future. In this sense, queer subjects' practices of seeking and maintaining their loving relationships encompassed the blurred discourses on romantic love and conjugal love, traditional values and modern lives. Big cities became sites for them to gain upward mobility and material recourses, keep a manageable distance from their natal families in their hometowns, and escape from marriage pressure or 'normative past'. Most importantly, they attempted to find pragmatic solutions to secure their same-sex loving relationship like many other queer couples in big cities.

Here, I relate *jiban* to Sahlins's idea of the 'mutuality of being' in which kinsmen are 'persons who belong to one another, who are members of one another, who are co-present in each other, whose lives are joined and interdependent' (2013, p 28). Such 'mutuality of being', as (Carsten, 2013) suggests, does not always carry a warm and positive vibe. *Jiban*, initially meaning that one is entangled and thus unable to leave (a relationship), seems to carry the double-edged qualities and uncertainty of kinship. Examining the strategies employed by queer couples to establish their *jiban*/mutuality through emotional, financial, and legal ties provides insights into the dynamics of kinship formation and dissolution over time, a concept characterized by the 'thickening' or 'thinning' of relationships (Carsten, 2013, p 247), which I will continuously revisit. Ultimately, for the queer couples discussed in this book, the concept of *jiban* is oriented towards building a secure, shared future.

Moreover, unlike the 'just-as-married' middle-aged queer couples, most young non-heterosexual people did not see themselves as successfully settled in Shenzhen/Guangzhou because they lived in rented shared flats and thus could not envision a long-lasting relationship in the big city. Narratives on queer conjugal love and urban citizenship hence reflect the rise of the 'enterprising/desiring self', which is maintained in terms of individual desires and is placed under the restricting authority of the Chinese state through the language of neoliberalism (Rofel, 2007; Kleinman et al, 2011). Chinese economic reform since the late 1970s has contributed to the growth of individual mobility and simultaneously formed unequal social stratums (Anagnost, 2008). Consequently, most Chinese individuals 'had to internalize the negative impacts of individualization by assuming more responsibilities, experiencing greater uncertainty and risk, and working harder' (Kleinman et al, 2011, p 15). In this sense, many Chinese queer citizen subjects had to come up with their own solution to cope with uncertainty and risk in their unprotected loving relationships. A private house owned by both was preferred among queer couples, for it ensured a stable living status and a legal secured bond under private law. Having children together was another key strategy queer couples used to establish *jiban* and thicken their loving relationships, which I will discuss further in the following chapters.

3

Queering Reproduction: Changing Moral Dilemmas for Chinese Non-heterosexual People

'You and your same-sex partner need to share a common bond for your relationship, and a child is the best bond!'

At a lesbian, gay, bisexual, and transgender (LGBT)-themed talkfest I attended in Guangzhou in 2019, a middle-aged representative speaker of a private assisted reproductive technology (ART) agency used this line to start his speech. The speaker then used his own experience as a gay father to validate his argument. According to the speaker, having a baby with his boyfriend was beneficial for their loving relationship. He concluded that a same-sex couple should plan to have children as soon as possible. His speech received a mixed response, as some young attendees murmured about the high cost of using ARTs and joked, "first we need a partner to do it together".

Both the speaker and the attendees talked about having children as a conjugal (and perhaps expensive) practice in a same-sex couple without mentioning family pressure. As I will show in this chapter, this kind of conversation was far from rare among my queer friend informants, and the way they framed having children varied. The act of having offspring carried significant weight in premodern China due to the patrilineal structure of ancestral lineage tracing and Confucian familism. One characteristic of the traditional Chinese kinship system was the patrilineal continuity that traces the family lineage through men, connecting men with both their male ancestors (*zuxian*) and descendants (*houdai*). Yang (1957) also points out that ancestor worship served to cultivate kinship values such as filial piety, family loyalty, and the continuity of the family lineage (p 278). Filial duty (*xiao*), a central moral principle in Confucian ideology, focuses on the continuation of the family line and the support, subordination, and obedience to elders (Ikels, 2004). Childlessness was a failure of filial duty to the family (Klein, 2017). Is it still the case today and with non-heterosexual people?

As a large-scale survey by the United Nations Development Programme (UNDP) (2016) indicates, nearly two thirds of LGBT respondents in mainland China felt under great pressure from their families of origin to enter heterosexual marriages and have children. While the survey result is revealing, it would be abridging for researchers to understand Chinese non-heterosexual people having children exclusively in the context of filial piety and parental authority. Hildebrandt (2018) reminds us to apply a social policy lens to family pressure felt by Chinese LGBT people as he points out the heteronormative features of the family-planning and elder care policies. The current generation of non-heterosexual people in mainland China born under the one-child policy (1979–2015) have no siblings to share the burden of labour and care work for their parents. In particular, the one-child policy has placed familial pressure solely on the only child, who is expected to excel in school, have a decent job, get married, continue the family line, and take primary responsibility for supporting the family elders. Additionally, due to the absence of robust public support systems, a substantial segment of the elderly population in China continues to rely on their children for financial and caregiving assistance in their later years (Yan, 2012; Xie, 2013). Such a structural disparity not only distinguishes contemporary Chinese perceptions and practices of kinship from those in the Euro-American contexts but also delineates a structural contrast between the prevalent family configuration in mainland China and that of other ethnic Chinese societies and diasporic communities (Wei, 2023). I begin this chapter by asking why and when non-heterosexual people in Guangdong have children. Rather than taking family pressure for granted, I want to highlight the dynamic interplay of socio-economic class, moral agency, and state policies that come to articulate queer kinship practices. To what extent does reproduction interrelate with the notions of future and risk in their lifeworlds? Furthermore, the important but yet to be asked question: how do they have children?

In this chapter, I explore the motivations and pathways for becoming parents in Chinese queer lifeworlds. To unpack this topic, I investigate decision-making processes that moved queer individuals or couples towards parenthood and those who chose not to pursue parenthood. Then, I document the existing practices for Chinese non-heterosexual people around having children and the moral and legal controversaries raised by these practices. This is followed by an elucidation of which practices were believed to be better in queer communities and how queer parents made their decisions to have children accordingly. Lastly, I stress the complexity of personhood and moral practices in queer lifeworlds.

Moving to parenthood

It is perhaps not surprising that parental expectations continued to be an important factor for many non-heterosexual people in having children. Several queer parents in their 30s or 40s told me explicitly that they were pressured by their rural families of origin to enter heterosexual marriages and have children. Urban youth, on the other hand, emphasized that their parents did not compel them; rather, they wanted their parents to be happy and satisfied. When I firstly met Zhenzhen, who was 24 years old, she was already preparing for in-vitro fertilization (IVF) treatment. I was surprised and said, "you are so young to have children!" Zhenzhen said: "I agree with you, but my womb is not in good condition. My body cannot wait. Besides, my parents are paying for all the IVF expenses. They are bored of their life in the small town, you know; they need a kid to kill their time."

Zhenzhen has come out to her parents, while her parents neither accepted her relationship with Fei nor objected to it. Zhenzhen and her 23-year-old girlfriend Fei were living in a flat purchased by Zhenzhen's parents. Zhenzhen's parents never asked Zhenzhen to marry a man. Nevertheless, Zhenzhen's mother urged her to have offspring after she was diagnosed with premature ovarian failure. Zhenzhen thought that, after her child was born, she could leave her child with her parents and continue to pursue her career. For Zhenzhen, having children was a win-win move.

Zhenzhen's situation was by no means unique. Zhenzhen and another middle-aged lesbian woman in my research clarified that they voluntarily chose to have children for the well-being of their parents. This decision was particularly pertinent for those who were only children born during the one-child policy era (1979–2015), as not having children often signified the end of the family lineage. Once more, the Confucian conception of filial duty stressed the importance of *chuanzongjiedai* (carrying on the family line) and strengthened parental authority. Borrowing the discourse on Confucian familism and ancestor worship, many non-heterosexual people held the opinion that not fulfilling one's family responsibility was a selfish thing to do. Commonly, I was told that, after children were born, they would have fulfilled family expectations and could then do all the things they wanted, including having same-sex relationships. Similarly, heterosexual marriages for queer women were phrased as not merely family pressure but a tactic for leaving families of origin to gain personal autonomy (Kam, 2013; Engebretsen, 2014). Having children, in Zhenzhen's narrative, became a moral accomplishment and a path to individual freedom.

Chen, the manager of a private ART agency, said she could tell if it was the clients themselves who wanted to be parents or the clients' parents who wanted to be grandparents. Contrary to Zhenzhen, Chen argued that fulfilling parental expectations through heterosexual marriage and having children was an act of cowardice and selfishness:

> 'Usually, if the clients' parents talk to us and pay for all the fees, I know the parents want a grandchild. These clients are irresponsible, like big kids, because they don't have their own motivation to be parents. They are just doing what their parents want so they can be free of family pressure. These kinds of clients probably leave the baby to their parents for babysitting after the child is born and continue to play around. I think it is not fair to the child coming to the world since the parent doesn't desire it.'

Chen felt that, in this context, the expected baby was merely a tool for the client to escape family pressure. To put it another way, Chen did not think people who had children for fulfilling parental expectations would be responsible parents themselves. Chen's opinion has become prevalent in online social media platforms like *Douban* and *Weibo*, which young users dominate.

Many people in my research highlighted that they had always wanted to be a parent. An, a gay father of three sons, said, "since I was young, I knew I wanted children and I had made plans. I planned to have mixed-race babies". Many lesbian mothers I met stressed that they loved children very much and desired their company in their life. One of my lesbian friends, Wen, said, "raising a child will give me the feeling of accomplishment". In this kind of description, queer intended parents did not mention their parents' expectations but rather concentrated on their own desires. A few queer intended parents mentioned that they would want children to support them in their elderly life, while they also stressed that it was not the key factor for them to have children. As I will return to shortly, the Chinese common saying 'raise children for the purpose of being looked after in old age (*yang'erfanglao*)' has been challenged by young queer urbanites, who no longer view parenting as a good investment.

Like the speaker mentioned at the beginning of this chapter, many queer parents described children as the most effective mutual bond (*jiban*) between two people in a couple. It must be noted that a child as a mutual bond/*jiban* in a same-sex couple only worked in certain situations. I will illustrate this with further individual accounts in Chapter 5.

Same-sex couples in this ethnography also described parenting as entering a more intimate and promising stage of their relationship. Pam, a 28-year-old queer woman, explained the reason for her and her partner Danny to have their child through a reciprocal IVF called '*A luan* (egg) *B huai* (pregnancy)', meaning Pam was going to give birth to the child using Danny's egg: "We have been enjoying time together. Naturally, we want our connection to be tighter. I can't think of anything else to bond us more tightly".

Pam believed that having children through *A luan B huai* could strengthen her relationship with Danny. At that time, Pam's mother had already accepted that her daughter was lesbian, and Danny planned to come out to her parents after Pam gave birth to the baby. According to Danny and Pam, no one would be hurt in this way. Sitting with Pam, Danny added:

'It is important to establish a *jiban* (mutual burden, mutuality) to make a relationship last. You two must plan a future together, otherwise it's just a repetition of eating and sleeping without the sense of a future life. When I was with my ex-girlfriend, she didn't have any clue about our future. I asked her whether she wanted to immigrate to foreign countries or stay in China and whether she wanted to marry me or have children; she just didn't know. I felt so insecure back then.'

Likewise, having children was frequently suggested as a strategy that increased the cost of separation (*fenshou chengben*), as a lesbian mother, Yanzi, illustrated: "When the two of you have children together, your girlfriend cannot just take the luggage and leave the house (*linbaozouren*) when you have a fight. You won't break up easily. She becomes the mother of your kid! It will be like an actual marriage".

In short, non-heterosexual people's drive for having children cannot be reduced to family pressure. They can also desire parenting as a lifestyle. Fulfilling parental expectations through entering marriages and having offspring is no longer the dominant factor in understanding one's moral worth, as Zhenzhen's account increasingly encounters criticism from other non-heterosexual people in Chinese cities. On the other hand, non-heterosexual people's motivations for having children are often unconsolidated and represented in both an individualistic sense as self-desire and a relational rhetoric as a conjugal technique. There is a generational tendency to present the desire for parenthood as an individualistic and voluntary choice free from traditional family pressure.

Lastly in this section, it is worth mentioning that raising a child in China, especially in first-tier cities, had increasingly become expensive and difficult, demonstrated by the continually falling fertility rate.[1] Most non-heterosexual as well as straight urbanites believed that, in order to raise a child, one had to own a school district apartment (*xuequ fang*) for children's future education. For many Chinese people, raising a child in a rented flat often implied instability and risk. Their desire for a privatized home was connected with the desire for a middle-class lifestyle that was marked by a prevailing sense of insecurity (Zhang, 2010). Within this framework, the act of parenting frequently became associated exclusively with the upper-middle class, a theme I will consistently revisit. My queer and straight friends in Shenzhen all stressed that buying a flat was unthinkable for those who had just worked for a few years. According to the Statistics Bureau of Shenzhen Municipality, the average annual income of 2018 in Shenzhen was ¥110,304/$15,130 for people working at non-private enterprises and ¥63,635/$8,730 for people working at private enterprises. In the meantime, the Shenzhen Real Estate Information Platform showed the average transaction price for housing property in 2018 was around ¥54,000/$7,407 per square metre.[2] The average housing price of a central and school district apartment was noticeably higher, usually exceeding ¥100,000/$13,718 per square metre. I frequently saw the following statement on online forums:

> If I didn't eat and didn't consume anything for a year, I might be able to afford to buy 1 square metre in Shenzhen. If I want to buy a flat by myself, I need to work for several decades without consuming anything. Do the math and think about it.

Therefore, many same-sex couples had no choice but to postpone their plans to have children, just like many straight married couples. As mentioned earlier, young people preferred to settle in big cities, and therefore they had to deal with the high housing prices. In Shenzhen, I heard many young people in their late 20s saying, "it is too early for me to think about having children". The overall trend of postponing childbirth among young Chinese urbanites also provided young non-heterosexual people with a convincing excuse to tell their parents whenever they were asked about their plans for having children. Moreover, the changing pattern of parent–child relations in urban China has shaped young non-heterosexual people's willingness to raise children, which I shall unpack in the next section.

"Having children is not worth it"

Sitting with my queer peers in a hot pot restaurant in the city centre of Shenzhen, I brought out the topic of my research: "I've been friends with you for long enough to know some of you don't want children. I wonder, do you like the idea of having children at all?"

Clara, a 27-year-old lesbian who was working as a financial consultant in Shenzhen, said:

> 'Getting married and having children is not a reliable option anymore. Nowadays, you must spend all your money on your children – buying imported milk powder, paying for school and tutorial lessons, supporting them financially for years after graduation – and they might not grow up as you hope. It is gambling. I'd rather save all these expenses for raising a child and go to a nice nursing home when I get old.'

Another lesbian friend of the same age laughed, "we just want to make money (*gaoqian*)!" Without mentioning the legal constraints of same-sex parenting or whether they liked kids or not, my peers concluded that they could not afford to parent and it was not a reliable investment for their future life. Clara told me she calculated how much parents need to spend on housing, healthcare, and education, and parenting for her was simply not worth it.

Other than the rising expense of having children, Clara's statement further implied changes around the idea of filial piety and elderly support. Chinese society has been experiencing rapid transformations in family structures and consumer culture (Ying, 2003). Although the de-collectivization of interests caused rural families to lose much of their economic autonomy, family (*jia*) remained an essential social unit (Cohen, 2005). Filial piety remains an essential moral practice, though the actual practice of it is 'situationally dependent and shaped by local circumstances of history, economics, social organization, and demography and by personal circumstances of wealth, gender, and family configuration' (Ikels, 2004, p 2). Children's education became an imperative type of family investment and an expression of parental affection (Fong, 2004; Kuan, 2015; Lin, 2019). Children's consumption has increased dramatically; at the same time, children bear their parents' hopes for financial support and class mobility (Fong, 2004). Since elderly care is strongly dependent on kinship norms under the existing Chinese welfare system, not having children could represent a profound concern for one's future life. Yet, an increasing number of young urbanites like Clara did not have faith in the Chinese common saying "raise children for the purpose of being looked after in old age (*yang'erfanglao*)". Relying on the notion of filial piety for one's care when elderly sounded unrealistic for them, as they had witnessed numerous urban Chinese parents spending all their life savings to buy apartments for the only children, which could never be repaid. In this context, the parent–child relation looked like the parents giving their resources out without receiving them back. As Clara and many young urbanites employed the rhetoric of financial investment and payback to think about parent–child relations, having offspring became increasingly linked to risk rather than security.

Perhaps another reason for her feelings was that Clara did not believe she successfully fulfilled her parents' expectations as an obedient daughter. When Clara came out to her mother, the latter ignored her. Clara rarely returned to her hometown in Yunnan Province. Whenever she talked with her parents through WeChat, they quarrelled about her life choices and her 'failure' in Shenzhen. As a *haigui* (overseas returnee) who spent years studying in Europe and returned to Shenzhen to work, Clara was anxious about returning her parents' investment in her education. After three years working in Shenzhen, her basic monthly salary had not exceeded ¥10,000/ $1,372. Living in the central district of Futian, half of Clara's salary was spent on rent. Her primary goal was to use her own money to purchase an apartment for herself in Shenzhen, yet this goal could only be attained for a few. When we walked by residential areas in Nanshan and Futian districts in Shenzhen, Clara often used her mobile phone to check the housing prices. All her dream apartments were priced over ¥100,000/$13,718 per square metre, which made her dissatisfied with her current earnings. She also mentioned that, if her parents ever tried to understand her situation, they might support her to pay the down payment on an apartment in Shenzhen, and their relationship would be smoother. Clara's argument resonated with Li's (2011) research on urban young Chinese families, which suggests that the urban youth understand filial piety as 'mutual respect' and 'equal relations' rather than 'obedience'.

Clara made it clear that she did not intend to be a model daughter in her parents' eyes. Not only did she think she could not afford childrearing but she also did not envision offspring as reliable support for elderly life. Furthering the discourse on filial duty, many Chinese urbanites in their 20s criticized the notion of seeing the continuation of the family line as one's moral responsibility. They frequently quoted a widespread statement from the internet: "Why is having offspring so important for some people? Must they have an inheritor to receive their throne or something?" By challenging the importance of continuing the family line (*chuanzongjiedai*), these young urbanites attempted to identify a distinction between modern and traditional values regarding having children.

While many young non-heterosexual people did not see parenting as an economically rewarding option and did not expect the coming generation of children to be fully obedient to their parents, some of my friend informants who were planning to or already had children also used a similar logic to validate their motivation for being parents. By stressing that they wanted no material return from their children, they described their motivation as pure (*chunjie*) and modern. Not a single queer parent in my research acknowledged continuing the family line or supporting their elderly life as their key motivation for being parents, even though these were often assumed to be the major reasons for having offspring in China.

To push this discussion further, the question of whether to reproduce or not is linked to queer relationality, reproduction, and, ultimately, debates surrounding queer futurity. We have heard too many times that 'children are the future', and 'queer sexualities are against nature because you cannot make children'. Following Bersani's definition of sex as 'anticommunal, antiegalitarian, antinurturing, antiloving' (1987, p 215) is the anti-relational turn in queer theory fuelled by Lee Edelman. As Edelman (2004) suggests, the conception of politics is linked to what he calls 'reproductive futurism' embodied in the figure of the child. In this sense, future is reduced to repetition. Fighting for the future is equated with 'fighting for children', while queerness 'names the side of those not "fighting for the children," the side outside the consensus by which all politics confirms the absolute value of reproductive futurism' (2004, p 3). Yet, Jack Halberstam (2008) points out that Edelman's version of queerness is apolitical rather than anti-politics. Unfolding tensions between same-sex and gender-variant traditions of queer activism and identification, Halberstam demonstrates that homosexuality has not always and everywhere been negative or anti-relational. José Muñoz (2009) suggests that queerness is also performative, meaning it is not only being but also doing for and towards the future. Patel (2006) suggests that the good neoliberal citizen, as an enterprise, cares for oneself and ensures a good sustainable life against risk by investing in the future. In resonance with Muñoz and Patel, I interpret the longing of queer individuals for children as an ideological endeavour rather than a submission to the politics of reproductive futurism. Similarly, the choice of queer individuals to forgo parenthood can be understood as a stance of non-investment in expensive parenting rather than an outright rejection of reproductive futurism. For my queer friend informants, the moral understanding of filial piety, the child's symbolic position in forming the cost of parenting, and the social policy in urban China together shape their ideas of risk and eco-sustainability and, ultimately, a good (queer) life.

It is also helpful to not assume reproduction as the only viable future within and beyond queer studies. Together with the ethnographic accounts, I make a call to re-examine the figure of the child in transforming Chinese society and beyond. Although family support remains the main resource for old-age support in China, the transforming socio-economic structure and parent–child relation appear to challenge the symbolic importance of the child, and this is especially visualized among young non-heterosexual people who refuse to have children. Still, not having children implied the need to have at least an alternative solution for elderly care and maintaining loving relationships. Clara hoped to earn enough money to support herself after retirement, as she spent most of her energy on excelling at work. When Zhao told me that he did not plan to have children, he acknowledged the fact that he and Ma were not worried about their elderly life as they were living a financially abundant life in Guangzhou. It could easily be observed that Zhao went to cafes and purchased decent kitchen appliances regularly. Zhao's parents never let Zhao send them money. Zhao was aware that his parents did not need his financial support. In 2019, Zhao had earned enough to buy an additional flat in Guangzhou. Zhao and Ma also kept a dog together, whom they referred to as their child.

The vanishing and the emerging pathways to parenthood

As mentioned earlier, my research includes a diverse group of queer parents, including but not limited to single and divorced queer parents, same-sex couples who use ARTs to have children, and gay–lesbian *xinghun* co-parents. Although the pathways to parenthood almost always implied moral judgement for my friend informants, I do not intend to make rigid classifications of Chinese queer parents; nor do I intend to rank the moral worth of these practices. Rather, by exploring how Chinese non-heterosexual people make and reflect on their choices in having children, I articulate a dynamic understanding of queer reproduction and moral landscape in recent years. Undeniably, there is more than one way to become a parent for Chinese non-heterosexual people, but they may not be recognized equally in the contexts of feasibility and morality.

Zhihun *(marrying a straight person)*

In Chinese queer communities, *zhihun* (*zhi* literally means straight and *hun* means marriage) is a commonly used slang term to describe non-heterosexual people marrying straight people. Several friend informants over 40 years old explained that they did not even realize their same-sex desires when they got married. While many non-heterosexual people who *zhihun* remained invisible to the public, an increasing number of queer parents, such as Joe, shared their experience of entering and leaving their heterosexual marriages, often with stories of parenting.

Joe got married in 1996 when he was 22 years old. Growing up in a rural area, Joe went to work at a factory in Guangdong Province after he finished junior high school. In 1996, Joe's relatives introduced him to a woman from his hometown. After the wedding, Joe came back to the factory and his wife stayed in the hometown. While being married, Joe was confused about his desire for men. After he read a journal article on LGBT issues, he was eager to talk to the author, Tommy. Joe exchanged emails with Tommy in the following months, and they met in person in the winter of 1997. They fell for each other, and Joe told Tommy everything about his family, including his pregnant wife in his hometown. The day after, Joe came back to his hometown and told his wife he liked men. Joe's wife was calm and they "divorced in peace". According to Joe, there was no romantic love between Joe and his ex-wife since their marriage was close to being an arranged marriage and they rarely spent any time with each other. Later, Joe's ex-wife gave birth to Jack in his rural hometown. Tommy and Joe took Jack to Guangzhou when Jack was 2 years old and the three of them started living together.

During interviews and daily conversations, people who *zhihun* often described their choice to enter heterosexual marriage as the only way they could fulfil their parents' expectations. Non-heterosexual people born in the 1970s and 1980s considered heterosexual marriage a family obligation that must be fulfilled. They clarified that staying in a heterosexual marriage was not the final solution to their parents' expectations; having offspring (sons, in some cases) was their parents' ultimate hope. We must not forget that both marriage and reproduction were central life experiences in Confucianist familism. Some middle-aged queer parents who entered a normative life pattern expressed mixed and even painful feelings. Mellow, a 43-year-old lesbian mother, had two ex-girlfriends before she intentionally married her male friend:

> 'I was 30 years old when I left the factory to open a flower shop. My ex-girlfriend generously supported me. However, the shop turned out to be a failure and I lost all our savings. My parents didn't push me to marry, but I knew they were worried about my situation. Back in the early 2000s, there was no advanced technology like IVF. Even if there was IVF, I didn't know if I could afford it. At that time, I made a terrible choice. I asked my best male friend from the factory to marry me, and we got married. My family was happy, but my ex-girlfriend was suffering and so was I. After two months, I found out I was pregnant. I couldn't pretend it anymore, so I came out to him and asked for a divorce. He didn't agree, and we went to court. The next year, we reached divorce by agreement. I felt very guilty and therefore didn't take any of his money. After I gave birth to a son, he wanted to take my son from me, and I eventually gave up the custody. Until my son turned 5 years old, he got married again and we (Mellow and her current girlfriend) took our son back to live with us.'

Countless debates were elevated regarding this practice in recent years. While a same-sex desiring person might claim that they got married without realizing their sexual orientation one or two decades ago, this kind of explanation would not be accepted anymore. Non-heterosexual people born after the late 1980s had the opportunity to learn terms such as 'tongxinglian', 'tongzhi', 'lala', 'gay', and 'lesbian' on the internet. Therefore, it was becoming rare that one could enter a conventional heterosexual marriage before realizing one's same-sex desires. Just like a gay friend informant said, "you can use *BlueD* (a gay dating app) everywhere".

Furthermore, emerging practices to deal with parental expectation such as *xinghun* marriage have gradually made a young non-heterosexual individual sound unconvincing when they claim they have no other choice. Mellow's practice to intentionally marry a straight man to have children was termed as *pianhun* (lying about one's same-sex desires to marry a straight person, or 'marriage fraud') in online discussions. The word '*pian*' (lie) signified that it was fundamentally an immoral practice. 'Marriage fraud' has been repeatedly denounced by LGBT organizations (Zhu, 2018). Almost all friend informants made it clear that they would not develop a friendship and an intimate relationship with someone who *pianhun*, as a lesbian friend informant reasoned:

'People who *pianhun* nowadays are either coward or selfish. I don't believe they have no other choice. Why must they listen to their parents? Why must they marry an innocent person to have offspring? They not only lie to their parents, but also hurt their straight spouse and eventually hurt our community!'

Pianhun was even more pronounced with the emerging issue of *tongqi* (literally meaning the wife of a homosexual man). At a Parents, Families, and Friends of Lesbians and Gays (PFLAG) event in 2018, a guest speaker, Weichen, gave a speech about her experience as a *tongqi*. Weichen said she was shocked when she found out about her ex-husband's affairs with men as she thought homosexual people would not enter a heterosexual marriage. There are roughly ten million straight women married to closeted gay men in China (Li et al, 2017). According to Weichen, her ex-husband not only lied about his sexual desires to marry Weichen but also borrowed a large amount of money without telling her. As a legally married couple, Weichen was responsible for paying her husband's debts. Consequently, Weichen had to go to court with her ex-husband to solve the financial dispute. According to my friend informants and online discussions on *Weibo*, *Douban*, and *Xiaohongshu*, *tongqi* women have been lied to and taken advantage of by their gay husbands in various ways, including being used as a shield against discrimination and exploited as a free surrogate mother for the gay husband. Many *tongqi* experienced physical and emotional domestic violence and lost custody of their children when they asked for divorce, since the divorce law favours men (Tsang, 2021). Mellow's narrative proves that queer women are also involved in the practice of *pianhun*, despite *tongfu* (husbands of homosexual women) being much less visible in mass media. Still, *tongqi* face worse gender discrimination and sexual health problems.

It should be noted that Xie, Joe, and Mellow are older than the majority of the friend informants in this research. Moreover, they chose to come out to their ex-spouses and parents at some point in their lives, while many other middle-aged non-heterosexual people remained married in a heteronormative family unit and would not participate in my research. Relationships with children from *zhihun* marriages, former marriage spouses, and same-sex partners varied. Xie, who had two children through previous *zhihun* and through ART with Hong, stressed that her older son, who was already studying at university, visited Xie and Hong frequently. "Gege (the older brother) accepts us quite well. I am even unhappy about the fact that Gege is always on Hong's side!" Xie joked. Xie did a good job of balancing her multiple kinship roles as a mother to her older son and as a partner to her girlfriend. Xie was not a caring daughter in her relatives' eyes, while she did not think her father deserved her care as well. Tommy and Joe maintained regular contact with Joe's ex-wife, who later moved to

Guangzhou as well. Tommy called Joe's ex-wife "Jack's mama" and regularly posted photos of Jack's mama with them at their home. On the other hand, Lin had rather divisive relationships with her separated husband, her son, and her girlfriend Mo, since she could not bring her school-aged son to Shenzhen to live with her and Mo.

In most circumstances, *zhihun* could be a neutral term, while *pianhun* was always negative in moral discourse. Being able to maintain harmonious relationships with one's former spouse, children, and current same-sex partner would make one sound more responsible and honest and less like *pianhun*. Tommy and Joe shared their story with thousands of blog readers because they believed that Joe's previous heterosexual marriage was not *pianhun*. Xie and Lin did not tell me a lot about their relationships with ex-husbands, while they implied that their ex-husbands did not marry them for love, so both parties were married with a purpose. In this sense, *pianhun* came into existence when someone not only lied about sexual desires and practices but also pretended to fall in love with a straight person. Xie and Lin further emphasized that they visited their children as much as they could. Mellow was aware of the criticisms about *pianhun*. When sharing her experience, Mellow repeated several times that she felt guilty, and she did not take financial advantage of her ex-husband. They also highlighted that they were honest with their same-sex partners. The different narratives of *zhihun* and *pianhun* complicate the dominant ethical discourse on 'marriage fraud' (Zhu, 2018). It would be accurate to suggest that *pianhun* was a vanishing practice among younger generations in big cities like Shenzhen due to the transforming attitudes towards entering heterosexual marriages and having children in queer communities.

Gay–lesbian xinghun/*contract marriage*

I became friends with Dae in 2015. After that, we regularly chatted via WeChat. Dae was born in 1982 and always saw herself as a T. When I first met her, she was playing football with her T friends before we went for a late-night dinner. When we met again in 2019, Dae kept her short T-style hair, while her colourful backpack with attached toy and cute water bottles somehow indicated her mother status. She joked that she was not only a single lesbian but also a divorced mother of twins. Dae's social circles were full of queer women and almost all her lesbian friends were in *xinghun* (contract marriages). *Xinghun*, short for *xingshi hunyin*, is also translated as nominal marriage, performative marriage, quasi-marriage, or a marriage of convenience between a gay man and a lesbian.

Dae married a gay man who was working in the army in 2012. They met each other through a *xinghun*-themed QQ group chat. At that time, like other non-heterosexual people when they reached 30 years old, Dae's parents expected her to marry. Dae chose *xinghun* to ease the pressure. I asked if her *xinghun* partner offered the apartment as bride price; she laughed and said, "my mother didn't ask for that. She was so happy that someone wanted to marry her old daughter!" Later, Dae made a difference between the 'just like real family' type of *xinghun* and the 'business/nominal' type of *xinghun*. According to Dae, her *xinghun* was more like the 'nominal' kind because there was no real exchange of bride price and dowry, and they did not live together.

For many non-heterosexual people desiring children, entering *xinghun* marriage was a necessary step towards being parents – it was against the planned-birth policy to have out-of-wedlock children. Intrauterine insemination (IUI) and IVF are only available to married couples in Chinese accredited hospitals. A marriage certificate means cheaper, easier access to IUI and IVF. If one is lucky enough, they may even have children through old-fashioned artificial insemination at home without going to a fertility clinic. Otherwise, unmarried people had to go overseas or choose private medical institutions in mainland China which were situated in legally grey areas. The lesbian and the gay man usually negotiate over how to pay betrothal gifts, how to behave in front of each other's parents, whether to get a marriage certificate and co-parent, and so on. They might have had a written *xinghun* contract which confirmed further details such as property and living arrangements, the length of the marriage, and parenting costs. Yet, they knew that such informal contracts had no legal force, and they could only count on each other's moral accountability. Even if both parties in a *xinghun* marriage signed a contract agreeing to not provide care for each other and to not share fostering rights, the agreements were legally invalid once they obtained a marriage certificate. In other words, non-heterosexual people in *xinghun* could not make a legally enforcing contract regarding personal issues including custody rights when such terms were against Chinese Marriage Law. *Xinghun* couples who chose to obtain marriage certificates in recent years preferred to sign a prenuptial property agreement and get it notarized, as they learned that the property agreement was the only legally valid contract in the case of *xinghun* marriage.

Dae's case suggested that financial capability sometimes was not the major reason non-heterosexual people chose to have children through *xinghun*. Some told me that they chose *xinghun* even though they could afford all the parenting costs. They were worried that if their children did not grow up with a father and a mother, they would suffer discrimination at school and enjoy a less accomplished childhood. The 'suitable' and desirable *xinghun* partner often need to be gender-conforming and hold a cosmopolitan middle-class status to fit the image of a socially recognized normative (Engebretsen, 2017). Having children with a *xinghun* partner meant that one needed to be even more choosy, since the *xinghun* partner would be the other biological parent and they might remain married for an extended period. My friend informants often joked that finding an ideal *xinghun* partner was even harder than finding a good same-sex partner. It is worth reiterating that entering a heterosexual marriage was never the ultimate hope of non-heterosexual people's parents – it would always involve having offspring. Therefore, *xinghun* should not be understood as merely a solution to ease marriage pressure from families of origin. By discussing *xinghun* in the context of queer parenting, I want to create a wider understanding of the practices of gay–lesbian *xinghun* and co-parenting. Non-heterosexual people's motivation for choosing *xinghun* could be linked not only to parental expectations but also to their desires to be 'legitimate' parents that complied with the image of the heteronormative family.

Dae and her *xinghun* partner obtained a marriage certificate once they agreed to co-parent. Yet, their plan to have children was postponed for several years until Dae broke up with her ex-girlfriend, who was also in a *xinghun* marriage. Dae and her *xinghun* partner went to the local public hospital to do IUI in 2016. In 2017, Dae gave birth to a son and a daughter.

I went over our chat history and found Dae's commentary on *xinghun* changed dramatically. When we met in 2015, Dae and Ju asserted that "*xinghun* is the most suitable tactic and perhaps the only tactic for Chinese sexual minorities now". What they implied was that *xinghun* could be a pragmatic solution for them to fulfil parental expectations and to enjoy freedom to have same-sex relationships. Soon after Dae's twins were born in 2017, she warned me, "If you can raise your children by your own or with your girlfriend, don't find a *xinghun* partner! *Xinghun* brings too many troubles and who knows if the kid really needs a father!"

At that time, Dae regretted that she chose to have children with her *xinghun* husband. She complained that her *xinghun* partner was not economically well off and was stingy with children. They also had an unpleasant argument when her *xinghun* partner proposed to take the children to the army with him. For Dae, co-parenting with her *xinghun* partner became unexpectedly problematic, and she wished she could raise children on her own even if it meant that she had to bear all the parenting costs and be recognized as a divorced single mother in public.

After Dae bought a bigger apartment herself in 2018, she got divorced from her *xinghun* partner to avoid future property disputes (Dae "confessed" that she used it as an excuse to get rid of the marriage certificate). Dae has been taking care of the newborn twins with her mother since the divorce. Her former legal husband had to stay in the army during weekdays and his parents were not healthy enough to take care of the children. Dae showed me the divorce agreement which indicated that she had full custody and her legal ex-husband needed to pay the stated alimony every month.

When we met again in person in 2019, Dae did not complain about anything. Instead, she mentioned that her *xinghun* partner came to her apartment every Saturday. Since her *xinghun* partner did not want to sleep at her home, he usually arrived before 8 am and left when the children fell asleep:

'My lesbian friends all told me that I am lucky because not every father is willing to spend time with his kid every weekend. My *xinghun* partner is a quiet person who doesn't like to play around with other gay men. He'd rather come to see and play with his kids.'

Dae's co-parenting experience with her *xinghun* partner reveals the complex interplay of legal policies, economic considerations, gender norms, and moral practices (Choi and Luo, 2016; Engebretsen, 2017; Wang, 2019; Lo, 2020; Ji et al, 2021). Although Dae said her *xinghun* was rather 'nominal' as she made an effort to avoid possible property disputes, she still had moral expectations of her *xinghun* partner based on their kin roles. In the later stages, Dae frequently called her *xinghun* ex-husband a 'father of twins'.

Wen, a 34-year-old lesbian, did not consider her *xinghun* marriage to be the result of parental pressure. Also, she did not equate getting *xinghun* married with being blindly obedient to her parents:

'I don't like to be pushed. If I felt I was being pushed to do something, I would fight. My parents never gave me any pressure to marry. I chose *xinghun* marriage not because I must do it but because I thought I could do it. Being married makes things convenient. I could use it as an excuse to avoid the after-work social activities with my boss and colleague. Maybe it sounds like a huge sacrifice to many others, but it was an easy task for me. Also, I want to have children because it was not a difficult thing for me to do.'

Wen spent some time emphasizing that she was not being used by her *xinghun* husband, nor did she ever use him. Another friend informant contended, "*xinghun* is just a lifestyle one chooses". Their narratives indicated that they refused to victimize themselves but rather to mobilize themselves as moral subjects who could fulfil their filial piety and manage their own life choices. Yet, after learning of other *xinghun* divorce cases in which the lesbian lost the custody of children, Wen was hesitating and thinking about having children by herself instead of co-parenting with her *xinghun* husband. In 2020, Wen and her *xinghun* husband divorced as they both decided to have children without a known opposite-sex partner.

As Dae has specified, there are many forms of *xinghun* marriage; some were more 'nominal' and some were more 'like real family'. An essentially 'nominal' *xinghun* means no legal or parenting bonds between two *xinghun* partners. When Danny looked for a *xinghun* husband to stop her parents and colleagues questioning her intimate life, she planned to only hold a wedding. As a lawyer, Danny did not want to get a marriage certificate because "it (legal marriage) involves property". Moreover, she did not want to co-parent with her *xinghun* husband because they "may scramble for children in the future". Some of their friends had what they called a 'like a real marriage' process: the *xinghun* bridegroom's parents provided an apartment as bride price and the *xinghun* bride's parents provided a car as a dowry, and the *xinghun* couple obtained an official marriage certificate and lived together in the matrimonial home. For queer women who were not economically independent enough to raise children on their own and queer men who wanted biological children but could not afford surrogacy, the division of labour in parenting could be 'like a real family'. The *xinghun* husband paid for the necessary parenting costs, and the *xinghun* wife paused her career for several years to raise the children. In this kind of comparison, the essence of marriage that made it 'real' was the gendered division of work rather than an affectionate and sexual relationship between husband and wife.

Whether one approves of the practice of *xinghun* or not, it has become increasingly visible in queer communities that *xinghun* is much more complicated than business deals; just like the saying frequently quoted when discussing *xinghun*: "marriage is never between two people, but between two families". People in *xinghun* marriages often had to comfort their parents-in-law, and both parties might feel wronged during such processes. When *xinghun* marriages came to an end, the custody of children often became the major divorce dispute, according to countless testimonials from my friend informants and online discussion forums. In recent years, I witnessed an increasing number of helplines and sharing sessions hosted by LGBT organizations to deal with the legal disputes raised by *xinghun*. I frequently hear my queer friends saying, "*Xinghun* will only solve the current problem and leave more problems for later". Some other friend informants argued that *xinghun* is also lying and therefore morally flawed. Young non-heterosexual people in cities contended that *xinghun* marriage fundamentally cheated parents and the queer community. Several LGBT organization workers said, "These people who choose *xinghun* won't be interested in doing anything to support our community. Do you know why it is so hard for us to come out? It is because of them".

In short, having children through the practice of *xinghun* and IUI/IVF technology was often considered a pragmatic and perhaps cost-saving option. Also, holding a marriage certificate permitted the *xinghun* couple the access to IUI and IVF in hospitals and ensured that the childbirth was lawful in mainland China. In this sense, *xinghun* was not seen as merely a solution to marriage pressure but also a solution to complying with the state regulation which tightly linked parenting to heterosexual marriage. The difference non-heterosexual people drew between 'nominal' and 'like real family' in the practice of *xinghun* was crucial for understanding marriage in Chinese society. The terms 'nominal' and 'like real' were used by my friend informants to compare different kinds of arrangements of *xinghun* marriage and demonstrated their understanding of a normative family in public eyes.

Furthermore, people who frame xi*nghun* as a personal choice that could be adjusted to resemble business cooperation neglect the roles of their financial capability and social status that enabled them such a negotiation. Both Dae and Wen have bought their own apartments that freed them from living with *xinghun* husbands and parents-in-law. Even in a *xinghun* marriage, men's and women's life trajectories are conditioned by gender norms (Engebretsen, 2009). While men could continue to pursue their careers, women's choices are limited as they are expected to focus on kids and chores. In the case of gay–lesbian co-parenting, the lesbians' living arrangements could be further limited if they lacked financial capability. This was illustrated in queer subjects' different experiences during *xinghun* marriage. Dae's ex-girlfriend was not economically independent and thus lacked negotiating power with her *xinghun* husband and *xinghun* parents-in-law. As a result, Dae's ex-girlfriend's living arrangement was significantly restricted, leaving her no room for being with Dae.

Guoji *(adopting from a family relative)*

I first met Tian at a Shenzhen PFLAG talkfest in 2019. He was with his 5-year-old son Xiaoyu and the father–son combination was admired by other attendees, with comments like "your son is so cute!" His son was wearing a rainbow name tag and playing with rainbow colour crayons. We had a brief talk when his son drew a rainbow line on my arm. No attendee asked how he 'had' his son; neither did I.

Tian was living in Dongguan, an industrial city close to both Shenzhen and Guangzhou. He was born in 1980 in Yongzhou, Hunan. After graduating from high school, he came to Guangdong as a migrant worker and stayed in multiple places in Guangdong including Dongguan, Guangzhou, and Zhuhai. He has worked at different factories and companies within the clothing industry. In 2008, he settled in Dongguan, and his family, including his brother, sister, and parents, moved to Dongguan to live in the same neighbourhood. His business mainly sold branded clothes on e-commerce sites since he had connections with clothing factories in Dongguan.

In 2014, Tian found a lesbian in a QQ chat group and got married in a rush under marriage pressure. They obtained a legal marriage certificate as they initially planned to co-parent. Tian's *xinghun* partner, a young lesbian who identified as P, wanted to marry urgently because she wanted to leave her family of origin and live with her girlfriend. The day after the wedding, she flew to Nanning to live with her girlfriend. Tian and his *xinghun* partner rarely met afterwards. They had an oral agreement on having children, while Tian's *xinghun* partner decided not to have children two years after. Tian was not sure why she changed her mind: "Maybe she was afraid that having children with me would affect her relationship with her girlfriend. I have heard many women will focus on their children rather than spouses after childbirth".

This was a myth that I frequently heard from both queer men and women. Tian's speculation revealed the gendered expectation placed on his *xinghun* ex-wife by wider society. As illustrated before, *xinghun* could be much more complicated than cooperative relationships and have an influence on a *xinghun* couple's intimate relationship with their same-sex partners. In 2016, Tian's *xinghun* partner flew to Dongguan to divorce Tian and flew back to Nanning the next day.

When Tian mentioned his experience of *xinghun*, I felt confused. If his 5-year-old son was not from his former *xinghun* marriage, how did he 'get' a son? Who was Xiaoyu's mother? I asked this question and Tian explained:

'My son Xiaoyu is my blood (*xueyuan*). My little brother has two sons. He and his ex-wife got divorced after their second son Xiaoyu was born. My little brother is with the older son, and I am with the little one now. My brother can't take care of two sons, so one is *guoji* (adopted from a family relative) by me.'

Tian's younger brother was a doctor and rarely had vacation time to be with his children. They reached an agreement that Tian could adopt Xiaoyu as his son. In this way, *guoji* transferred Tian's kin role from being the uncle to the father of Xiaoyu. Several clarifications need to be made here. *Guoji* was far from an often-mentioned pathway to parenthood in queer lifeworlds, especially among lesbians. There were two other gay friend informants who *guoji*-adopted sons from their siblings in my research. No lesbian friend informants mentioned *guoji* adoption, and it appeared that few daughters were *guoji*-adopted. In fact, many one-child generation queer individuals had no siblings. Also, no friend informants ever talked about *lingyang* (a general word for adoption) as a desirable option for having children.[3]

Guoji adoption has had a long history since ancient China and was a desirable option for families without sons until the late 1960s under communist rules (Cohen, 2005, p 117). Patrilineal kinship and blood ties remained the dominating factors in apprehending parent–child relations in the practice of *guoji* adoption. We must not ignore the fact that the men in late Imperial China (1368–1911) who adopted sons to maintain the continuity of the family line strongly preferred to select heirs from their closest male siblings with the same surname. *Guoji* could be translated as 'agnatic adoption', while its traditional aim was to ensure the adopted male heir cared for his adoptive parents and worshipped them after their death (Cohen 2005, p 116; see also Watson, 1982; Szonyi, 2002). Thus, the adopted heir should have been old enough to know what was going on and be aware of his filial obligation to his adoptive parents. For Tian and the other two friend informants, the main purpose of *guoji* was not to ensure the continuity of the family line but to have a companion in their life. What Tian and other gay fathers meant by '*guoji*' was not the same as its traditional meaning. Tian also stated that he did not adopt Xiaoyu for elder support, and his brother could "take Xiaoyu back" in the future if he wanted.

The process of formally adopting Xiaoyu did not go smoothly. To be legally recognized as Xiaoyu's father, Tian had to obtain the signature of Xiaoyu's biological parents (Tian's brother and former sister-in-law). However, Xiaoyu's mother refused to sign the adoption document. Because of that, Tian had not completed the legal process at the time of our interview in 2019, which meant Xiaoyu was not legally recognized as his son. Tian seemed to not be worried about that. He simply said, "Well, if my younger brother or Xiaoyu's mother want to have Xiaoyu as their son in the future, I will return Xiaoyu; but I believe Xiaoyu's *qinsheng* (biological/own) parents would want to give the child a better life, wouldn't they?"

Xiaoyu calls Tian '*baba*' (dad) and calls Xiaoyu's little brother '*xiao baba*' (little dad). Xiaoyu was aware that he had two dads and a big brother. Tian undoubtedly had spent the most father–son time with Xiaoyu. He held all the financial responsibilities as a father, such as paying for Xiaoyu's education. Also, Tian had the authority to take Xiaoyu to different LGBT events.

As Xiaoyu was going to elementary school, his *hukou* (residence/household) was still with Tian's brother in Yongzhou, Hunan. This meant he could not register with the public elementary school in Dongguan. If Xiaoyu was Tian's legal son, Xiaoyu would not have any problem since Tian had already obtained Dongguan *hukou*. At that point, I understood what Tian meant by a 'better' life. Dongguan certainly had better educational resources than rural areas in Youngzhou, Hunan. Therefore, Tian displayed disappointment that Xiaoyu's mother did not give her son the opportunity to receive a better education. Moreover, taking Xiaoyu to travel each summer was also something Xiaoyu's mother could not afford to do. In fact, Xiaoyu's mother rarely visited Xiaoyu. Tian's statement implied that Xiaoyu's mother was selfish because she refused to let Xiaoyu gain better qualifications to give Xiaoyu a decent life.

In the case of non-heterosexual people adopting children, biological ties with these children could still be essentially important, as the legal policy of adoption did not recognize non-heterosexual people as morally suitable parents. The practice of *guoji* adoption had skipped the first stage of gaining the permission of the child welfare centre as a state institution and it eliminated public moral dispute. Tian was Xiaoyu's uncle in genetic and conventional kinship terminology. The adoption negotiations happened between relatives instead of strangers. When Tian explained that Xiaoyu was his brother's son, he used the specific term *guoji* instead of the general word *lingyang*/adoption to legitimate his fatherhood through the conception of *xueyuan* (blood tie). In this way, he also mobilized the kinship terminology, transforming his kin role from uncle to father.

Despite Tian's continued efforts to highlight his moral and financial agency to parent Xiaoyu, legal procedures might still produce discomfort and confusion around parenthood for queer parents. The other gay father I interviewed had also described that, as an unmarried man, he could not risk his gay identity being found out by the Department of Civil Affairs during the adoption process.

ARTs alone without entering heterosexual marriage

If both *zhihun* and *xinghun* are morally flawed practices, and adoption and childbirth outside heterosexual marriage is restricted, how to have children – in the 'right' way – has become a burning question among queer intended parents. When I started my fieldwork in 2018, many queer friend informants recommended me to check out the WeChat public page 'Rainbow Baby' (*caihong baobao*). This public account was created by a lesbian couple in 2015 who had mixed-race twin babies through the *A luan* (egg) *B huai* (conceive) process overseas. The process of *A luan B huai* is practically the same as what is termed reciprocal IVF, in which one partner (person A) supplies the eggs to the other (person B), who becomes the gestational carrier of the pregnancy. The lesbian co-mothers, owning a kindergarten themselves, had been sharing their life with hundreds of followers.

ART terms such as artificial insemination and *A luan* (egg) *B huai* (conceive) have emerged in lesbian communities since the 2010s. In some cases, one might bear two children using both of their eggs, referred to as *AB luan B huai*. This required the assistance of IVF-EF (in-vitro fertilization-embryo freezing) technology, which was far more expensive than doing IUI. Many desiring lesbian mothers reasoned that the *A luan B huai* process would make the lesbian couple feel that the child was consanguineously bonded to both. According to them, the child carried the T's DNA and was in the P's uterus to absorb nutrients from the P's body.

For queer women who wanted to do IUI or IVF procedures without getting married, they might either go to an overseas hospital (with or without a Chinese agency) or a private medical centre in mainland China which charged higher amounts than a public hospital. Although buying sperm from a sperm bank and doing IUI/IVF were lawful in China, these were not available to unmarried people. In other words, if Chinese non-heterosexual people wanted to have children without getting married and without getting into legally grey areas, they had to do so overseas.

Among gay intended fathers, surrogacy was the desired option, as an emerging number of gay icons in China publicly posted their children online and did not hide how they had their children overseas. I got to meet Professor Min at a Shenzhen PFLAG talkfest. Min gave a speech at the talkfest, encouraging attendees to "be yourself". After the speech, a lot of gay attendees went to Min for advice. I heard people calling Min a role model, knowing that he was respected not just because of his position as a university professor but because of his 13-year relationship with his boyfriend and two sons through surrogacy. Min had overseas experience in the United States, where he realized and embraced his gay identity. After attending a few blind dates arranged by family relatives, Min felt he could not hurt a woman by marrying her. Min then came out to his parents, telling them he would never enter heterosexual marriages. After being together with Shan, a Hong Kong-based businessman, for more than a decade, Min thought that their intimate relationship could be tightened by being co-fathers. They flew to California twice: the first time to sign a contract and have sperm retrieval treatment, and the second time to bring their sons back.

Surrogacy was illegal in China, though there was an increasing number of private reproductive medical centres and ART agencies associated with the underground market in surrogacy. Some non-heterosexual people decided to do ART in mainland China since it was cheaper and less time-consuming. People who worked as employees often could not get enough vacation time to do it overseas. Yet, these private ART businesses were not legitimate in China and thus could raise legal issues and human rights debates. I will discuss further the use of ART and ART business in the next chapter.

Despite the sky-high costs of ART, especially surrogacy, it was undoubtedly the most recent and most desirable option among Chinese non-heterosexual people. For many queer (intended) parents, not only could ART be done without the fuss raised by heterosexual marriage, being able to choose an unrelated egg/sperm donor was a vital point. In addition, this was often considered the ideal practice for a same-sex couple to have children 'together' as their mutual bond, while the previously mentioned practices always involved another heterosexual marriage and another opposite-sex parent outside their queer intimate relationships. As discussed earlier, even the claimed-to-be-nominal *xinghun* could produce unequal relations based on given kinship roles and pose restrictions to living arrangements unless both parties had equal negotiating power. Recalling Chen's statement that some of her gay and lesbian clients come with their parents – we must not ignore that – ART also becomes a desirable option for non-heterosexual people's parents to have biological grandchildren. For many, it was having biological offspring that helped them to gain parental acceptance of a same-sex partnership.

Understanding queer individuals' moral decisions

There are several implications non-heterosexual people emphasized when discussing their motivations for and approaches to having children. The first one was morality. As non-heterosexual people living in a society where having offspring has been a significant aspect of filial piety and only heterosexual married couples are granted legal rights to have children, their desires and pathways to parenthood were central to moral discourse. In premodern China, the ritual practice of ancestor worship and the Confucian conceptions of filial piety both placed emphasis on the continuation of patrilineal lineage. While some queer parents, especially the post-80s and post-70s generations, explained that they had no choice but to have children to please their parents or to expect elderly support as a return from children (as *yang'erfanglao*), many non-heterosexual people disconnected their desire for children from the notions of familial duty and instead framed their motivation for being parents as a positive and voluntary act. Also, a generational shift in understanding filial piety from 'obedience' and 'duty' to 'mutual respect' and 'equal relations' is emerging (Riley, 1994; Yan, 2003; Xie, 2013). The transforming family structures have also mobilized queer individuals' relationships with their families of origin, which I shall explore in Chapter 6. In addition, the increasing housing and living costs have discouraged the urban youth from being parents and inevitably shaped how they envision their future care relationships. For these reasons, fewer and fewer queer urbanites mention having children as an ultimate solution to fulfil family obligations and to ensure one's elderly support. In this sense, Chinese young non-heterosexual people stressed a moral–immoral divide as well as a modern–traditional divide. By deeming the Confucian tradition of continuing the family line as no longer economically rewarding and morally praiseworthy, the young generation in urban China has created a new discourse on what is moral and what is not. Moreover, non-heterosexual people's investment in parenting should not be interpreted as being exclusively traditional or modern as their practices do not occupy such a binary. Emerging research on queer kinship and families in various contexts suggests that investment in queer parenting can be both connected to the traditional/patrilineal family form and very queer/subversive (Mamo, 2007; Folger, 2008; Ryan-Flood and Jamieson, 2009; Murphy, 2013; Sorainen, 2015; Lo et al, 2016; Patton-Imani, 2020; Yao et al, 2023). Therefore, queerness should not be simply seen as resistant or against heteronormative norms of reproduction; my friend informants' moves to parenthood can be both linked to conventional family values (pleasing parents) and queer relationality (bonding same-sex relationships).

Moreover, the tendency in online and offline queer communities to morally evaluate non-heterosexual people's pathways to parenthood is notable. There are many ways to become a parent for Chinese non-heterosexual people, but they may not be recognized equally in terms of feasibility and moral values. When making their decisions to have children and when reflecting on such decisions, queer parents measure their self-interests and interpret their actions in a proper relational manner with other people involved, so they may maintain moral accountability in their social circles. The discourse of the moral–immoral divide is vital for understanding the complexity of sexuality/ sexualness and selfhood in the transforming Chinese society. The Chinese 'self' can be 'divided by a number of "dividers," such as past versus present, public versus private, moral versus immoral, and so on' (Kleinman et al, 2011, p 5). Yan (2017) has furthered the discussion on the divided selfhood and suggests a tripartite approach to understanding Chinese personhood as both a statement and an action. Yan argues that, in the dynamic process of 'doing personhood' (*zuoren*), the moralist self is employed to control the desiring individual for the purpose of making oneself the proper relational person (2017, p 3). A person's moral accountability is achieved through cultivating good relations with other people. Building on Yan's argument that personhood is a process of becoming, I suggest that we take all three components – the moralist self, the desiring individual, and the relational person – to unpack Chinese queer subjects' moral practices. Min's speech on "be yourself" (*zuoziji*) provides a vivid example, as he argues that "be yourself is not static". To be able to "be yourself", as Min suggested, one needs to gain economic independency and build social networks. For Min and his folks, "being yourself" involves more than the act of coming out or embracing an openly queer lifestyle – it is about the constant negotiation between personal desires and moral obligations in order to achieve good reputation both within queer communities and in the wider society.

At the same time, this chapter's personal accounts demonstrate that there is no one consistent moral stand for Chinese non-heterosexual people to maintain. The discourse on the moral–immoral divide is always manifold and dynamic. For instance, Zhenzhen used the prevalent discourse on filial piety to explain her intention to have children as reasonable and morally good, whereas Danny and Pam would blame Zhenzhen for being a selfish person and claim that they would never have children for that purpose. Xie had a son from her previous heterosexual marriage almost two decades ago, so her choice to get married would receive fewer moral criticisms than same-sex desiring people who marry straight people today. When *xinghun* marriages were morally unacceptable in some young non-heterosexual people's eyes, some queer parents like Dae describe *xinghun* as a practical tactic to raise children and to form a socially recognizable normative family. The emerging queer communities have also played an increasingly remarkable role in apprehending Chinese non-heterosexual people's moral sense of self. For the younger generation of non-heterosexual people in urban China, being an out and honest person in intimate relationships and friend circles can be as significant as being a virtuous child in their parents' eyes. The moral worth of one's practice is relationally evaluated by their parents, their partners, their colleagues, their friends, and themselves in a temporal and spatial context.

The other two factors that arise here within the moral–immoral discourse are law and finance, which I will take up again throughout the book. In addition to moral measurements, queer individuals' ability to cope with the state policy and the rising costs of being parents undoubtedly shaped their decisions regarding having offspring. In short, having children is a morally, legally, and financially charged process. This is particularly evident in *xinghun* partners who co-parent. Co-parenting with one's *xinghun* partner reveals the complex interplay of legal policies, gender norms, and moral values, as non-heterosexual people in *xinghun* marriages struggle to walk the blurred line between 'nominal' and 'real' marriage. The practice of *guoji* adoption from family relatives raises less fuss compared to formal adoption, despite that going through the relevant legal procedures can still produce discomfort and confusion around parenthood for queer parents. Against this backdrop, using ART alone without entering any form of heterosexual marriage has emerged as the seemingly ideal option for queer intended parents, especially same-sex couples, when it comes to having children. Rather than hoping for the existing marriage and adoption law to change, most queer Chinese citizen subjects hoped to gain personal agency and purchasing power to justify their queer and reproductive desires. For non-heterosexual people who have children without entering a heterosexual marriage, the legal challenges they face are, in many ways, similar to people who have 'out-of-wedlock childbirths', which I will discuss further in moving to Chinese non-heterosexual people's participation in assisted reproduction. As we shall see in the next chapter, the use of ART has raised further debates on gender inequalities and social stratifications.

4

Queering Technology: Becoming Queer Parents through Assisted Reproductive Technologies

In summer 2018, I got to meet An, a 33-year-old gay father living in Shenzhen. An was the owner of an investment company. He and his boyfriend Ye have mixed-race triplets and their story of having children through surrogacy overseas has been reported by several news websites, which made them known to the online gay community. An's *Weibo* was full of admiring comments by other gay men. Many commenters said they would follow An's path to having children.

An and Ye started to plan for having children in 2011. They decided to use An's sperm since Ye was not in a good health condition. According to An, he has put a lot of effort into ensuring they would have 'good' children. An did research on surrogacy and in-vitro fertilization (IVF) legal policies and visited hospitals in Thailand, Russia, and China. He finally chose a Russian clinic specializing in IVF and surrogacy and later invested in it. An selected a good-looking German model to be the egg donor since he always wanted to have mixed-race babies. An also lost 15 kilograms to achieve his best health condition: "I kept tracking my semen quality. In 2013, my sperm vitality had improved to 78 per cent, so I started the process". An explained that he was a Hong Kong resident and the surrogate mother stayed in the Hyatt hotel with them for three months. In 2014, An's three babies were born in a private hospital in Hong Kong. Since all procedures were done outside mainland China, An did not need a marriage certificate to register the childbirth. According to him, he spent $620,000 towards having children from 2011 to 2014. An ended his description with an emotional sentence: "After they were born, I was very excited! They are exactly what I imagined!"

An gave precise narratives on how he had children overseas, knowing that his description of having children was powerful proof of his privileged social class. An used the online visibility of his gay family to promote his transnational assisted reproductive technologies (ARTs) business. During my stay in Guangdong, I found an increasing number of not only queer parents who employed ART but also lesbian, gay, bisexual, and transgender (LGBT)-identified people working in the ART industry.

This chapter focuses on the interplay of queer networks and the emerging private ART companies in urban China. ARTs such as intrauterine insemination (IUI) and IVF were initially developed to overcome infertility problems for heterosexual couples. According to Franklin, IVF discloses 'our biological relativity in the form of a technology employed to create biological relatives, thus changing how we understand the adjective "biological"' (2013, p 28). She points out that the pursuit of IVF as a popular conjugal technology is not necessarily driven by the desire to have children but is embodied in the sense of centring one's life around reproduction, aligned within the institutional norms of both heterosexuality and marriage. To put it another way, the pursuit of reproductive technologies involves not only the desire to reproduce but also the desire to belong to certain social groups, such as groups of mothers and queer reproductive families. After IVF, 'reproduction has become a matter of technique, and mere biology has become an oxymoron' (Franklin, 2013, p 33).

If ART such as IVF has become normative, what is its position in queer relationships in China? How do non-heterosexual people understand the emerging ART, and who tends to employ ART? As many may observe, ART provides an example par excellence of stratified reproduction, namely, 'the power relations by which some categories of people are empowered to nurture and reproduce, while others are disempowered' (Ginsburg and Rapp, 1995, p 3). Despite the presence of inequities and ethical dilemmas in using ART, LGBT people's inclusion in biological reproduction around the world represents hope for the potential of queer reproduction, family forms, and kinship (Inhorn and Birenbaum-Carmeli, 2008; Cadoret, 2009; Mamo and Alston-Stepnitz, 2015). Thus, the concerns that must be addressed include not only issues around sexuality and kinship but also how the ART market is organized (Carvalho et al, 2019). This chapter illustrates how ART companies and queer organizations sponsored by them continue to shape the ideals of reproduction and future in queer lifeworlds. I use data from government documents, mass media, and online discussions on ART to articulate the legal and moral context of ART in Chinese society. Individuals from different genders, ages, and classes interpreted the legal and moral issues regarding human gamete selling and surrogacy in diverse ways. I then provide narratives regarding how Chinese queer (intended) parents employ ART services to have children.

IVF, human gamete donation, and surrogacy in China

The first baby conceived from in-vitro fertilization and embryo transfer (IVF-ET) was born at the Third Hospital of Peking University in Beijing in 1988, which marked the beginning of the history of ART in Chinese society. The use of ART in China is strongly connected with its unique birth-planning policy and socio-cultural emphasis on reproduction (Klein, 2017). Methods to deal with childlessness such as concubinage and *guoji* adoption from close relatives have been documented throughout Chinese history. In recent decades, ART has become a vital alternative to deal with infertility.

In 2001, the Ministry of Health[1] of the People's Republic of China issued Order No. 14, the Management Measures of Human Assisted Reproduction Technology, and No. 15, the Regulations for the Administration of Sperm Banks. They came in line with the national family-planning policy, meaning that ART, including IUI and IVF, were only available to married, infertile couples. Order No. 14 states that medical facilities and medical personnel must not perform any surrogacy procedures.[2] Meanwhile, the two orders prohibit any form of buying and selling of human sperm, eggs, and embryos. In 2003, the Ministry of Health issued a notice concerning the revision of the norms, standards, and ethical principles for ART and sperm banks. The notice stipulates that medical personnel must not apply ART to couples and single women who do not comply with the National Population and Family Planning Law and must not choose the sex of the child. In 2006, the Ministry of Health issued Order No. 44 regarding the regulation of ART and accreditation of human sperm banks, which requires that every infertility centre's licence be renewed every two years. If requirements are not met, the service is suspended.

In this context, sperm banking and ART have become important technologies of birth control (Wahlberg, 2018). Although IUI and IVF are lawful practices and available in over a hundred accredited medical facilities, unmarried Chinese citizens are not legally permitted to undertake ART or obtain human gametes from these accredited medical facilities. The existing state regulation on the use of ART thus denied parenthood to single and non-heterosexual people and further limited their ability to produce families.

The National Health and Family Planning Commission has reiterated that surrogacy is an illegal practice and has launched special procedures to punish the practice of commercial surrogacy. On the other hand, surrogacy is literally not mentioned in the National Population and Family Planning Law,[3] which has created ambiguity among the public. Performing surgery for surrogacy is certainly unlawful in China. Nevertheless, people working for private ART companies have argued that the surrogacy business is in the 'grey area' rather than completely banned by state law. Many salespeople at ART companies used the 2015-revised Population and Family Planning Law as evidence to tell me that "there is no state legislation prohibiting surrogacy". Although the National Health and Family Planning Commission prescribed administrative penalties for surrogacy, the criminal sanction for surrogacy was not specified and was not associated with criminal law charges in China. In this sense, the law existed in a complex relation to surrogacy, as it did not simply regulate the practice of surrogacy but caused more ambiguities within it. Based on observations in India and the global surrogacy market, Rudrappa (2018) argues that the 2016 ban against commercial surrogacy was brought forward to protect surrogacy, but it would deepen working-class women's exploitation in India and other countries, especially in Southeast Asia. *Legal Daily* released an 'Investigation on the Surrogacy Black Industry Chain' on 17 July 2019, which claimed that the underground surrogacy industry chain in China was relatively complete, including the entrusting party, the surrogacy intermediary, the surrogacy mother, the medical personnel or clinics implementing the surrogacy technology, and the device providers of the surrogacy.

Against this background, I want to clarify the meaning of 'Chinese ART companies' in this chapter. These could roughly be divided into two groups. One type of Chinese ART company is the ultimate service provider that owns direct access to a complete (underground) industry chain, including doctors and medical centres inside mainland China. Another type is an intermediary agency that has office space and some salespeople who take clients to the actual service providers in either mainland China or overseas. The latter comprises the majority of Chinese ART businesses.

Online debates over ART: the image of a wealthy gay couple and a poor surrogate mother?

Commercial surrogacy and the selling of human gametes have long been disputed within the mass media and internet communities. Since the appearance of surrogacy in China, major journals have reported on women losing their uteruses and even lives during egg retrieval or surrogacy. On 16 February 2017, Jiemian.com published a news article entitled 'Renting out the Womb: The Underground Production Line of Chinese Surrogacy Market' (Liu and Luo, 2017). This article detailed the story of a 27-year-old woman, Wang Jialan, who became a surrogate mother to ease her family's financial pressure. Before becoming a surrogate, Jialan was an apprentice at a beauty salon. For Jialan, working as a surrogate mother was a way to make quick money and was unlike prostitution. Jialan received ¥150,000/$2,0577 from a private ART agency after she gave birth to a child, which helped her family to deal with their financial problems. Meanwhile, the clients who want children through surrogacy usually pay the private agency a total of ¥350,000/$48,012 to over ¥1,500,000/$20,576. The article points out that the administrative policy banning commercial surrogacy did not restrain the development of underground surrogacy markets. Furthermore, the growing surrogacy underground chain made surrogates vulnerable as they lacked negotiating power.

On 5 August 2018, Thepaper.cn published a news article entitled 'Investigation of Underground Black Chain Surrogacy Business: 14-Year-Old Teenage Girl Being Tricked into Selling Her Eggs, 850,000 RMB for Guaranteed One-Stop Service'. At the beginning of the article, the journalist described the experience of a 14-year-old girl, Xiaojuan, who dropped out of school and went to Guangzhou. A web friend talked Xiaojuan into selling her eggs to a private agency. The agency pushed Xiaojuan to complete the egg retrieval operation in a rented apartment. The unsanitary and unprofessional procedure triggered ovarian hyperstimulation syndrome for her. Similar news articles appeared on news websites and TV every once in a while. In these appearances, the surrogates and egg sellers were represented as unenlightened victims who did not know the possible emotional and physical distress caused by these procedures, and the private ART companies were referred to as 'underground/black businesses' that cheated and exploited working-class women from rural China.[4]

In the mass media, the clients of commercial surrogacy and underground gamete selling were usually desperate couples who were either infertile or had lost their only children and could not find other options to have children. *Legal Daily*'s new report in 2019 showed that 10 to 15 per cent of married couples in China have fertility problems, and about 20 per cent of them need to employ ART to get pregnant. The universal two-child policy, allowing all married couples in China to have a second child, became effective in 2016 and notably encouraged the birth of a second child (Song, 2019; Zhang et al, 2019). At the same time, older couples who were eager to have a second child realized that they were either infertile or too old to bear a child. Furthermore, the shortage of available human sperm in accredited sperm banks seemed to leave infertile couples no other choice except turning to the underground ART market. Since 2016, the growing number of older couples desiring a second child has stimulated the booming underground market for informal human gamete trading and surrogacy agencies (He, 2017).[5]

The mass media coverage of the illegal practices of egg selling and surrogacy has caused some unexpected consequences. An increasing number of people get to know of the existence of ART and become clients of private ART agencies through the news, even where ART agencies are portrayed in a negative light. Chen, the manager of a private ART company in Guangzhou, said, "Some parents of gay men didn't know about surrogacy. Once they saw the terrible news about the poor surrogate mothers on TV, they realized that their son could do this to have children instead of marrying a straight woman!"

The online discourse on ART, especially surrogacy, has become a battlefield where gender inequality issues have been visualized. Many female users of Chinese social media platforms have actively condemned the underground market in egg donation and surrogacy. Meanwhile, people who supported egg donation and surrogacy remained an ambiguous group. Although the mass media platforms, especially TV news, rarely mentioned Chinese LGBT people as the clients of underground ART businesses, gay fathers who employed ART had more online visibility than heterosexual couples who adopted ART to have children. Edison is one of the gay-identified influencers who chose to have a mixed-race son through surrogacy outside China. His son was born in the United States in November 2017. Unlike most gay internet celebrities who had high visibility within online gay communities but were otherwise not known by the public, Edison joined one of the most popular online talk shows in 2015, making him famous to the general audience. Some gay fathers who employed surrogacy have become known in online gay communities, including one of my friend informants, An. It should be noted that Edison, An, and other gay fathers who openly shared their lives with their children all used agencies in countries outside mainland China. These celebrated gay fathers within online gay communities have arguably co-constructed surrogacy as the most desirable strategy for Chinese gay men to have children. Compared to these gay fathers, heterosexual couples who have children through surrogacy, either inside mainland China or overseas, kept their practice to a much lower profile to avoid gossip (He, 2017).

On 20 December 2019, the Standing Committee of the National People's Congress announced that they had received 237,057 online suggestions and 5,635 letters on the draft book of marriage and family, including legalizing same-sex marriage. The announcement by the Chinese governing body fuelled numerous polls and open debates on social media. Shortly after that, debates on same-sex marriage turned to the topic of surrogacy. A female user, whose web name was A-Yan, posted on the *Douban* group forum:

> I voted against the legalisation of same-sex marriage at *Ifeng.com*.[6] Do you really believe that if same-sex marriage is legalised, there will be no *tongqi* (wives of homosexual men) women? There is no such thing. Gay men still want to have children, so whether it is legal or illegal, same-sex marriage does not prevent them from *pianhun* (lying about one's sexual desires to marry a straight person) to have children. Moreover, when same-sex marriage becomes legal, gay men will fight for the legalisation of surrogacy as their next stage. Gay men want to promote the legalisation of surrogacy by legalising same-sex marriage. Look at Taiwan and the United States; we know that women's status will become even lower when surrogacy becomes legal. Not only

there will be chaos caused by surrogacy, cases of *pianhun* fraud won't be reduced, because not every gay man has the economic conditions to afford commercial surrogacy and they are going to continue to *pianhun*. (A-Yan, posted 22 December 2019)[7]

A-Yan's post, which received more than 400 replies, was not a rare one. Many discussants showed similar worries that supporting same-sex marriage equals supporting surrogacy. Their worries were rooted in the belief that Chinese men would always want a child of their own, regardless of their sexualities. Since the issue of *tongqi* appeared, many women have come to realize that the main reason for gay men marrying straight women – *pianhun* – was to use the *tongqi* wife to continue their family line. In this sense, gay men who marry straight women used their innocent wives as not only tools for passing as straight but also surrogates for having children. A-Yan's post entails an underlying understanding that gay men were not worthy of sympathy for their use of women's eggs and wombs to reproduce.

An online survey conducted by Ding and Gayspot in 2018 showed that 71 per cent of the gay respondents wanted to have children through surrogacy and 76 per cent of respondents hoped commercial surrogacy would become legal in China.[8] What worried the female readers of the survey most was that 56 per cent of gay respondents considered China to be their desired area for commercial surrogacy. A-Yan and other women on social media repeatedly quoted the survey result to prove their argument. Moreover, I suggest that the increasing online visibility of gay fathers whose lifestyles were endorsed by other gay men has not only strengthened the reliability of the survey result but also intensified the conflict between the image of gay men as wealthy clients and all women as potential victims. In A-Yan's post, for example, many discussants expressed their anger when they saw gay fathers describe how they select '*luanmei*' (literally meaning 'egg girl') and '*daimu*' (literally meaning surrogate). To cite from another heated thread titled 'I even start to doubt the rise of the male homosexual right will be the primary suppressing power to women' with hundreds of replies:

> You can tell that these gay men don't respect surrogate mothers and egg donors at all by their words. They treat these women like animals and products without sympathy. I never seemed to feel the kindness of gay men towards women. On the one hand, they want people to understand them and demand social progress to accept homosexuality; on the other hand, they still say 'I need to continue my family line'. If you are gay, you should accept being childless. (Rizhaoyaojin, posted 17 May 2019)[9]

As a female researcher, I could not disregard these voices from women like A-Yan on this matter. During fieldwork, I frequently heard gay men saying, "I am envious of you lesbians. You have a uterus. Having children for you is no trouble". For them, surrogacy was more expensive than IUI/IVF, so lesbians could spend less on having children and thus had less 'trouble'. This assumption was not factual, though it unpacked the moral and economic aspects within the practice of having children. The use of ART is undoubtedly always linked with the woman's body. In IVF, the woman's ovaries 'are artificially forced to ripen extra eggs, which are then surgically extracted' (Greely, 2016, p 9). Moreover, IVF is often combined with other procedures in the case of same-sex couples having children. For instance, a lesbian couple would need donated/sold sperm, and a gay couple would need donated/sold eggs and a surrogate to have children. Egg retrieval operations and surrogacy cause more physical and emotional discomfort for women, and in some cases, these procedures can even be life-threatening.

For A-Yan, Rizhaoyaojin, and many other young women against the practice of surrogacy, Chinese gay men, rather than heterosexual couples (who remain the major clients of underground surrogacy businesses), are the main supporters of legalizing surrogacy in China due to their gender, their role as sons in a patrilineal family, and their desire for biological offspring. Chinese gay men having children would always involve the issue of a *tongqi* being used as a free surrogate, a disadvantaged lesbian in a *xinghun* marriage, or a poor surrogate being exploited. In this discourse, *tongqi*, surrogate mothers, and women selling their eggs were exploited by gay men and dehumanized as instruments for having children. Following this argument, the legalization of same-sex marriage became a threat to women's social status and rights, as it might lead to the legalization of surrogacy.

In addition, a great number of queer women in my research compared *xinghun* marriage to surrogacy. Many young queer women assured me that they would never co-parent with gay men. One young queer woman said, "Gay men want *xinghun* marriage because they can't afford doing surrogacy in countries where surrogacy is legal. They don't want to pay for having children, so they turned to us thinking we can be free surrogates for them!"

It should be noted that, compared to lesbian mothers who used ART, gay fathers were more prone to moral criticism for their use of gestational surrogacy. Yet, it did not mean that lesbian mothers' use of ART was ethically acceptable in public discourse. Rather, lesbian mothers' presence was peripheral in public discourse. There were a lot more gay-identified micro-celebrities than lesbian-identified influencers in Chinese mainstream social media platforms. To put it another way, gay men's use of surrogacy attracted much more public attention than lesbians' use of IUI and IVF. Hence, queer women and queer men did not deal with the same moral criticisms when they became clients of ART businesses.

In short, the major platforms for mass media (which seemed to represent the state's attitude due to censorship) portrayed the practices of human gamete trading and commercial surrogacy as not only illegal but also unethical. At the same time, they displayed an ambiguous attitude towards the clients of private ART companies rather than blaming them. Online debates about the practice of surrogacy have often been linked to issues of gender inequality, which further expanded to issues of gay parenting and same-sex marriage. For many young women in urban China who were concerned about the gender privilege gay men held, gay men were not a threat to women's rights only when they did not desire reproduction and abandoned their existing gender privilege. In these debates, gay men's ethical right to pursue biological reproduction was held in question. The emerging practice of commercial surrogacy has shaped young women's attitudes towards gay men and LGBT communities. In this context, it is worth scrutinizing the relations between queer communities and ART companies and exploring how practices of ART are apprehended in Chinese queer lives.

The only true sponsor? ART companies and their marketing strategies

On 18 August 2018, I walked into a hotel away from the city centre in Shenzhen to attend an annual talkfest held by one of the largest LGBT non-profit organizations, Parents, Families, and Friends of Lesbians and Gays (PFLAG) China. PFLAG China holds talkfests in dozens of cities around China, at times with more than 300 attendees. Their WeChat page stated that their talkfests' purpose was to 'fix parent–child relationships, support family harmony, and build a harmonious society together'. On my way from the subway station to the hotel, I met at least 20 volunteers waving small rainbow flags and giving attendees directions. Stepping out of the elevator on the seventh floor, I found the corridor and meeting room full of people and rainbow accessories. More than 300 people attended this event. I also noticed a large roll-up banner of an ART agency named HH Company and flyers of the same company on my chair.

The annual talkfest started with a short video introducing PFLAG China and 'love, understanding, responsibility, family' as its theme. There were four hosts, two identifying as gay men and two identifying as lesbians. The last guest speaker, Chen, talked on the topic of 'having and raising children'. Before that, other speakers had shared their experience of coming out and strongly discouraged attendees from entering any form of heterosexual marriage. Chen was the founder of HH Company, which sponsored this talkfest. Chen introduced the ART services HH Company provided. She then revealed that she and her girlfriend had had twins through ART. Finally, she promised that clients from the talkfest would enjoy LGBT-exclusive discounts and service packages.

From 2018 to 2020, I attended six PFLAG China events in Shenzhen, Dongguan, and Guangzhou. The number of attendees ranged from around 50 to above 300. It became impossible for me to ignore that all these LGBT events were sponsored by private ART companies. In every event poster, there was a logo of an ART company and a small line such as 'dear child, you are my beloved gift'. There was always more than one representative from ART companies giving speeches on their experiences of having children. In fact, LGBT people talking about having children has become a fixed part of the programme at events held by PFLAG China. There were promotional banners and information booths in every talkfest for potential LGBT clients. It appeared that these LGBT events became not only social events for Chinese queer people and their families but also entry tickets to pink money markets for ART companies. By attending the events, I got to know Zhao and Chen, two of my friend informants who worked closely with both LGBT organizations and ART businesses.

After moving to Guangzhou to live with his boyfriend, Zhao started to work at PFLAG China. Not long after, he took on the new challenge of becoming the fundraising manager. He had tried to raise funds from various enterprises selling consumer goods. Nevertheless, few of the companies were willing to sponsor LGBT events directly. For instance, some cosmetics and sex toy companies offered coupons and samples as gifts for attendees. On the other hand, the ART agencies gave positive responses to Zhao's request:

> 'These ART services are almost the only business that supports us (PFLAG China) with real money (*zhenjinbaiyin*). At first, we worked with foreign ART organizations and agencies assisting clients in having children in the United States. Now, you see, we are sponsored mostly by the Chinese ART companies because the overseas ART organizations are too expansive. Many overseas ART organizations thought they didn't attract clients from PFLAG China and therefore stopped supporting our events. Furthermore, we believe the Chinese ART companies are more affordable for most Chinese LGBT people.'

In 2018, Zhao resigned from his position at PFLAG China. His previous business contact, Chen, reached out to him and offered him a job position at HH Company. Since then, Zhao has worked as a sales and marketing consultant at the company. He told me that he had thought about finding a new job in another LGBT non-profit organization, but he then thought that "working in these private ART companies can also help LGBT people". He soon acquired two clients through his queer friends.

On 15 December 2018, I attended a 'rainbow family sharing salon' held by HH Company. Zhao was the main organizer. The salon was advertised in the *xinghun* marriage/queer parenting WeChat groups and was held in the office of ZT (pseudonym), a Guangzhou-based LGBT non-profit organization focusing on gay health rights. Besides me, all the 13 attendees were planning on having children. The ZT worker gave a brief speech introducing the role of the ZT organization and Zhao, followed by a warm-up open discussion about coming out. They proposed an interesting angle as they asked not only how to come out to one's parents as a queer child but also to society as a queer parent. The attendees generally believed that Guangzhou and other big Chinese cities were becoming tolerant towards out-of-wedlock parenting. After the warm-up discussion, Zhao played an English video about queer families. He then explained the history of artificial insemination and IVF in China. The attendees asked questions about legal policies and disputes rather than the procedures. Like many ART company representatives at the PFLAG events, Zhao also emphasized that LGBT clients get discounts because "life is not easy for us (*douburongyi*)".

Two months after exchanging WeChat messages with Chen, I had the chance to visit HH Company's main office in a commercial building in Guangzhou. HH Company had become the major title sponsor of PFLAG China annual talkfests. When I arrived in the afternoon, Chen was chatting with a middle-aged heterosexual couple and a potential egg provider. I waited in her office with her two lesbian friends. The lesbian couple had known Chen for a long time and were considering opening a branch of the HH Company in Shenzhen. An hour later, Chen finished her conversation and came back to the office to chat with us. Her office looked typical of most Chinese entrepreneurs, with a tea table big enough for six people to talk while drinking tea. After her friends finished reading the document of HH Company, Chen handed it to me and said:

'You must know many rich gay and lesbian people. If you introduce customers to us, you will get a percentage of the sales as well! You can cooperate with us like my two friends. You know you can trust my company as we sponsored many LGBT events. Feel free to look at our service packages and ask questions!'

I quickly went over the document and thanked Chen for her trust. As someone with lots of queer contacts, Chen saw me as a potential sales agent. However, due to my awareness of legal and ethical complexities, I euphemistically declined the offer. We chatted and had several cups of tea. After Chen's friends and colleagues left the office, she started to talk about how she entered the ART industry.

Chen referred to herself as a typical T. She was born in 1985 in Zhuzhou, Hunan. She came to Guangzhou at an early age for better job opportunities and romantic relationships. Chen met her partner Liu eight years ago. According to Chen, Liu was a very capable and strong-minded woman.

Liu was divorced and lived with her son before Chen '*baiwan*' (made someone gay) Liu. Chen then started working as Liu's assistant. Two years after moving in together, they thought about having children together. For Chen, the process to have children was easy thanks to Liu's manager position in one of the earliest Chinese ART companies: "Before meeting Liu, I never knew that I could have children without marrying a man! Liu's career offered us a chance to get enough information and resources to have children through IVF".

Chen and Liu had two children using their eggs and the same man's sperm. This is called '*AB luan* (egg) *A huai* (conceive)', a developed version of *A luan B huai*, and required better medical techniques. Liu gave birth to their twins in 2015 and became a housewife.

In 2017, Chen founded HH Company with a doctor she previously worked with. Chen was responsible for the sales part and the co-founder specialized in the IVF procedures. According to Chen, there were more than 150 IVF/surrogacy agencies in Guangzhou by 2018, while few of these agencies own actual medical clinics. She confirmed that every surgery was performed in their "medical lab" in Guangzhou, including test-tube surrogacy.[10] In other words, Chen's company was the actual service provider in the industry, and she was hoping to make connections with ART agencies from all over the country. Chen's statement about the number of ART companies was rather honest. Yang and Yan's (2012) report indicates four to five hundred IVF/surrogacy companies in China: one tenth of them in Guangzhou alone. *Legal Daily*'s report in 2019 also estimates that there were over 400 surrogacy agencies in China. Chen was aware that the business was in the grey area, while she seemed not to be worried about being shut down by state authorities. According to her, Guangdong was far from Beijing, so "the policy is more relaxed". Her company was expanding vigorously across China during and after my fieldwork.

Similar to other Chinese ART companies, Chen's company offered two basic IVF and two surrogacy service packages for clients. The IVF basic package was around ¥150,000/$20,577 and the basic surrogacy package was around ¥600,000/$82,307, excluding the cost of buying human gametes. Choosing the more expensive package meant the client could choose the sex of their children (usually for people who wanted sons). HH Company divided their target market into six groups, including families who had lost their only child (*shidu jiating*), couples who wanted sons, couples who were too old to bear a second child after the two-child policy became effective in 2015, couples suffering infertility problems, wives who did not want pregnancy to 'ruin' their bodies, and LGBT people who wanted children. During my fieldwork, Chen's company established a 'Rainbow Business Division' with a special rainbow logo and continued to develop their strategies to attract Chinese LGBT intended parents.

In 2018, Chen hired Zhao and several other gay men from different LGBT organizations as salespersons. The rest of the HH Company employees were relatives of the other main partner of the company. Regardless of their gender and sexual identities, the HH Company employees were aware of the strategies for locating LGBT potential clients through social media platforms. Once, during my visit to HH Company's office, a young male employee, Chen's nephew, was educating other employees about *BlueD* (a gay socializing app). Chen taught her nephew to source LGBT clients through organizing *xinghun* WeChat groups in same-sex online communities. The tactic of organizing *xinghun* chat groups was based upon their knowledge of queer daily lives. As mentioned before, one purpose for Chinese non-heterosexual people to enter heterosexual *xinghun* marriages was to have children. In other words, people who were interested in *xinghun* were usually interested in employing ART to have children as the following step.

Not long after they started sponsoring LGBT events, HH Company's 'Rainbow Business Division' established a WeChat public account named 'Rainbow Studio'. Likewise, some Chinese ART agencies offering IVF/surrogacy-related ART services own WeChat public accounts named '(company name) Rainbow Baby', emphasizing that they are LGBT-friendly. These WeChat public accounts share news and useful information on LGBT rights and the development of ART, and implicitly market their services in the contents.

Chen told me her LGBT clients doubled in 2018 thanks to her marketing strategies with LGBT organizations. Other factors included the relaxation of family-planning policies and the information circulation about ART. In major Chinese cities, single parents were no longer required to pay the high social maintenance fees. The State Council published a decision in 2021 that allowed a married couple to have three children and abolished social maintenance fees. Still, heterosexual married couples constituted the majority of Chen's clients.

Since I became familiar with the employees who identified as straight and did not work directly at its 'Rainbow Business Division', I learned that their clients were mostly from their social circles in their hometown. According to them, there were many desperate wives who "would give their lives for having a son". For the five groups of potential straight clients, they used a poster (Figure 4.1) which described their scope of services as 'test-tube babies (*shiguan ying'er*), guaranteed surrogacy (*daiyun baosheng*), guaranteed baby boys (*baosheng nanhai*), sperm and eggs provider (*gongjing gongluan*)'. The poster also shows their genetic testing and sex identification of the foetus services. Based on HH Company's sales experience, services like biological sex selection were popular among all types of clients.

The historical practice of prenatal sex selection in China is deeply rooted in the cultural preference for male offspring.[11] In premodern China, family

Figure 4.1: Flyer for HH Company

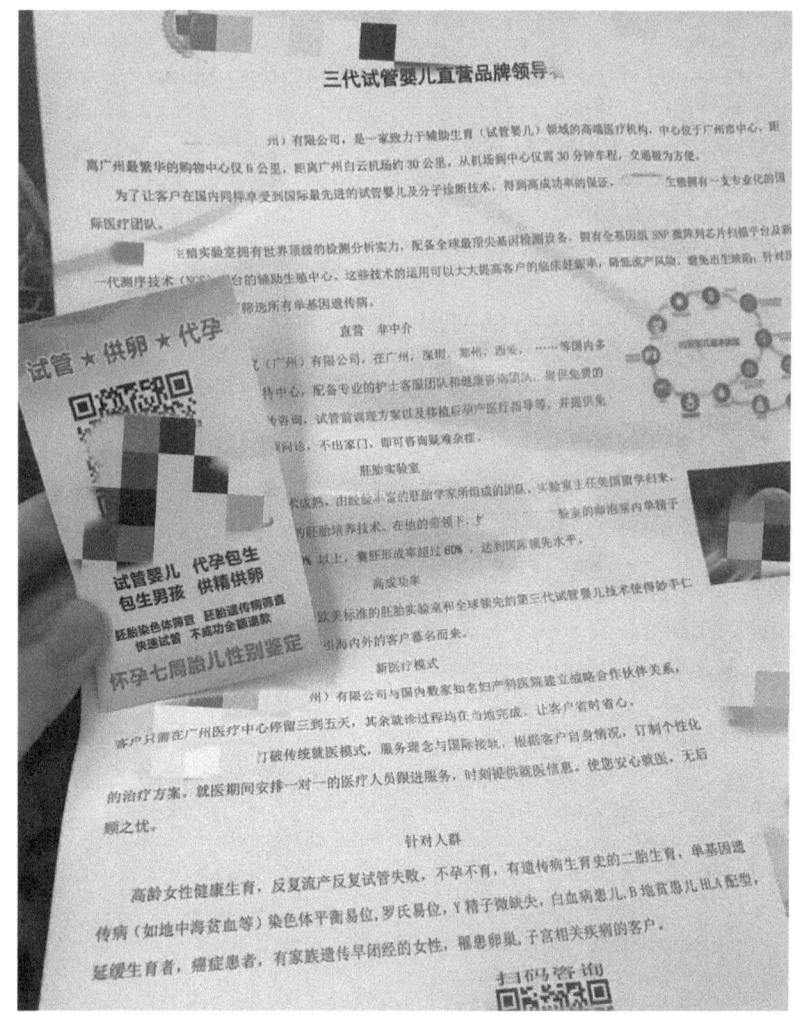

Source: Author's own

was a closed and unitary group consisting of living and deceased men sharing the same origin and surname. While sons were permanent members of the family, daughters were considered temporary members who would 'marry out'. Both the belief of ancestor worship and Confucian familism have enforced patrilineal ideology by emphasizing the importance of having male offspring (Walker, 1996; Xie, 2013). Research conducted outside Asia indicates that the process of modernization, enhanced economic conditions, and elevated women's social standing can undermine the traditional gender norms and son preference. However, the situation in East Asia appears to be more intricate (Greenhalgh, 1985; Chu, 2001; Zhou et al, 2012). The

Chinese government has taken a number of policy measures to tackle the disproportionately high sex ratio. Yet, sex-selective abortion is very accessible despite it being legally forbidden (Zhou et al, 2012).

HH Company's sales and marketing strategies towards its queer and straight potential clients were remarkable. As Mamo and many other scholars point out, while same-sex desires were being constructed as non-procreative, ART medical specialities were portrayed as curing (heterosexual) childlessness, and their legitimate clients were portrayed as childless heterosexual people. In this way, ART would 'reproduce not only human beings, but also natural women and natural families' (Mamo, 2007, p 130). China's legal policies reinforced this kind of reproduction and normalized parenthood as exclusively legitimate for heterosexual married couples. At the same time, private ART centres like the HH Company have emerged in China, marketing ART as both challenging and strengthening normative family forms and kinship norms.

Queer parents working for ART companies

In 2018, I met Fei in a lesbian online forum, where we discussed the issues lesbian mothers might have and I told her about my research. We quickly arranged a Friday night to have dinner together with her girlfriend Zhenzhen. Both Zhenzhen and Fei were from other parts of Guangdong Province and went to colleges in Shenzhen. At the time we met, Zhenzhen was undergoing IVF. Out of curiosity, I asked about Zhenzhen's job. Zhenzhen hesitated for at least five minutes before telling me she had recently changed her job to work at an ART agency, which assisted her in her visit to a Thai hospital. "I am grateful for this experience because it inspired me to a new career path," Zhenzhen said. She also persuaded Fei to apply for an administrative job at the same agency to work with her. Being aware of the debates over ART, Zhenzhen was worried that telling others about her job at an ART agency would make others judge her morality.

After working at the first IVF agency for half a year, Zhenzhen and Fei made a leap to another IVF agency and worked as channel managers. They said their working experience in this industry gave them the negotiating power to double their salaries. Again, Zhenzhen claimed that her new employer was certified and directly associated with the Thai hospital. Their role was to establish contact with doctors in public hospitals, so these contacts could recommend their agency to patients whose needs could not be met by public hospitals – for example, couples wanting to choose the sex of their child and couples who could not conceive at all and could only use surrogacy to have children. Zhenzhen and Fei were passionate about working in the ART industry. As they have learned, there were not many experienced people in this industry, straight or queer. Zhenzhen believed this was a growing industry with plentiful opportunities for upward mobility. They told me they had done some research on the salary levels in their jobs and were confident their income would soon rise again. Zhenzhen added, "Once I have a baby myself, I will have an unbeatable professional advantage as a lesbian mother".

Apparently, Zhenzhen was one of the queer parents who sensed the marvellous potential market of the ART industry in Chinese queer communities. For Zhenzhen, her gender, queerness, and expected pregnancy turned from career disadvantages to career advantages in this industry. Later in 2019, Zhenzhen made another leap to a famous ART agency in Shenzhen founded by a gay man and increased her income once again.

When Zhenzhen was expecting her children as well as a bright career life, there was a rising number of lesbian mothers and gay fathers doing what she planned to do – sourcing clients through same-sex socializing apps. They frequently posted photos of their babies born through *A luan B huai* (reciprocal IVF) or surrogacy. As experienced queer parents, they were willing to give suggestions to their queer clients about whether to have a mixed-race 'rainbow' baby, how to come out to others as queer parents, and how to cope with the existing family-planning policy on single parenting. Several of my friend informants chose to purchase the IVF package recommended by a lesbian couple on the *Rela* app; their decision was motivated by the kind and positive role model that the couple portrayed. The image of a loving same-sex couple with their own children symbolized the potential for non-heterosexual individuals in China to maintain lasting relationships and openly build harmonious queer families while embracing their same-sex desires.

These queer parents were undoubtedly seen as model Chinese non-heterosexual citizens by their followers, though were not yet representative. Over the last few years, gay and lesbian influencers, LGBT organizations, and private ART companies in China have come to include references to both 'rainbow family' (*caihong jiating*) and 'rainbow baby' (*caihong baobao*) in Chinese LGBT slang. For another example, the host at the 2019 PFLAG China talkfest asked the guest speaker, "why do you want a rainbow baby?" The term 'rainbow baby' initially referred to a baby born after the loss of a previous baby due to miscarriage, stillbirth, or infant loss. In Chinese queer communities, 'rainbow baby' has become a term exclusively for babies born through ART and free from association with hetero-reproductive relationships.

Regardless of the categories of Chinese ART companies and the ambiguous legal policies and reinforcing acts regarding the business, all private ART agencies tended to frame their work in positive language. Since An has invested in a Russian clinic, he told me (and clients) that, in European societies, women choose to be surrogate mothers not only because they want money but because they want to help others. Chen, on the other hand, explained that the surrogate mothers her company recruited enjoyed a relatively "cushy" job and generous financial rewards compared to working in a factory. Her colleagues usually distributed small recruitment cards outside the factories around Shenzhen. Chen let me stay in the office once a candidate for becoming a surrogate mother walked in. Chen's colleague asked the candidate, "Does your husband agree with this?" The candidate said yes and explained her situation. Her family borrowed money from underground parties and had no other way to pay the interest. She had given birth to two sons, which qualified her for the job. After finding out she could not leave Guangzhou to visit her family during pregnancy, she said she needed to discuss the issue with her husband. The fact that Chen and her colleagues did not hide their hiring process with surrogates and egg donors from me revealed something about their understanding of their work. Nor did they conceal their income from me. One of Chen's colleagues bought a luxury car within one year of joining the HH Company. Chen and her girlfriend had two more children and a bigger flat in 2020. The seemingly highly profitable and promising market kept attracting non-heterosexual people including queer parents into the ART business. HH Company claimed that they did not abuse surrogates/egg providers; nor did they overcharge their clients; instead, they paid surrogates/egg providers a higher rate than their factory work and they charged LGBT clients a lower rate than overseas ART agencies. HH Company and other ART agencies who described them as LGBT-friendly came up with special discount service packages for same-sex couples. Chen once said, "Doing business is the greatest charity work (*shangye jiushi zuidade gongyi*)", which resonated with Zhao's statement: "working in these private ART companies can also help LGBT people".

As a rising number of non-heterosexual people joined ART companies and attempted to frame their work as a good deed, it is hard to ignore the issues raised by the underground ART market. In HH Company, surrogates could not leave the apartment without obtaining permission and were not allowed to have contact with clients. Chen explained that if surrogates went out casually during pregnancy, they might lose the baby; and if surrogates met the clients, they might extort money from clients. Also, the clients could 'interview' the eggs/sperm providers and look at their backgrounds, while the eggs/sperm providers would not be able to get any of the clients' information. According to ART companies in China, these rules were set out primarily to protect clients' privacy and rights. Such practices inevitably intensify the unequal relations between surrogates/gamete providers and IVF/surrogacy agencies and clients. The reduction of IVF/surrogacy to merely a 'womb-for-rent' business continued to impact the moral image of queer parents, especially gay fathers, in China. Moreover, the unregulated market leaves concerns of donor anonymity and children's rights.

PFLAG China volunteers expressed mixed feelings towards Zhao and other queer people who jumped into the ART industry and turned their LGBT contacts into potential clients. Many lesbian volunteers believed that people like Zhao were attracted by the high commission possibilities in the ART industry rather than motivated by the desire to help LGBT people. In the group dinner after a PFLAG conference, a young lesbian said in anger, "How can an LGBT organization, a civil organisation for human rights, promote surrogacy? It hurts women!" Paradoxically, we sat with two mothers (*mama*) of gay men who were guest speakers in the conference, and I recall that one *mama* mentioned ART in her speech: "The posterity issue (for non-heterosexual people) is now easily solved; it's just a matter of technology and method".

Consuming ART; choosing own children

At this point, it is vital to take a closer look at the actual process of queer intended parents using ART. Although ART was often seen as "the ideal choice" among queer intended parents, my friend informants revealed that employing ART to have children took much longer than they expected. Many of them changed their initial schedule, their ART agencies and hospitals, the egg/sperm donors, and surrogates due to health, legal, and economic reasons.

Unmarried individuals in China are not legally permitted to use ART services in accredited clinics. As a result, those who wish to employ ART without getting married and without entering a legally uncertain situation have to turn to cross-border reproductive tourism. Gay fathers I have met were aware that women choosing to be surrogate mothers and egg providers in China were in need of money and this was often their only possible motivation. Such motivations inevitably turned surrogacy into an unequal business since the surrogate mothers and egg providers had less negotiating power. Min, who has twin sons with his boyfriend through surrogacy in California, told me that the surrogate mother of their children was a religious, White woman. Min felt his choice in having children was morally acceptable since the agent told him the surrogate mother chose her job for good reasons. In this way, Min felt the choice hurt no one as the surrogate mother enjoyed her job. Min and Shan spent $231,000 in total to have two children. For queer women who want to employ ART in Euro-American or Southeast Asian countries, the costs can be high as well. While some single lesbians may choose to employ IUI, middle-aged women often found the success rate of IUI unsatisfying and turned to IVF. A lesbian couple who shared their reproductive experience on a public page said they had spent $65,000 on an *AB luan B huai* process in California.

Many non-heterosexual people doubted the reliability of Chinese ART companies. Although a large amount of money circulates in the Chinese ART industry, contracts between private ART companies and clients are invalid under Chinese law. The commercial surrogacy contract is generally seen as involved in a violation of 'public interest', which is a question of social morality (Ding, 2015). In most cases, such contracts were 'gentleman's agreements' that solely depended on mutual trust. Disputes over the contract and the custody of children related to reciprocal IVF and surrogacy are brought to the courts from time to time, and courts have delivered inconsistent views in these disputes. An attendant of a 'rainbow family sharing salon' in Guangzhou commented, "I'd rather pay more to foreign ART companies to avoid disputes".

While some queer parents were fluent in English and could travel overseas by themselves, other queer reproductive tourists were assisted by Chinese ART agencies due to information gaps or language barriers. Tian, a gay father of two, said he simply did not trust Chinese businessmen even though he belonged to this group. Tian owned an online shop and most of its merchandise was cheap international branded clothing direct from local factories. He reasoned that Chinese businessmen did not have religion and therefore had low moral standards. It should be noted that the primary reason he did not choose a Chinese surrogacy company was a lack of trust. Eventually, Tian signed a surrogacy contract with a Thai agency with Chinese-Thai translators, though the contract between these kinds of agencies and clients was legally flawed as well. Tian had to travel to Laos and then Cambodia after the agency told him that Thailand had banned surrogacy for foreigners.

In countries where commercial surrogacy and compensated gamete donation are legal and available to LGBT tourists, the cost of ART procedures is remarkably high. In the USA, a single IVF cycle can range from approximately $8,000 to $15,000, while the expenses associated with surrogacy often surpass $100,000 (Thompson, 2016), excluding indirect costs. Consequently, reproductive tourists may travel to the Middle East, East Europe, or elsewhere in Asia for cheaper ART services (Twine, 2015). Though many non-heterosexual people did not consider doing ART inside China as a satisfactory option, some queer intended parents became clients of Chinese ART companies for their competitive price packages and convenient location. After I had known Wen for two years, she started researching Guangzhou ART companies and asked me if I knew any good ones. She was eager to conceive before she reached 40. Wen did a lot of research on the pricing and the marketing of IUI and IVF services. Although she had little trust in Chinese ART companies, they remained the only affordable and practical option for her. Wen's job would not allow her to take a long overseas trip, and the Chinese agency offered her a cheaper IUI package for less than ¥80,000 ($10,974).

As I mentioned in the previous chapter, being able to freely choose egg/sperm donors was a vital preference many friend informants emphasized. Each queer parent who employed ART gave me a detailed elucidation of how they made their investigations and final decisions in selecting the suitable sperm/egg donor or surrogate mother. They looked at the egg/sperm donor's skin colour, height, educational background, career, health condition, and other characteristics. Zhenzhen showed me the photos of candidates of sperm donors when we talked about her trip to Thailand to prepare for IVF cycles. All photos had the candidates' personal information attached. Zhenzhen explained how she selected the sperm donor:

> 'These candidates are all good-looking! I interviewed them for a whole day. One of them is a TV actor in Thailand and he came with his broker, but I doubt he was wearing heightening insoles to fake his height. You need to meet candidates in person, so you know if they lied about their height or anything.'

Zhenzhen's words reflected her perspective on human gamete providers, which was prevalent among people who used ART-related services: one must be suspicious of ART agencies and people involved as they could lie. During my time in Chen's ART company, I noticed that interviewing the egg/sperm donors and asking a series of personal questions was generally preferred by clients, even if they needed to pay an extra price for it. Zhenzhen emphasized that the sperm donor must not know any of her information.

Whether to have mixed-race babies has also become a seemingly available choice to queer clients. Min and his partner bought an ovum from a Chinese student studying in the US. According to Min, the average price of an ovum was $8,000–10,000, while they paid $15,000 for an ovum since Asian ova were rare in the US. Min was willing to pay a higher price for an Asian ovum because he wanted Chinese babies rather than mixed-race babies. As a university professor, Min did not want his children to attract attention from others. His concerns resonate with several lesbian friend informants' statements on having mixed-race children: having a mixed-race baby meant other people would always be curious about the baby's other biological parent and even ask rude questions, which might trouble one's career.

Contrary to Min, An, as an openly gay father of three sons and an entrepreneur, welcomed public attention to his gay family rather than being afraid of it. When the other researcher and I arrived at An's company for our first interview, we found two cameramen with professional video equipment waiting for us. An was aware that the news about his mixed-race sons helped him gain much attention and fuelled his Russia-based ART agency. During and after my fieldwork, An sent his mixed-race sons to numerous talent classes and variety shows.

Furthermore, the ability to cruise the legal 'grey area' freely has become a key personal skill for both ART companies and desiring queer parents in China. For the HH Company, it was the ability not to be fined or shut down by the local authorities that made their business survive. Chen and her peers were extremely careful to avoid drawing any attention from state authorities, and they changed their social media profile information regularly. Chen never sent me any typed messages and, whenever I had questions about her business, she would tell me to visit her company to talk in person.

Queer parents who employed ART without entering legal marriages had to cope with the legal ambiguity and sometimes difficulties that went along with their unmarried status and out-of-wedlock children. Without two married parents who comply with birth regulations, registering the birth for the newborn can be troublesome. Within a stratified system in China, only the privileged elite find it possible to circumvent birth regulations and legitimate their 'unplanned' extra births (Shi, 2017). Queer parents who used ART were only able to register their 'unplanned' children after paying a considerable amount of money or through social relations *(guanxi)* with officials. Due to their 'unique' situation, they often encountered conflicting advice from various local departments and dedicated weeks, or even months, to gather the necessary documentation as demanded by officials. It has only been recently that major cities have stopped charging social maintenance fees for out-of-wedlock births. Still, in most parts of mainland China, unmarried parents had to pay more money and go through more bureaucratic processes to get proof of paternity and other legal certificates. The State Council published a decision in July 2021 to promote long-term and balanced population development; this decision allowed a married couple to have three children and abolished social maintenance fees and other penalties on *hukou* registration. That said, although the penalties for 'unplanned' births have been removed, unmarried Chinese citizens are still not allowed to use ART in accredited hospitals and are not entitled to maternity benefits.

Gender norms often came to shape queer parents' experiences as unmarried parents. Lesbian mothers I know tended to worry more about explaining their pregnancy and newborn child to others as unmarried women. This was because being acknowledged as an unmarried parent in the workplace and community could pose more challenges for women. Gay fathers I met did not think it was an immensely difficult task to explain where the child came from to others, while they often needed to provide officials with a made-up story when they registered birth and *hukou* information for their newborn. For instance, Tian pretended to be a single heterosexual man who had a romantic affair with a foreign woman and an 'unexpected' child. When he went to the airport and the police station with his little son, he told the governmental officials repeatedly that the mother did not want the child and showed them a written claim by the mother. The written claim was provided by the ART agency, which included it as part of their service package. These alleged 'tactics of convenience' were used frequently by other gay clients and circulated in queer communities.

Reproduction without sex – a desirable future or unaffordable hope?

Since IVF appeared, it has been realized as the crucial method that will lead to the end of sex as the only way to conceive (Greely, 2016). By this time, IVF and IVF-related reproductive technologies have become a 'better-established and widely available consumer option, and itself a more normalized and naturalized activity' (Franklin, 2013, p 228). IVF ultimately transformed our understanding of biological relations and points to the future of reproduction and kinship (Franklin, 2013). For queer parents in this chapter, ART has been envisioned as enabling queer biological parenthood. The unstoppable trend of using ART to have a biological child and the emergence of Chinese ART companies in queer communities have led to new forms of queer reproductive paths and families. From the very beginning, *A/AB luan B huai* emerged as an ideal technological device for lesbian couples in urban China to form co-motherhood rather than to overcome infertility. Unlike Mamo's (2007) lesbian interviewees in California, who turned to advanced technologies only if other technologies failed, many lesbian couples I met in Guangdong actively sought out reciprocal IVF as their first choice. In this sense, Chinese lesbian couples' use of IVF has queered the heteronormative knowledge of reproductive technologies and parenthood, even if they did not intend to challenge the cultural norms. It becomes vital to read ART as an emerging conjugal – and thus not merely biological – technology among queer people that involves the remaking of identities, relationships, and social groups. The reproductive decisions of Chinese queer (intended) parents are moulded by the prevailing socio-legal environment and a developing comprehension of desired queer futures. As mentioned earlier, Chinese queer people's desire to have children is closely bonded with the ever-changing notions of filial piety, elder care, and individual choice.

In Guangdong, the emergence of LGBT-friendly private ART companies aimed to appeal to queer clients by displaying support for LGBT organizations, projecting a 'rainbow' image, and promoting ART as a means to facilitate queer reproduction. It became palpable that these queer parents and ART companies co-constructed ART as the ideal way for Chinese non-heterosexual people to have 'children of their own'. The tension between being the 'only sponsor of Chinese queer social events' and 'an industry chain that exploits women' was embodied in the ART companies' marketing strategies towards their target clients. In addition to making possible single and queer parenthood, the Chinese private ART companies that presented an LGBT-friendly image fuelled sex selection and gender inequalities that have long existed in China. The relationship between LGBT organizations and the ART industry therefore encompasses not only sexuality but class, kinship, and gender concerns.

This chapter closely engages with other scholarship that problematizes the language of choice and individuality both in queer family making and assisted reproduction (Dempsey, 2010; Gabrielson, 2011; Murphy, 2013; Gammeltoft, 2014; Lo, 2020; Patton-Imani, 2020). With the emergence of Chinese ART companies and their marketing strategies towards queer communities, queer intended parents appeared to have more choices as they could have access to ART either in foreign countries or in mainland China. My friend informants' personal accounts are immersed in the language of choice, including how they chose the ART agency and service packages, how they selected the eggs/sperm providers, how they decided to have mixed-race babies or not, and how they exercised such choices with their family members. In this sense, choice is constituted as an individualistic and bourgeois notion that is naturalized by consumer culture (Weston, 1991; Strathern, 1992a). Mamo's research on lesbian mothers illustrates how American societies deliver the idea that individuals with agency can surmount constraints through the appropriate attitude, knowledge, determination, and choices (2007, p 230). The language of choice, free will, and self-determination risks 'concealing the structural forces and inequalities that shape reproductive decisions' (Gammeltoft, 2014, p 16). In other words, emphasizing 'choice' made by individuals rather than the ways governmental systems shape access to reproductive and family-making rights 'creates an illusion of equality' (Patton-Imani, 2020, p 13). For Povinelli, the choice is perceived as if it is the 'only real choice available to us' made between these discourses of individual freedom and social constraint in our everyday lives (2006, p 6); yet, individual freedom and social constraint are co-constituted, and, in some situations, they could mean the same thing. What becomes clear is that we cannot examine the alleged personal choices and social constraints as self-evident and mutually exclusive conceptions, for the 'legibility of choice is contingent on social, economic and cultural capital' (Richardson, 2017, p 217). This chapter, together with the previous ones, delineates how glocal market and economic conditions shaped queer individuals' decisions regarding whether, when, and how to have children in addition to state and cultural conventions. Their financial capability to employ ART and navigate the restrictive birth-planning policies again highlights the material construction of sexual citizenship and its relation to consumption (Evans, 2013), gender, and class (Taylor, 2010). As the consumer of medical services, queer (intended) parents' practices were marked by social stratification along knowledge, resources, nationalities, and power (Wei, 2022). What is more, being upper-middle-class customers, non-heterosexual people's practices of choosing egg/sperm donors and surrogates risked commodifying the disadvantaged latter group and reinforcing social stratification.

In brief, the experience of these queer parents who employed ART has echoed Chen's saying, which is: "Wait until you are wealthy enough to have children". This rhetoric aligns with the narrative of being a good sexual citizen by being a good consumer (Rofel, 2007; Evans, 2013; Wei, 2020). As Bell and Binnie (2000) remind us, while we are all sexual citizens, we are not all equal sexual citizens. Few friend informants in their 20s had the financial confidence to consume ART services and raise children by themselves. Rather, they told me that they needed to have a stable conjugal relationship and generous income to have children and form a perfect queer nuclear family. The freedom of choosing a reliable and 'personalized' ART service and thus a desired biological child of one's own were only available to people like An. We must note that under China's intense neoliberal restructures, it is increasingly difficult for the young generation to achieve upward mobility in big cities. The emphasis on ART as the ultimate solution in queer lifeworlds reconsiders and requalifies the concept of queer sexualities as reproductive. In the context of ART, queer futures are simultaneously made possible and normalized. With the assistance of IVF-related ART, queer individuals and couples may have biological children without sexual intercourse and without entering any form of heterosexual marriage, but the high costs of IVF and the required extensive timeframe for such procedures arguably enable capitalist reproduction in queer sexual citizenship. As Mamo points out, 'the history of assisted reproduction is a history of the enforcement of biopower' (2007, p 57). Queer parents' participation in assisted reproduction has enacted stratified reproduction, that is, the medical support only available to certain groups. As many studies indicate, ART remains restricted to the global elite class (Mamo and Alston-Stepnitz, 2015; Twine, 2015; Wei, 2022). The personal narratives in this chapter have demonstrated that this seemingly ideal practice was only available to the upper-middle-class subject who could afford the high cost of childbirth and parenting and whose career was unlikely to be affected by unmarried births.

Furthermore, as all my friend informants stated, the cost of ART services was small compared to further parenting costs. In the case of same-sex couples having children together through ART, the children could only be legally registered with one parent, an issue which they had to strategically overcome to address their needs. The next chapter moves to explore the interference between ideas of 'blood relatives' and 'queer relations' and the construction of good parenting in Chinese queer lifeworlds.

5

Queering Parenting: Raising 'Our Children'

During a get-together dinner, I had the following conversation with Wen, a 34-year-old lesbian who was planning to have a child:

Me: I had dinner with a lesbian couple Xie and Hong last weekend. They have a lovely baby boy whose nickname is Doudou.
Wen: I am so jealous that they have children together! It would be the best way. Are they a T–P couple?
Me: Yes, Xie is T and Hong is P.
Wen: Do their parents accept their relationship? Doudou is Xie's (biological) son, right? Do Hong's parents acknowledge Doudou as their grandson?
Me: They used Hong's egg. Hong got pregnant via artificial insemination.
Wen: Doudou and Xie are not blood ties?
Me: The sperm they used was from Xie's brother.
Wen: Oh, that also works.

When I mentioned that Xie and Hong have a son, Wen immediately assumed their son was biologically linked to Xie (the T) and was given birth to by Hong (the P). This process was commonly referred to as *A luan B huai*. Otherwise, Wen would not have thought the baby was their son. The confusion raised in our conversation indicated the ambiguous link between blood ties and parenthood in today's queer world. Such conversations were a common occurrence during my fieldwork in Guangdong, China, as the arrangement of same-sex co-parenting is not always readily apparent to others.

As this book has documented, queer parents have children through previous heterosexual marriages, *xinghun* marriages, *guoji* adoptions, or assisted reproductive technologies (ARTs) only; they are single, divorced parents or they co-parent with their same-sex partners. For queer couples, having children together has increasingly become a key strategy to strengthen their conjugal relationship. Yet, the recognition of the child as 'our child' and thereby a durable mutual bond between people in same-sex couples only works under certain situations and with certain strategies and resources. In other circumstances, it could work the opposite way. What continually came to my attention during my fieldwork was how my friend informants distinguished between 'my children', 'my partner's children', and 'our children', and how they integrated such distinctions into their relationships with partners, families of origin, and wider society. Strathern raises the question of whether the reproduction model leads to the reproduction of relationships, as she mentions that, unlike maternity, the father's role is always less visible and has to be symbolically or socially constructed, yet the very invisibility of parenthood is a social construction (1992a, pp 52–55). While individuals reproduce individuals, 'relations don't reproduce relations' (1992a, pp 52–55). In other words, parenthood must be constructed. The categories of biological relative (for example, egg donor), as Strathern argues, result in a distinction between social and biological parenthood (1992b, p 19). Within the landscape of queer parenting in China, where same-sex marriage and joint custody are absent, this situation further created a perceived distinction between biological, social, and legal parenthood. Building upon Howell's concept of 'kinning' as 'the process by which a foetus or newborn child (or a previously unconnected person) is brought into a significant and permanent relationship with a group of people that is expressed in a kin idiom' (2003, p 466), I am intrigued by how same-sex co-parents in urban China navigate the construction and visibility of their co-parenthood. This exploration is particularly relevant in light of prevailing state regulations and dominant family norms that often negate non-heteronormative reproductive relationships and unconventional family structures.

This chapter reveals the complexity of defining the boundaries between blood relative and queer kin. The cases of single queer parents and queer couples having children together amplify their understanding of blood ties and children's position in sustaining conjugal love and a protected future. In this chapter, I do not dwell on what constitutes kinship or 'authentic' forms of kinship. Rather, my purpose is to make visible how my friend informants make claims on parenthood and kinship as their social facts and what they do with them. As the ethnographic accounts will show, the idea of blood and biology still holds its centrality in Chinese family life, while it has also been proved to have elastic potentialities for queer couples who desire joint parenthood. Moreover, this chapter explores how Chinese queer parents understand their role as parents and non-heterosexual subjects with relation to legal concerns, conventional patrilineal family norms, and material resources.

The harmonious coexistence between 'my children' and a same-sex partner

I have known Dae for years. Dae had twins through a *xinghun* marriage, later divorced, and remained co-parents with her former *xinghun* partner. Born in 1982, Dae sees herself as more 'traditional' (*chuantong*) and more focused on family than younger generations. Dae immediately started seeking girlfriends after her twins were born. Even though these women often stayed in Dae's apartment, Dae's parents, who moved in to help care for the twins, never questioned Dae's relationships, and nor did Dae say anything. Like many other friend informants, Dae interpreted her parents' response as 'silent acceptance' (*moren*) of her same-sex relationship.

Still, Dae complained to me about her intimate relationships. She told me that ever since she had had children, the dates she met through same-sex socializing apps were constantly jealous of her children, causing numerous quarrels. For Dae, her children were her major focus, and she spent the most time with her children rather than with girlfriends. One of Dae's dates, who was in her mid-20s, once told Dae that "if you treat your children so well, you should treat me the same". Yet, Dae felt uncomfortable with such a comparison. She admitted that she could not spend the same amount of time and money on any future girlfriend as compared to her children. Furthermore, Dae referred to her children as her blood and family, whereas she never referred to her ex-girlfriends as her family members.

Dae's statement mirrored her experience with her ex-girlfriend, whom she was with from 2009 to 2015. They split due to her ex-girlfriend prioritizing her *xinghun* family over Dae. Dae's ex-girlfriend had been living with her *xinghun* husband and parents-in-law after the wedding. After giving birth to a son, Dae's ex-girlfriend stayed with her *xinghun* family and rarely went out. Dae felt like an outsider to her ex-girlfriend's *xinghun* family and she told me she could not even give her ex-girlfriend's child a nickname. Dae did not become the co-mother of her ex-girlfriend's child, although she expected she would do. As a result, Dae felt her ex-girlfriend formed stronger kin relations with her *xinghun* reproductive family than with Dae. They eventually broke up over the phone. According to Dae, her ex-girlfriend was too cowardly and dependent. Dae concluded her experience with her ex-girlfriend as a lesson learned: "If you are weak, your *xinghun* marriage becomes a real marriage, and you become a real wife". It was at this point that Dae determined she would have biological children instead of counting on lesbian co-motherhood.

After Dae started co-parenting with her *xinghun* partner, she realized that her children were so crucial to both her and her *xinghun* partner that she would never expect her future girlfriend to see her children in the same way. Dae prioritized her relations with her parents and children as blood ties while expecting her girlfriends to accept the arrangement that Dae had 'another' part of her life with her children. Dae anticipated that her blood relatives would be the key support resource in her elderly life, while she did not think a girlfriend would accompany her when she grew old. In this sense, same-sex dating became a time-limited, vulnerable relation for her. Dae asked me to introduce potential girlfriends to her, although I never managed to do so. Among young lesbians I have met in urban Chinese cities, Dae's views about children and same-sex relationships were morally contradictory, if not selfish.

Having children has drastically altered Dae's romantic relationships, although she once claimed that "children and girlfriend are separable, so they don't affect each other". She couldn't let her girlfriend stay over for more than a few days, since she lived with her two children and parents. Also, Dae's *xinghun* partner still visited their children on a weekly basis despite their being divorced. Therefore, Dae's claim, or her effort to 'separate' her children and girlfriend into two different relationships, did not lead to the result she desired. Rather, the disconnection between her children and girlfriend has limited her capacity to maintain a lasting same-sex relationship. Additionally, Dae's tactic to not explicitly introduce her romantic relationship with her girlfriend to her parents again limited the possibility of building connections between her family of origin and partners.

Dae's personal experience renders the often-talked-about myth in same-sex communities about the harmonious coexistence between 'my children' and a same-sex partner for a queer parent. People often referenced a common notion that mothers were more attentive to their children than anyone else. Simultaneously, those I encountered during my research shared a prevailing view that gay fathers faced less pressure in parenting, presumed to be less concerned since societal expectations did not require them to be primary caregivers at home. Many Chinese non-heterosexual people, including Dae, who had their biological children, doubted that they could find a same-sex partner who treated the children as their own. The hope of having both a blood-related child (especially through heterosexual marriage) and a same-sex partner was increasingly perceived as selfish among queer youth, as they believed that a loving partner should not be treated as less important than blood relatives. In this sense, it became intolerable if their queer partners placed more emphasis on their biological children than them. This was what Dae's young girlfriend expressed when she asked Dae to spend more time with her. The underlying logic of this statement symbolizes resistance to the Confucianist hierarchical order of kin relations where conjugal relations were less important than parent–child relations.

This emerging opinion among young lesbians had led to older lesbian mothers like Dae complaining that there was little chance of them finding a girlfriend. Some lesbian mothers claimed to their potential dates that their children were "left" with grandparents and that they were free from parenting responsibilities. Such statements also seem to suggest the competing relations between blood children and queer partners, revealing the perception that a queer subject needed to cut loose the relation with their children and *xinghun* spouse (sometimes together with the family of origin) to pursue romantic relationships. Furthermore, some non-heterosexual people tended to use their same-sex partners' negotiations with blood ties and partners as a significant criterion for their loving relationships. Mo, who was living with her girlfriend Lin in Shenzhen, strongly refused to see or live with Lin's school-age son. When Lin tried to divorce her legal husband, who she only saw once a year, he asked Lin to take custody of their son. Mo told Lin that she hated taking care of little children, especially boys. Eventually, Lin gave up trying to bring her son to Shenzhen. Lin's son stayed in rural Anhui with his grandparents. Mo told me that she was satisfied with Lin's decision as it showed that Lin prioritized her feelings rather than those of other kin relatives.

"It's their blood, not mine"

Even when same-sex couples were in the process of planning for parenthood, the acknowledgement of their roles as single or co-parents remained a subject of ongoing negotiation. Tian, a gay father of two sons, broke up with his ex-boyfriend when he was planning to have his second child. Reflecting on this, Tian stated:

> 'We have been together for years. He showed no interest when I asked him if he wanted children with me, so I did it using my sperm. He said he was fine with it, but his indifferent attitude annoyed me. He should have at least asked about the surrogacy progress. He seemed to never care about my sons. What's the point if my partner didn't want to be involved in my life with my children? I felt lonely, so we separated.'

Despite this, he remained hopeful for a lasting relationship. "It's best to have three children," Tian told me. "I want to have my third child with my future partner; we can use his sperm."

Zhenzhen once said, "I am not going to take care of other people's children" during one of our conversations on the relationship between ART and same-sex co-parenthood. Just turned 24 years old, Zhenzhen planned to have her own child while living with her girlfriend Fei in Shenzhen. Zhenzhen expressed her desire to have children through surrogacy:

> 'I don't want to waste my youth in pregnancy. The previous (egg retrieval) surgeries I did have already frightened me. I am considering

surrogacy, but it is very expensive. I really want Fei to carry my baby, but she is too skinny. Also, my mother and I think it is unfair to her. She would be just like a surrogate since the baby would be my legal child.'

I asked Zhenzhen, "but if Fei gave birth to your child, she could be the child's legal mother?" I said this to Zhenzhen since, by that time, I had known the *A luan* (egg) *B huai* (conceive) method and assumed Zhenzhen and Fei could follow this trend to obtain joint parenthood. Zhenzhen answered:

'No, the child has to be my legal child and be in my *hukouben* (household register booklet). That's why I think this is unfair to Fei. If she left me, she would lose her times and she would be an unmarried woman who had given birth in other people's eyes.'

Zhenzhen compared the *A luan B huai* method to surrogacy, as she thought if she asked Fei to carry a baby using her egg, Fei would be like a surrogate without receiving any benefits. Zhenzhen's statement further implies that pregnancy can be reduced to mere labour in their eyes. The key factor why they did not consider *A luan B huai* as a desirable method was Zhenzhen's insistence on registering the expected baby as her legal child rather than Fei's child. Thus, the child would be biologically and legally Zhenzhen's, whereas Fei's connection with this child would be held in question.

From Zhenzhen's words, it was obvious that Zhenzhen valued her mother's opinion. It was Zhenzhen's mother who encouraged Zhenzhen to have a biological and legal child. To further complicate this matter, as queer individuals choose to have children with or without their same-sex partners, whether their parents recognized their children as grandchildren was a significant issue to be taken into consideration. Zhenzhen and Fei told me that, although Zhenzhen had never mentioned her lesbian desires to her parents, Zhenzhen's mother was alerted and showed suspicion and discontent when she found out that her daughter was living with a woman. However, after they lived together for more than a year, Zhenzhen's mother started to 'silently acquiesce' in the fact that her daughter was not going to marry a man and instead hoped Zhenzhen would have offspring. This is not unique in Chinese non-heterosexual people's experiences, as offspring are often seen as the trade-off for the acceptance of a same-sex partnership. To put it another way, parental acceptance of same-sex desires/relationships does not necessarily eliminate the pressure to marry and have children for many Chinese queer children.

Against this background, Zhenzhen confirmed that her child had to be legally registered with her *hukou* so that the child would be legally the grandchild of Zhenzhen's parents. During another chat, Fei explained:

'Zhenzhen accused me of being half-hearted towards her parenting plan. I honestly don't know what she expects from me. I just graduated from university; I am not ready to be pregnant or be a parent. I am her girlfriend, not her wife. Her mother won't think me as her wife as well.'

When Zhenzhen was preparing to be a mother, Fei had not yet come out to her parents. For Fei, Zhenzhen's expected child could never be accepted by Zhenzhen's parents as a grandchild. Due to the restricted international travel under the Covid-19 situation, Zhenzhen had to give up her travel plans to Thailand and restarted the in-vitro fertilization (IVF) process with a private Chinese ART company. However, after several IVF attempts failed, Zhenzhen had to postpone her parenting plan. Fei, on the other hand, told me she felt relieved because she was not ready. From 2018 to 2022, I heard Fei reassure Zhenzhen many times that she was willing to parent Zhenzhen's child, but their co-parenting plan was never settled between them and their families of origin.

The question of how one should treat same-sex partners' children remained highly controversial in queer communities. Many non-heterosexual people stressed that they could not treat their partners' children as their own simply because "it's their blood (*xueyuan*), not mine". In this sense, the notion of blood and biology is not excluded from queer kinship but rather becomes the locus of queer (co-)parenthood and *jiban*/mutuality. Blood is a dominant signifier for apprehending parentage and kin relations, and the absence of shared blood can be a problem. Yet, blood is not always reliable. What are often neglected are the affective, financial, legal, and biomedical factors that come to articulate the nuanced interpretation of blood in everyday life. We must not ignore the existing legal implications of queer intimacies and parenthood in China which interact with the notion of blood, as the child can be legally bonded to only one mother and one father. In reality, queer individuals' decisions to participate in childrearing with their same-sex partners were shaped by various social factors and private interests. They also envisioned a distinction between reversible and irreversible relations in queer kinship, believing that while they could break up with their same-sex partners and cut their relations completely, they could not do the same with their biological children. Like Simpson (1994, p 837) suggests, the history of divorce in Euro-American society is a history of the growing reversibility of affinal relationships. One might be an ex-husband but not an ex-father. In this sense, the high reversibility of Chinese same-sex conjugal relationships seems to be knotty to address for many.

In addition to legal uncertainty, a central question to be negotiated among queer couples was: would my families of origin accept this child as my/our offspring? Against this backdrop, one's parenthood was only unquestioned when using one's own eggs/sperm. Yet, such distinctions, based on the notion of blood and biology, make it problematic for a single/divorced queer parent to seek and maintain same-sex conjugal relationships, whether intentionally or unintentionally.

The stories of 'failure' to establish recognizable parenthood are not new. The practice of concubines in late Imperial China suggests complexity in Chinese kinship, as concubines were neither recognized as the wife in the house nor the legal mother of their biological children. Concubines' biological children could only call the legal wife 'mother' and were raised by the wife; concubines could not address their children by their name but only with appropriate titles. Walker (1996) thus suggests concubines failed to form bonds of kinship in the way that legal marriages could. In other words, parenthood could not always be created through the alleged romance or even the biological fact of procreation when other authoritative institutions were lacking.

The conceptions of biology/blood and family line, together with the legal implications of joint parentage/custody, have shaped the distinction between 'my own children' and 'my partner's children' and created challenges for queer parents to balance their kinship roles as children, parents, and partners. Some non-heterosexual people therefore maintain that biological parent–child relations (blood ties) are stronger than intimate relationships. Their partner's children, just like their partner, could not be biologically and legally recognized as their family, and thus such relations became reversible. The underlying logic was that their partner's children were by no means their future and therefore not worth any investment. As these child-related issues have been increasingly discernible in queer communities, queer couples attempted to identify suitable strategies for achieving joint parenthood, so they could strengthen their relationships instead of weakening them.

'Our children'

As revealed earlier, *A luan B huai* has emerged as a popular strategy among Chinese lesbian couples to have children together since the 2010s. Made possible by IVF-EF (in-vitro fertilization-embryo freezing) technology, *A luan B huai* enables a woman to conceive a baby with the egg from her same-sex partner. During the last few years, numerous Chinese queer women I have met in person and online have endorsed *A luan B huai* as the ideal strategy to 'solve all problems' including having offspring and establishing *jiban* (mutual bonds) with same-sex partners. Danny and Pam, a couple who chose *A luan B huai* as their most desirable path to joint parenthood, decided to use Danny's eggs to have children. Pam, who was due to give birth in 2020 at the time of my fieldwork, once said, "imagine a baby comes from my body and looks like Danny; isn't that wonderful?" In other words, Pam felt she was connected to the baby as she was the one who bore them.

Neither emphasizing nor negating biological relatedness, Pam employed the notion of 'body' and 'appearance' to validate such mutual connections. In this way, they also naturalized Pam's motherhood with the Chinese adjective *qinsheng* (own birth). Literally meaning giving birth by oneself, *qinsheng* was normally used to refer to one's own children/parents. With reciprocal IVF, Pam gave birth to the baby and described it as *qinsheng*, and therefore the baby as her own, blurring gestational/genetic motherhood.

At the same time, many queer women, especially those in their 20s, expressed worries about the potentially unequal positions involved in *A luan B huai* childrearing. *A luan B huai* is sometimes called *T luan P huai*, since person A (the genetic mother) is usually a self-identified T, and person B (the gestational mother) is usually a P and more economically dependent in their relationship. People who were against the practice of *A luan B huai* argued that person B, who gave birth to the baby, was no more than a surrogate being exploited by person A. To support their opinion, they shared stories of their (web) friends, who were usually P and had given birth to their T girlfriends' biological children, eventually losing both their house and custody of children after breaking up with said girlfriends. In these stories, the key point was always who the baby was legally registered with. In the case of *A luan B huai*, it is possible to either register person A[1] or person B as the child's legal mother, but not both. Based on my observation in field sites and online platforms, most queer women believed it was unfair to register the child's legal identification with person A, as person B would have neither biological nor legal connections with the child. In this sense, many queer women treated gestational motherhood as vulnerable and needed to be protected by legal registration, which is different from many Euro-American societies (Strathern, 2011).

Being aware of these legal and ethical concerns regarding *A luan B huai*, Danny and Pam were going to register their expected child as Pam's child. Also, Danny and Pam had made plans to "explain" where the baby was from to their parents. Pam's parents already knew about their daughter being with a woman, and Pam was confident that her parents would be satisfied to see her being recognized by others as a single mother rather than a childless lesbian. On the other hand, Danny was in a *xinghun* marriage, but she planned to divorce her *xinghun* husband and come out to her parents once the baby was born, so she could tell her parents that they had a biological grandchild. They bought sperm from a private ART company instead of using sperm from Danny's *xinghun* husband. Danny believed they must not raise children with her *xinghun* partner or their children would have too many parents and grandparents involved.

Xie further emphasized the vital role of biological connection in authenticating one's parenthood. As mentioned in previous chapters, Xie already had a son from a previous heterosexual marriage, while Hong had no offspring. Xie prevented Hong from having children through entering a *xinghun* marriage, as she warned us, "having children with the *xinghun* partner means you two are bonded for a lifetime!" Dae's and many other's *xinghun* co-parenting experiences resonate with Xie's statement. As a result, Xie and Hong decided to use Xie's brother's sperm since Xie wanted the child to be her blood as well. Xie's brother, who lived in Hunan Province, agreed to help them. Since Xie was an experienced nurse, they did intrauterine insemination (IUI) in a hotel room. In 2018, Hong gave birth to a baby boy and registered as the child's legal mother. By that time, the procedure of a single mother registering a baby in Shenzhen had been relaxed, according to their experience. For Xie and Hong, no matter who the baby was registered with, the baby was 'their' child and their *xueyuan*/blood. Both Xie's and Hong's parents went to see their offspring and slowly acquiesced in their cohabitating relationship. The fact that Xie and Hong were always able to take their little son to hang out with other lesbians reinforced their co-parenting status and closeness that is recognizable in queer communities. When Hong and Xie shared their experience with me and another lesbian couple, the younger couple immediately started discussing which male family relative they could "borrow" for having children. The most secure solution, as regarded by the lesbian couple, was to make sure the child was tied by blood to both.

This idea of 'borrowed fertility from a relative' is not unique and happened among several other queer couples I met. What seems to be happening here is that one form of kinship is being used to establish another; in this case, a brother is a way of producing a mother, and, in a way, also reverses the kin roles and blood ties of uncle, aunt, and father. In this sense, these queer couples not only made legible their co-parenthood around the central position of the blood tie but also mobilized the idea of blood and kinship terminology.

Making sure the children are biologically linked to both people in a gay couple has been somehow made possible by IVF-EF technology as well. After being with Shang for more than ten years, Min desired children as he wanted to bring new life into their intimate relationship. They decided to have two babies through surrogacy using both their sperm and an egg from the same egg donor. Half of the embryos were fertilized with Min's sperm, and the other half were fertilized with Shang's. As a result, their twins would be blood brothers with different fathers but the same mother. Moreover, their twin sons were named after both fathers, as they shared a surname with Min and were given first names that included Shang's surname.[2]

According to Min, his father, who never liked Shang, saw both twins as his grandchildren and cared for the twin babies very much. Min found out that his father watched the twin boys through the house surveillance camera almost every day. After the twins turned 2 years old, Min's father started to visit Min in Shenzhen once in a while, mostly to play with grandsons. Min even started to feel that he could persuade his father to move from Northern China to Shenzhen. In this context, Chinese non-heterosexual people's practice of co-parenting cannot be grasped without realizing the symbolic patrilineal tradition of family lines. Another gay couple, An and Ye, had a similar experience as An's mother moved in with them to take care of the grandchildren. Ye and An addressed each other's mothers as '*popo*' (mother-in-law). Ye's mother, who was already from Shenzhen, occasionally visited them.

Here, I link the Confucian conception of the family line with the discussion of queer parenthood in Chinese society. In Min's case, his father saw the twins – rather than one of the twins – as grandchildren, as the twins were inseparable blood brothers. Because of that, having twins using a shared egg donor allowed Min and Shang to not only become biological fathers of one child each but also become 'blood-related' co-fathers of two twin brothers. As many same-sex couples have realized, parents of non-heterosexual people may slowly and silently accept their children's same-sex cohabiting relationships without necessarily acknowledging their same-sex desires, especially after knowing they have grandchildren. The grandchild played a vital role, making the same-sex couple co-parents and the grandparent–grandchild bond recognizable. Therefore, same-sex couples may strategically utilize the family line's symbolic importance to make their natal families accept their same-sex partner as a family member that was similar to a son/daughter-in-law.

By exploring the use of emerging ART, which are seen as both enabling and interfering with nature, Strathern (1992a) points out that the very ground for nature to be seen as a distinct domain from culture has become questionable as nature needs to be protected by technology. Hayden's research (1995) on lesbian mothers has suggested that biology is mobilized from a singular category to various meanings and biology itself is no longer a self-evident symbol. Their research findings from Euro-American societies indeed brought insights for this research. The notion of biology/blood tie played a central role in the construction of parenthood for Chinese non-heterosexual people, while it was not essentially fixed or interpretable. Rather, it might be mobilized to create the feeling of *jiban* (mutual bond) and joint parenthood among same-sex couples with the assistance of ART. In other words, the queer parents in my research did not construct lesbian/gay parenthood through all-out distinction from the centrality in biology and blood ties. Weston does not exclude 'blood and biology' from queer kinship since chosen families are 'defined through contrast with biological or blood family, making biology a key feature of the opposing term that conditions the meaning of gay kinship' (1991, p 211). The question being elicited here is: is this strategy, made possible by ART, the only solution to constructing joint parenthood for a same-sex couple in urban China? How is the social parenthood described by Strathern (1992b) being anticipated by Chinese non-heterosexual people in the era of ART?

'If my encounter with Joe is our destiny, the arrival of Jack is a gift from God.' This is quoted from Tommy's blog 'Three Men under One Roof' (*sannanyizhai*), through which he has been sharing his life with his partner Joe and their son Jack since 2005. As a journalist who writes both accessibly and exquisitely, Tommy's 'Three Men under One Roof' blog has received lots of attention, and his family has frequently been referred to as the 'Chinese version of the *tongzhi* family' by journal reporters and queer activists in China. During our first meeting, Tommy's mobile phone screen lit up and he pointed out the wallpaper of his phone to me: "look, my son Jack".

Tommy never hid the fact that he and Jack were not biologically related. Tommy's partner Joe was Jack's biological father and legal guardian. Joe's ex-wife gave birth to Jack before Joe divorced her and moved in with Tommy. It was obvious from Tommy's blog and from his words during our interview that he treated Jack as 'our child' rather than 'my partner's child'. When Jack turned 2 years old, Tommy and Joe brought Jack to Guangzhou and started to live together. Tommy emphasized many times that it was holding little Jack in his arms that gave him the feeling of family. He emphasized that having a mutual life goal was what made an intimate relationship long-lasting. For Tommy and Joe, raising Jack was their mutual goal. Jack always calls Joe '*Baba*' (Dad) and Tommy 'Daddy' inside and outside the home. Tommy was the major breadwinner for the family, and Joe worked as a house husband. Though Tommy worked in Yunnan and Thailand for years, he was proud to tell me that he never missed important moments as Jack grew up. In every parent meeting in school, Tommy came as Jack's godfather and Joe came as his father. The teachers and other parents never asked anything. "It feels very natural," said Tommy.

Tommy and Joe came out to Jack when Jack was 11. Tommy described this in his blog as one of the most important days in his life. When he finished work and came back home, Jack opened the door and asked him, "Daddy, are you *tongxinglian* (homosexual)?" Tommy suddenly froze and did not know how to respond. Jack laughed, "Dad told me you are both homosexual. He told me you love him very much, don't you?" Tommy saw Joe surfing the net and Jack holding his PSP gaming console; everything seemed smooth. He smiled and answered, "Yes, I love your dad, and I love you too. Tell me what you want for your birthday". Joe stopped Tommy and said, "don't bribe Jack. He is fine". Tommy advised that other gay fathers ought to come out to their children when they were 8 to 10 years old, as he reasoned, "If they are younger, they may not understand what their father is saying; if they are older, they may have already heard homophobic statements in school".

Tommy joked that their son had a big heart that Jack told his girlfriend in high school about his family.

Tommy used his personal experience to tell other gay men that affective bonds are as important as blood relationships. The three of them have been living together since Jack was 2 years old, and Jack treats both as his father. It should be noted that Tommy was never Jack's legal guardian or adoptive father. Tommy has spent more than 15 years trying to make his parents accept his relationship with Joe and Jack. After Tommy's father passed away, Tommy's distant relatives in his hometown continued to curse him for "not getting married and having offspring". Jack accompanied Tommy to the farewell ceremony and the following family dinner, when one of Tommy's uncles questioned, "He (Jack) is not your blood; can you put his name on your father's gravestone?" Eventually, Joe and Tommy decided to put Jack's name on Tommy's father's gravestone, prefixed with 'grandson'.

When Jack was preparing for his F-1 visa in 2018 for an American college exchange programme, Tommy encountered a problem that he never thought about before. As a college student who did not have an income, Jack needed to submit his parents' financial statement. However, as Jack's legal father, Joe did not have a stable income or property certificate to prove that he was able to afford Jack's tuition and living costs overseas. Tommy said:

> 'If I were the one to provide the financial statement, it would be so much easier. I have held an executive position in a private company and have satisfactory bank statements and property certificates. But how can I prove my relationship with Jack? Jack's teachers and my colleagues all know my family. Jack has called me "Daddy" for 18 years. We believe we have been doing fine just like other families even though we don't have a marriage certificate. Nevertheless, this little legal certificate suddenly becomes necessary.'

Unlike adoptive parenthood, Tommy's status as Jack's father was not recognized by the law and thus created difficulties that were more powerful than their neighbours and schoolteachers. Tommy actively used his influence as a journalist-blogger and his financial capability to deal with most troubles he encountered. In 2012, Tommy and Joe's 15th anniversary, they signed a heritage claim notarized by their friends. In this claim, Tommy wrote that if anything happened to him, his godson Jack would inherit his property, and Joe, as Jack's legal father, could handle his property. After his father's funeral, Tommy never came back to meet his distant relatives from his hometown. Eventually, Jack's F-1 Visa application passed fine with Joe's financial statement but left Tommy and fellow gay fathers worried. What else could happen if they failed to prove their parental status to officials? For most people, the troubles Tommy and Joe have encountered seemed to be insurmountable without adequate resources, thus making such queer 'social parenthood' unprotected and vulnerable. In this sense, Tommy's parenting practices were often seen by non-heterosexual people like Xie as selfless behaviour while not desirable. My friend informants' narratives reveal that they may or may not be the 'co-mother/father', 'second mother/father', or 'chosen father/mother' of their same-sex partner's biological child. Yet, if Tommy did not treat Jack as a 'our child', he would not have a mutual life goal and eventually would not establish *jiban*/mutuality with Joe. Tommy has been managing several WeChat groups with nearly 200 members calling themselves gay fathers. As Tommy mentioned, the number of gay fathers has been steadily rising as more and more gay men became aware of ART.

The dynamic interrelations in same-sex intimate relationships and queer co-parenting practices elicit questions about the elasticity and uncertainty of kinship relations in today's urban China. The personal experience of my friend informants successfully achieving co-parenting relationships and thus tightening their conjugal intimacy have demonstrated the possibility of mobilizing the dominant centrality in biology and the Confucian conception of blood ties. As some queer parents and their natal families attempted to define the boundary between kinship and non-kinship relations through a social–biological distinction, the existence of such a boundary became an oxymoron. The recognition of biological ties and chosen ties is further voiced in the use of the language of love and care in queer intimate and familial lives.

"Children will accept us if they feel enough care and love"

> 'Daddy, I am willing to give you all my pocket money; you can take it from my drawer without asking me.'

Bei, a gay man in his 40s, told every queer participant in a meet-up that his 5-year-old son said this to him the other day when he joked that he had no money to buy food for the family. Bei started living with his partner 13 years ago, and they adopted the second child of his partner's brother as their son. In other words, Bei's partner was the child's *shushu* (uncle) in conventional Chinese kinship terminology. Unlike Tian's ex-boyfriend, Bei had always wanted a son, and he felt connected to the baby boy when he saw him the first time. Thus, Bei's partner *guoji* adopted the boy from his brother, who felt overwhelmed by raising two sons. Bei was touched by his son's generosity and thought his son learned from him to express his affection. For Bei, his son showed him love and care through the will to give him his pocket money. Moreover, Bei knew that his son recognized him as a warm father from daily conversations like the one previously mentioned.

Because of that, Bei was positive about their son's attitude towards having two fathers. Bei's parenting experience again echoes Tommy's argument on the importance of affective bonds. What intrigued me in the narrative was their expression of affection and its material underpinning.

In this research, every friend informant with children has indicated that love for children is the most important thing for one to qualify as a decent parent. In the meantime, the most frequent topics being brought out in interviews and daily conversations on parenting were companionship and education.

Tian and his friends visited several pride parades in Europe last year. On the last night of the trip, a middle-aged gay father cried during their talks and Tian was touched:

'This gay man is my *laoxiang* (person from one's fellow town). He got married and had a child before knowing he was gay. He told us that he felt sorry for his grown-up child. His child never left Yongzhou until college. Think about it. His child must have faced a lot of discrimination growing up in that small town. I felt for him.'

After hearing his *laoxiang*'s story, Tian decided that he would not let his child Xiaoyu grow up in a small town. Tian planned to get Xiaoyu into the private international school in Dongguan, which did not require Dongguan *hukou* (residence), while being far more expensive than public school. Tian asked me many questions as he could not decide whether to send his son to a private boarding school or a day school. During a talking session, Tian mentioned that his son Xiaoyu was diagnosed with autism two years ago. He immediately took Xiaoyu to seek treatment. Tian took Xiaoyu to the same doctor recently, and the doctor said his 6-year-old son was "normal" with no sign of autism. Tian emphasized that love and companionship were the most important things for a child to grow up happily. He said, "some heterosexual couples don't spend enough time with their children. The left-behind children (*liushou er'tong*) are poor".

Each weekend, Tian took Xiaoyu to meet other gay and lesbian parents and their children for hiking, picnics, or casual gatherings at each other's houses. Tian explained to me that he and other parents were intentionally doing it for their children. "Because I am a man, I want Xiaoyu to grow up with some women like his mom's role in his life. I collaborate with a lesbian mom very well." Just like Tian, other queer parents who were willing to participate in my studies were confident that they "are doing better than the heterosexual parents" by showing other people the material and educational resources and "healthy" childhood experience they have provided for their children.

An stressed in the interview that he and Ye would never hesitate to spend for their sons. After their three mixed-race children were born, they hired several babysitters and each of them stayed at home for half of the year. Also, An's mother moved to Shenzhen to babysit her grandsons and had lived with them since then. An never explicitly came out to his mother, who did not say anything about their cohabitating status. An's mother and Ye got along fine as they often went to the local food market together. The children call Ye '*Abi*', since they could not pronounce '*Babi*' (an alternative of Daddy). Ye spent a lot more time playing with their sons, while An was not so patient with the children. One day, the kids came back home and suddenly called Ye 'Mom'; An and Ye explained to their sons that their mom was in Germany, and they may see her when they grow up. An and Ye's three sons were going to an international kindergarten and taking weekly interest classes. An planned to send three sons to the Harrow International Boarding School in Hong Kong, which he believed to be an exclusive school for the elite class.

Chen and her girlfriend Liu's children were attending a bilingual kindergarten as well. After hearing my educational background, Chen often mentioned her philosophy towards child education:

> 'Whenever my children have vacations, Liu or I take them travelling. They have been to many places so far. Last summer, my partner took them on a road trip to Tibet. This year they went to Japan. We don't think it is too early to take them to the Himalaya Mountains. They learn a lot from travelling. We want to provide them with the best we can.'

Chen also told me that their home was decorated like an amusement park. Liu filled the entire second floor of their house with numerous toys. They had added a small swimming pool in their bathroom.

> 'My children's kindergarten classmates love our house! The moment they entered our living room, they usually ask my children, "is it really your home? You are living in a fairyland!" When they left our house, they always asked if they could come back again. Some kids even told their partners to make their house like ours.'

Chen was proud that other kids admired her children's home. Chen and Liu were planning to move to a larger house as they thought they would soon need a larger swimming pool. Although Chen and Liu never explicitly mentioned their relationship to other parents at kindergarten, the parents, according to Chen, were *gao-suzhi* (high quality) and smart enough that they never asked 'embarrassing questions' or let their kids do so.

It is worth re-mentioning the trend among queer parents for choosing Euro-American egg/sperm donors to have mixed-race babies. When I first met Chen, she felt that such a choice could possibly hurt the child because people might get curious and gossip about the child's biological parents. Still, Chen frequently encountered young gay and lesbian clients who wanted mixed-race children. A year later, Chen changed her opinion and had a little mixed-race daughter. In urban China, a Euro-Asian mixed-race appearance was always related to positive descriptions like good looking (*gaoyanzhi*) and high class (*gaoji*). Against this background, giving children a Euro-Asian mixed-race appearance also means giving them a better-looking, and thus a better, future.

Tian, An, and Chen have arguably endorsed and followed similar good parenting models promoted by the mass media and consumer culture. Lin and Li (2011) identify a trend towards the nuclear family characterized by two parents and an only child. Families with an only child have exhibited children-oriented consumption, spending more money on the child rather than the adults in the household (Yin, 2003). Chinese parents see fulfilling children's material desires as an approach to purchasing happiness for them and expressing parental love (Fong, 2004; Lin, 2019). After the only-child generation became parents themselves, their consumer behaviours continued to affect how they treated their children. The consumption market for children has expanded and is not limited to dietary supplements, toys, clothing, and education. On the other hand, investments in children's education have been closely linked to the anxieties of intergenerational class mobility (Fong, 2004; Kuan, 2015; Lin, 2019). Among queer parents, the relations between children, family, and consumer markets are further layered with the uncertainty of queer kinship. Zhenzhen once expressed her worries to me: "If a heterosexual couple didn't educate their child well, no one would say anything. But if a same-sex couple's child didn't grow up to a decent person, people may comment that 'homosexual people can't raise kids'".

Besides providing material and educational resources, it has become a crucial aspect in queer parents' lives to construct a loving family atmosphere for their children. As many of my friend informants clarified, children could still receive enough parental love even though they did not grow up in a "whole" family. Their personal experiences with their families of origin also inevitably shaped their conception of what constituted a good family.

When Xie heard about my research, she said she was surveying T's relations with parents and concluded none of her T-identified friends felt parental love from their fathers. Later, I realized that the criterion of 'love' for Xie was closely associated with material resources and gender relations. Xie was born in 1975 during the period of the Great Proletarian Cultural Revolution. According to Xie, her mother was from a *dizhu jiating* (literally meaning landlord family, which was the target of violent denunciation campaigns). To erase the capitalist background for herself and her offspring, Xie's mother married a farmer with a "clean (farmer) background" and had a son and a daughter. Her father only valued the male child and never listened to Xie's requests. Xie once said:

> 'No matter what form of a family is, love is what the kid needs most. My family is complete with a mom and a dad, but I didn't feel love growing up. My parents prefer men over women. As women, we couldn't have meals at the table. I never received the same amount of care as the men growing up in that family.'

When Xie graduated from junior high school, she went to nursing school although her father could have afforded to send her to a public high school, which might have led to better career opportunities. Xie's father ignored Xie's complaints and later persuaded her to enter marriage. Years after leaving her family of origin and hometown, Xie has been doing business and started enjoying a well-off life. She supposed she had the braveness to leave her previous heterosexual marriage, come out to her parents, and gain economic independence partly because of her T role and masculine style (the T role was widely believed to be more independent and have more personal agency). Still, Xie was not satisfied with her educational background as she knew she could do better if she went to college. During a get-together, she said to me and another lesbian couple in their early 30s, "You can't do anything without education nowadays. We are going to provide our children with the finest educational resources we can".

Xie's accounts reflect the generational changes around the conception of parental love and filial piety. Cohen (2005) points out that the de-collectivization of interests has caused rural families to lose much of their economic autonomy, while family (*jia*) remains an essential social unit. The traditional disadvantaged positions, women and youth, have gained increased individual freedom. The rise of 'romantic/free love' and the rejection of arranged marriage in the last century are closely linked to the sense of modernity, freedom, and individual autonomy (Yan, 2003; Lee, 2006; Pan, 2015). The relationship between romantic love and filial piety 'became an important site on which new modes of subjectivity and sociality were worked out' (Lee, 2006, p 16). Being raised in a rural family that treated her as someone who did not merit material investment, Xie felt disappointed and cut her parents out so she could pursue her desired romantic relationships.

Xie made it clear that having a complete natal family with a mother and a father did not mean the family provided good quality of care for children. The changing attitudes towards the 'complete' family and parental love did not happen inside queer circles but in wider society. Xie's opinion resonates with the younger generations, who have shown a growing rejection of simple-minded filial piety (*yuxiao*) and an endorsement of mutual respect and equal relations between parents and children. In this sense, reciprocity in parent–child relations is emphasized: only if you love your children and care for them as they grow up are you a good parent who can enjoy their love and care in return. Xie and Hong talked with other lesbian mothers about coming out to their children and were confident that their children would accept them when they felt enough love and care. Just like Chen said, she once joked with their children, asking them if they wanted a father to replace her. "The kids cried and yelled 'no' to me and Liu," Chen confessed. "I immediately regret my words but feel happy in the meantime."

Although Tommy, Chen, Min, Xie, and An never detailed their income to me, owning several housing properties in first-tier cities like Shenzhen undoubtedly placed them in the upper-middle classes. They were living in well-managed neighbourhoods, usually located near elite elementary schools. One cannot neglect the material underpinning of their alleged higher-than-standard parenting choices. The rhetoric of chosen families and love leads us again to evaluate the notion of individuality and personal choice. The individual person, as Strathern explains, exercises choices as they do style, while their motivations are neither private nor public (1992a, p 166) and style itself is 'an imitative act' (p 177). In this sense, choice has become 'naturalised by the aesthetic and constraints by consumer culture' (Strathern, 1992a, p 162). Under rapid social and family transformations, what constitute 'a good grandparent, a good parent, or a good child have been redefined' (Yan, 2021, p 4; see also Kuan, 2015). What my friend informants meant by "being a good parent and giving children the best life" could be explicated in a similar manner: protecting their children by avoiding 'low-*suzhi*' (quality) homophobic neighbours and schoolteachers, giving them the most comfortable living arrangements, providing them with the best educational resources, and spending quality leisure time with them. Consequently, saving money and purchasing housing property in a tolerant neighbourhood have become essential steps for becoming a reliable parent, queer and straight alike. Even for young non-heterosexual people like Clara and Zhao who did not want kids at all, these steps were desirable for maintaining a lasting same-sex relationship and having a better chance of being accepted by their parents. Hence, non-heterosexual people's choices to move to cosmopolitan, open-minded cities for upward mobility are closely linked with the existing practices of love and care and their visions of a desirable future.

Blood ties and queer relations

Overall, this chapter reveals the complexity in defining the boundaries between kin and non-kin, biological ties and chosen ties. As the division of biological and social facts appeared in the discussion of kinship, it has firstly become clear to anthropologists that kinship is not reducible to biology. At the same time, scholars have pointed out that kinship is a lumpy, contagious connection, and is not always positive in the sense of bringing warmth to its members (Das, 1995; Carsten, 2013; Meinert and Grøn, 2019). Kinship relationships are rarely severed nor end completely, and even the breakdown of relationships, as with divorce, can lead to the reordering of social continuities (Simpson, 1994; Strathern, 1996). For queer parents who shared their life experiences in this chapter, blood ties and affective bonds seem to sometimes be threatening and sometimes reinforce each other's positions.

First of all, my friend informants in this chapter expressed incompatible views on the issue of alleged biological, legal, and social parenthood. Dae and many other queer parents conceptualized blood ties as the most central and authentic form of kin relations, and they tended to view non-heterosexual conjugal relations and non-biological parent–child relations as non-kin or 'less-kin' relations. The young urbanites, on the other hand, highlighted the central position of conjugal love in their kinship value system in comparison with the traditional patrilineal parent–child relation. Moreover, non-heterosexual people's natal families rarely acknowledged their queer partners' children as their offspring. Consequently, some queer parents had to make tough choices between their blood kins and their chosen tie. Dae chose her blood relations over her girlfriend, and Lin chose to live with her girlfriend Mo instead of her son. In an extreme circumstance, Xie left her natal family and her biological child in her hometown to chase upward mobility and romantic relationships in a modern city.

As described earlier, most non-heterosexual people perceived their same-sex partners' children as non-relatives not solely because they were not blood relatives; rather, their decisions to participate in childrearing with their same-sex partners were shaped by various social, economic, and legal considerations. A queer individual could not establish a legally recognizable tie with the biological child of their same-sex partner. Here, the legal domains included not only Marriage Law but house registration, family-planning policies, ART regulations, and other mechanisms for producing recognizable kinship and citizenships (Kim and Friedman, 2021). Queer co-parents in my research had to present themselves as single parents when dealing with local *hukou* registration authorities and, in some cases, lied about how they had their children. They registered as single parents, meaning one of the co-fathers/mothers must give up legal parenthood and bear the risks and uncertainties around unrecognized custody themselves. Hence, social parenthood in Chinese queer lifeworlds could hardly equal legally recognizable parenthood like adoptive parenthood or step-parenthood in heterosexual households, and even the idea of social parenthood became questionable for many non-heterosexual people. While desiring same-sex marriage and joint custody as legal protection, many Chinese same-sex couples may only count on material recourses to navigate uncertainties of queer parenthood.

What Dae and other non-heterosexual people often stated was the alleged irreversibility of consanguineal relations and reversibility of affinal relationships (see Simpson, 1994), as a person might be an ex-husband but not an ex-father. The high reversibility of Chinese same-sex conjugal relationships is especially problematic since they do not go through legal marriages and divorces. In Dae's case, she found out she might cut out relations with her ex-girlfriend completely, but she might never cut her relationship with her blood ties and *xinghun* ex-husband, who was the other blood and legal parent of her children. Just like the lawyer speaker in a non-profit workshop said, "non-heterosexual couples don't even qualify as *feifa tongju* (illegal cohabitation) in legal terms". For this reason, co-parenting in *xinghun* marriages might form durable mutual bonds between the lesbian 'wife/mother' and the gay 'husband/father' with gendered roles, whether they expected it or not. Some non-heterosexual people therefore argued that biological parent–child relations are stronger than same-sex intimate relationships. Yet, we must acknowledge that their belief that "blood is thicker than water" is configured by existing social and legal institutions.

To discuss this matter further, many non-heterosexual people in this book reason that establishing parent–child relations with the biological child of one's queer partner, non-heteronormative/queer relationship is risky, as the person has no blood or legal ties with the child. Such a kind of parenthood can rely on affective recognition as the other two perceived authoritative recognitions – blood and law – are absent. Queer co-parenting practices raised further concerns about the potentially unequal family relations, as the housewife/house husband role in same-sex relationships was not protected by law, and therefore the person in this role was at higher risk of losing custody. Against this backdrop, many Chinese same-sex couples desired legal marriage and joint custody as protection against risks. The very uncertainty between state legislation and queer kinship shaped non-heterosexual people's perceived nature of queer relations, including queer conjugal relations and queer non-biological parenthood (Borneman, 1997; Goodfellow, 2015; Kim and Friedman, 2021). The interaction between law and family prompts a nuanced consideration of the dynamic between the state and culture. Opposition to same-sex marriage and queer parenting exposes a discourse regarding the state's role in recognizing relationships, underscoring political fears around the openness of kinship (Butler, 2002). Butler thus stresses how state legitimacy can be a site for both laying claim to recognizability and articulating cultural denial of queer kinship (2002, p 28).

It appears that Tommy held a view on queer parenting quite contrary to Dae who embraced seemingly conventional kinship values; Tommy's life choice was radically innovative. Although Tommy was aware that he might never be legally recognized as Jack's father, he chose to co-parent with his same-sex partner Joe. Tommy's parental status and his relations with Joe and Jack were acknowledged by his friends and colleagues in their everyday life with several prerequisites. The biological mother of Jack had already divorced Joe and did not request custody of Jack. Moreover, Tommy's job as a journalist and his considerable income level in a big city allowed him to express his queerness in a relatively free manner. Yet, Tommy had to negotiate with the uncertainties of his father status caused by the legalities of custody, and handle his distant relatives' attitudes towards his same-sex co-parenting relationships. In this way, Tommy's statement that the "affective bond was as important as the blood relationship" was also shaped by legal concerns, conventional patrilineal family norms, and material resources. One's gender, social status, financial ability, age, and distance from families of origin all come into play.

Against this background, using ART without entering any form of heterosexual relationships has emerged as the seemingly ideal way for queer couples to become co-parents, mostly because these practices cause less legal risk about parenthood in their eyes. Like many of my friend informants explained, there would be no fighting for custody with an opposite-sex *zhihun/xinghun* partner. In the case of *A luan B huai* (reciprocal IVF) among lesbian couples and surrogacy among gay couples, the position of biological relatedness was often put together with the role of bodily experience and affective bond in constructing the couple's co-parenthood. Some friend informants chose to have two children or use the sperm/egg of their partners' opposite-sex relatives to make sure that their children were biologically related to both, thereby mobilizing the kin categories and terminologies. Either way, the success or failure in achieving queer couples' co-parenting status in their everyday lives unsettle the notions of blood and biology, making them contingent features in queer kinning processes.

Finally, queer parents' reflective accounts in this chapter reveal the generational changes in conceptions of parental love and care. Developed from the previous chapters, I suggest that both the expression of parental love and conjugal love were conditioned by one's material resources. At the same time, the changing understanding of love and care signifies transforming Chinese family values, which I will further detail in the next chapter. I suggest that the idea of blood and biology still holds its centrality in Chinese family life, while it has also been proved to have elastic potentialities for queer couples who want to establish same-sex joint parenthood. The various arrangements of queer co-parenting demonstrate the mobilizing possibilities beyond 'blood' ties and kinship terminology, that is, (co-)parenthood being constructed and strengthened using the language of bodily experience and affective recognition. This chapter finds that the notions of biology and patrilineal family line alone does not work to construct or deny queer co-parenting relationships; rather, it is the queer subject's capacity to eliminate the involvement of a third biological or legal parent outside their queer conjugal relationship, to navigate uncertainties caused by heteronormative legal terms, to secure educational and housing resources in big cities, and to handle their parents' attitude towards their queer nuclear families.

6

Queering Family: Modern Rainbow Families

In the 2018 Parents, Families, and Friends of Lesbians and Gays (PFLAG) China Shenzhen talkfest, the host asked everyone, "what is the best way to express 'I love you' in Chinese?" Then, she answered herself: "I think the Chinese version of 'I love you' is 'my parents have approved us'". The host's speech in this PFLAG event demonstrates the strong wish for the coexistence of romantic love and parental harmony during the emergence of queer subjectivities. Indeed, parent–child relations have been the most important relationships in Confucian Chinese society and still hold their significance in today's China. Moreover, the host's words stress the hope for a harmonious negotiation between the families of origin and non-normative sexualities. In the Chinese language, '*jia*' (family/home) refers to not only a group of people but also a mental space that refers to the ultimate home and roots one belongs to (Chou, 2001, p 35). In most Chinese social studies and queer communities, family/*jia* was always perceived as the most essential and powerful social unit that affected queer personal life (Chou, 2001; Engebretsen, 2009, 2014; Kam, 2013; Song, 2022). Huang and Brouwer suggest 'the most profound struggle that Chinese queer subjects face is, hence, not in a "public," socio-political domain; instead, it is located in their "private" lives – in the precarious, lasting negotiations with their intimate families, especially their parents' (2018, p 101). As discussed in Chapter 3, seeing family of origin as the central heteronormative unit in queer life could limit the possibility of realizing the heteronormative features in the socio-legal domain. Not all anti-heteronormative sexual relationships are anti-family, and the notion of family is constantly being reconstructed (Bose and Bhattacharyya, 2007, xxvi; see also Luo, 2020). I thus begin this chapter by exploring how the changing notion and scope of 'family/*jia*' has constantly interacted with queer kinship practices and life aspirations.

Developed from the previous chapters, I also document the various forms of non-heterosexual families I encountered during the fieldwork. While the conventional definition of family and the lack of legal recognition continue to create constraints for non-normative forms of families, queer subjects and their family relatives have also concretized the queer/*tongzhi*/rainbow family in urban China. Lesbian, gay, bisexual, and transgender (LGBT)/ non-heterosexual families are often delineated through the language of 'fictive/chosen families' in contrast with 'biological/blood' families, and such discourse assumes that LGBT families are creative and innovative in their structure (Weston, 1991; Dempsey, 2010). Meanwhile, emerging research on LGBT families in non-Euro-American societies as 'families of choice' has been challenging the dominant Western knowledge of queer chosen families and coming-out politics (Mizielińska and Stasińska, 2017; Lo, 2020). Thus, I do not intend to narrow down the definition of Chinese queer families as there is not only one model of these. In this chapter, I investigate how different forms of queer family are recognized in different times and spaces by queer individuals, communities, and the wider society. This book treats family as a contested field. Through ethnographic accounts and reflections, I complicate the transgressive–assimilative, visible–invisible, out–passing dualities in Chinese queer relationships.

Coming big home, coming small home

The month of the Chinese New Year sees a peak in passenger transport as urban migrants return to their hometowns to reunite with their families. Celebrating the Spring Festival Eve with the whole family has been a nationwide tradition in China,[1] constituting the most important family gathering of the year. In the days following the Spring Festival Eve, relatives began to visit each other. China's rapid economic restructuring has driven a growing number of individuals to seek better educational and career opportunities in different cities or countries. For many (queer) migrants, Spring Festival may be the only time to have face-to-face communication with their parents and extended families. Such home-leaving and home-reunion processes have inevitably complicated the once close kinship tie. The connections between people and their natal families are often stretched – not only by the physical separation but also by underlying emotional detachment, the dynamic process of negotiating kinship, the stressed feeling experienced in kinship practices, and the time constraints on top of spatial separation (Wei, 2020). In the last decade, Spring Festival has become the peak time for coming out, as many non-heterosexual people could not stand the intense marriage pressure from parents and relatives when they returned from migrant cities (Lin and Xu, 2013). Chou (2001) advocates for an indigenous 'coming-home' approach, an artful integration of one's same-sex partners into the familial context without explicitly disclosing sexualities, in contrast to the Western confrontational coming-out strategy. The emphasis on 'coming home' has been critiqued in recent years, as scholars argue this strategy can be culturally essentializing (Wong, 2007), insufficient (Huang and Brouwer, 2018), and even impossible (Wei, 2020, 2023). I thus concur with Wei (2020) that in the context of stretched kinship connections, there cannot be a universal 'coming-out/coming-home' strategy for Chinese queer people, as each strategy entails risk and uncertainties that necessitate delicate negotiation (p 40). In light of these considerations, I detail how my friend informants negotiated their queer relationships with their parents and relatives during the Chinese New Year through various means.

Young queer couples who had not come out to parents often went back to their home alone as single persons. They described it to me as *"gehuigejia"* (each to one's own home). Many non-heterosexual people in this research were in-betweens. Their parents might have already known about their same-sex relationship status but they either sidestepped it or refused to talk about it. Non-heterosexual people who had come out to parents may have gone back to their hometowns with their same-sex partners. Some of my friends living in Shenzhen did not go back to their hometowns during the Chinese New Year holiday. Instead, their parents went to Shenzhen and stayed for a few days. 'Reverse reunion' is becoming popular in first-tier cities like Shenzhen among young migrants. *China News* and other news websites have reported 'reverse spring rush/reverse reunion' as the newfangled trend since 2018. The reason more and more young migrants choose not to go back to their hometowns seems obvious: the price for train/flight/coach tickets from migrant cities to other parts of China is much higher than the other way around, and it is easier for their parents to go to Shenzhen. Despite the obvious factor, young non-heterosexual people have more subtle reasons to stay in the city and more complicated experiences with their families of origin during the Chinese New Year.

Alice and her girlfriend Fiona were from Chengdu, the capital city of Sichuan Province. They met each other in college and their relationship was entering into its seventh year in 2018. They had been living in Shenzhen for three years. Both of their parents had noticed their conjugal relationship, showing neither approval nor fury. In 2018, Alice and Fiona each went back to their own parents' homes in Chengdu during Spring Festival. Their relatives still asked them about their plans for marriage and other personal questions. Moreover, the aunts and uncles assumed that working in Chengdu was better than working in Shenzhen and continued to encourage Alice and Fiona to come back to live in Chengdu. In 2019, Fiona went back to her parents' home in Chengdu while Alice stayed in Shenzhen. This time, Alice told me she had a much better experience.

Several months before the holiday, Alice asked her parents if they wanted to visit her in Shenzhen because she did not want to hear her relatives asking her about her work and relationship status anymore. To her surprise,

Alice's parents responded positively. The day after Fiona flew back to Chengdu, Alice's parents arrived in Shenzhen. Alice let her parents stay in her rented apartment:

> 'At first, I was going to book a hotel room for Mom and Dad. Then, I realized they have figured out my relationship with Fiona anyway. What is the big deal if they are staying in our apartment and see Fiona's things! There is no need to cover up the fact that we are living together.'

Alice and her parents lived together in her rented flat for two weeks and visited the city. Alice's parents had a great time and stopped asking Alice to go back to Chengdu. Alice told me she and her parents were all glad they had spent Chinese New Year together and, at the same time, far from other relatives:

> 'I had some sincere chats with my mom and realised that she was not unhappy with my relationship (with Fiona), but rather worried about confronting the relatives. She cares so much about how others think of us. Therefore, I am going to take her to travel next Spring Festival as well.'

Before this Spring Festival holiday, Alice spent years subtly mentioning her same-sex relationship to her parents. After that, she realized the key issue was her uncles' and aunts' traditional family values. In a large extended family, members from different age groups, social classes, and educational backgrounds could have dramatically conflicting values; however, they might feel morally obliged to show care for each other's personal life because they are linked by the patrilineal ideas of blood (*xueyuan*) and family clan (*jiazu*). Alice's unmarried status was a failure in some relatives' eyes, which made her mother anxious.

Alice tried to distance her mom from her relatives, and she was optimistic about her strategy. Alice and Fiona both held master's degrees from top universities and were able to secure satisfactory income in Shenzhen. After working in Shenzhen for some years, Alice's mother began to take her words into account rather than her relatives. Also, Alice's mother had two female friends who were a couple and had had a child together recently. Alice's mother certainly knew her friends were a *lala* couple as she told Alice that the baby was born through reciprocal in-vitro fertilization (IVF). Alice thought it was also a reason that her mother changed attitude towards same-sex relationships. For Alice, her parents spending the Chinese New Year with only her, in a family of three, was a positive sign. Alice expressed her hope that she would settle in Shenzhen with Fiona, so their parents could come to Shenzhen and therefore be away from their relatives' gossip for good. Fiona agreed with Alice and said she had another unpleasant holiday back in Chengdu:

> 'I had to give the younger relatives a lot of red pocket money, and the aunts and uncles drove me mad. One day, my aunt rebuked her husband when they were preparing dinner. I tried to ease the tension, while my aunt suddenly turned to me and said they would stop quarrelling if I got married! What's wrong with her? ... So, I have offended almost everyone (in the extended family) to make them shut up. When they ask me how much my salary in Shenzhen is, I ask them how much their house loans are. When they ask me when I will get married, I ask them when they will divorce.'

Fiona's statement is the epitome of many young urbanites' attitudes towards annoying questions from distant relatives, queer and straight alike. Fiona also planned to spend the next Spring Festival somewhere else with only her parents. She believed that the 'reverse reunion' and travelling during Spring Festival would be the future:

> 'The reason why we are still going back to the hometown and having dinner with all the relatives is because the family elders want us to do so. The grandparents can't travel long distances and they are the only people who unite the big family. However, when the elders are gone, the big family (*dajia*) will disperse, and only small families (*xiaojia*) remain.'

In Fiona's words, the "big family" refers to the Confucian patrilineal family or family clan, and the "small family" refers to the nuclear family with one's parents included. It becomes clear that the increase of the 'reverse Spring Festival reunion' in urban cities reflects the changing understanding of 'family' and 'relative', and such changes have a nuanced influence on queer intimate and family relationships. In a family in which one's parents were close to a large number of siblings and relatives, coming out was tricky as one felt one's private life became a subject of moral judgement for all distant aunts and uncles. As Brainer's (2019) research on Taiwan LGBT families of origin indicates, siblings' rejection could be a profound concern when queer children and their parents made decisions to address issues of gender and sexuality. That is one reason 'coming out' and 'parental acceptance' are slow and ambiguous: one's parents may accept their child being queer but not in queer relationship; in some cases, one's parents may accept their child being in a queer relationship but not being unmarried and childless. Some friend informants who chose to enter *xinghun* marriages told me that they had already come out to their parents; still, they got married to protect their parents' moral reputation (*mianzi*) in the 'big family'. In other words, their parents might fail the 'big family' test if their offspring did not embrace a heteronormative lifestyle.

Fiona and Alice's experience reflects the increasingly perceptible distinction between the 'big family' and the 'small family' in Chinese private life. Since living in Shenzhen, I have found a noticeable number of parents of young non-heterosexual people who now prefer smaller family gatherings during traditional family reunion events. In conversations with my peers, I often heard stories of their parents who were once close to their cousins and felt obliged to help each other through lending money or business collaboration. However, instances of relatives taking advantage of their generosity led their parents to distance themselves. These widely shared narratives among young people demonstrate that they did not think blood relatedness or sharing the same male ancestor would automatically produce thick, trusting relations. Many young Chinese urbanites do not include their relatives in their scope of family anymore. Furthermore, some young non-heterosexual people mentioned that their parents tended to "escape" from relatives after knowing their children's queer desires, since they did not want their relatives to gossip about them.

In short, many friend informants contended that, nowadays, "the big family is becoming the small family (*dajia bian xiaojia*)". This was happening generally among Chinese young urbanites as they were becoming estranged from distant relatives. In other words, the nuclear family is becoming more important than the extended family under rapid social change and market reforms. The decrease in small-scale family cooperation and the emergence of the free labour market were crucial factors. Young queer couples might settle into a place away from parents and relatives and eliminate their shared interests. As Schroeder (2012) observes, being able to choose leisure activities and to choose who to spend free time with have become vital for exercising individual autonomy. What is more, relatives were no longer seen as part of one's family by young non-heterosexual people, especially if they did not feel emotionally close with their relatives. Therefore, one was no longer morally obligated to always spend time with relatives and please them. In this case, the importance of a patrilineal family clan, or a common male ancestor, has decreased. Still, urban young non-heterosexual people in this research showed a strong desire for parental acceptance. In the cases of middle-aged queer parents, such as Tian and An, their mothers left their hometowns to live with their sons' queer families and silently acknowledged their sons' same-sex relationships. Many young non-heterosexual people therefore expressed a strong desire to gain enough resources to settle in a big city and facilitate their parents moving away from their relatives and traditional kinship values.

Furthermore, we must not only focus on young non-heterosexual people solely as if they are the only social group undergoing transformations. In many cases here, parents of non-heterosexual people revised their kinship values and supported their children's life choices. Mama Qin, a PFLAG volunteer whose daughter was queer, suggested to other young non-heterosexual people: "Getting parental acceptance is just a matter of time since your parents love you. You need to accompany them more and make both of you strong. I want you to remember that your *jiazu* (patrilineal family clan) has nothing to do with you; don't let them hold you back."

Many parents of non-heterosexual people have described their experience of acknowledging their children's queer relationships as "coming out" as well. Moreover, they became their children's spokespeople in the 'big family' and focused on their children's well-being rather than their moral reputation in the Confucian patrilineal family. As the conventional definition and scope of family/*jia* has been destabilized, it is useful to realize the elasticity in Chinese family values that provides negotiating space for Chinese non-heterosexual people to balance their multiple kin relations.

The role-model rainbow (reproductive) family

In a 2019 LGBT-themed talkfest, Tian shared that he came out to his mother after his second son, a 'rainbow baby', was born. He felt his coming-out experience sounded like a fake one:

> 'My mom was not angry after I told her I was gay. She even started to speculate about my friends and said, "oh, is that guy who is very tall and muscular homosexual as well?" I thought my mom would not sleep that night; it turned out I was the one who couldn't sleep.'

Most attendees seemed unsurprised, as they supposed that Tian's mother had no more reason to be angry about Tian's same-sex desires. Tian had brought biological and legally recognized offspring into the family and therefore fulfilled his familial duty. As mentioned before, having offspring was often viewed as aiding one's coming out to families of origin. A man sitting near me signed, "He (Tian) must be rich!" Tian's adopted first son Xiaoyu was never called a 'rainbow baby' by others, which implied that the birth of Tian's second child was innovative and different from normative reproductive relationships. How does this relate to the emerging forms of queer family in today's urban China?

A rainbow family is generally defined as a same-sex or LGBTIQA+-parented family in Euro-American societies and this term has lately been adopted by Asia-Pacific regions. Over the last few years, the terms 'rainbow family' (*caihong jiating*) and 'rainbow baby' (*caihong baobao*) have been increasingly mentioned in Chinese queer communities, principally by LGBT organizations, gay and lesbian bloggers, and private assisted reproductive technology (ART) companies.

The discussions on whether a family might call themselves a 'rainbow family' and their child a 'rainbow baby' in queer communities always involved a moral evaluation of one's marriage and parenting practices. From my experience with my friend informants, ART agencies, and LGBT communities, only the babies born through a way that was free from association with heterosexual marriage and sexual intercourse belonged to the category of rainbow babies. Lesbian mothers and gay fathers were hesitant to refer to their children from previous *zhihun* (heterosexual marriages with heterosexual-identified spouses) as rainbow babies. Also, queer parents in *xinghun* (gay–lesbian contract marriages) rarely referred to their co-parenting status with opposite-sex *xinghun* partners as a rainbow family, nor would they join such WeChat groups. In this sense, the endorsement of the emerging 'successful' rainbow families and rainbow babies concentrated more on the individual's capabilities rather than the person's non-normative gender and sexual relationships.

Not long after I discovered Tommy's 'Three Men under One Roof' blog, several lesbians recommended a well-known WeChat public account named '*Caihong Baobao*' (Rainbow Babies). This public account was created by a *lala* couple in 2015 who had mixed-race twin babies through the *A luan B huai* process overseas. The *lala* couple, owning a kindergarten themselves, had been sharing their family life and collecting stories of other "non-*xinghun tongzhi* families with children", which they later termed "rainbow families". Many lesbians endorsed them as the model lesbian/rainbow family. As the public account attracted thousands of followers, the *lala* couple organized online support chat groups for non-heterosexual people who wanted to have or had children to exchange experiences and resources. Moreover, the *lala* couple described their choice to have a rainbow family as a resistant and aggressive move. They stated that they chose to set their lifestyle in opposition to obedience and compromise. In this way, they appeared to embrace the Western-originated coming-out advocacy and acknowledged the rainbow family as a lifestyle that attacked the normative heterosexual family.

In addition to online social media platforms, the 'rainbow family' and the 'rainbow baby' have been increasingly acknowledged in offline queer communities. PFLAG China states that they focus on family issues including parental acceptance, queer parenting, and elderly care. While aiming to promote family and social harmony, they have demonstrably contributed to the standardized discourse on the Chinese rainbow family or role-model LGBT family. In each PFLAG China event, there were several types of themes and guest speakers that were never absent. Firstly, the events usually began with the topic of self-acceptance. The guest speakers were gay men and lesbians who had 'completely come out' and devoted themselves to the LGBT community. 'Coming out and family acceptance' was one of the most emotional themes when the parents of gay men and lesbians shared their feelings and experiences after knowing their children were not straight. They were addressed as *"Mama/Papa"* and were surrounded by young non-heterosexual people who wanted advice on coming out to their parents. At least one same-sex couple would share their love stories and advice on maintaining a "lasting relationship". Queer parents who had children without entering heterosexual marriages were also the necessary guest speakers in the 'having children' section. When the hosts began to introduce the same-sex couples and queer parents, the screen would display a photo of a sweet moment between them. The themes were selected by organizers to encourage participants to come out to their parents, avoid entering any form of heterosexual marriage, have a lasting same-sex intimate relationship, build a network of elder support, and take part in LGBT activities.

Organizers nominated the guest speakers as role models who gave guidance to curious attendees. Invited guest speakers were mostly considered successful individuals by the public, including doctors, professors, entrepreneurs, and so on. After these same-sex couples and queer parents walked off the stage, there were always some attendees approaching them and asking for their WeChat or phone numbers. It should be noted that the majority of attendees in these LGBT talkfest events were self-identified gay men, some were self-identified lesbians, and only a few identified as transgender or bisexual or other gender and sexual categories.

Certainly, guest speakers' personal characteristics and resources were often admired by attendees and seen as the reason they were so successful in both their careers and familial life. In the meantime, the selected guest speakers and themes have discouraged attendees from expressing themselves from disadvantaged backgrounds even though PFLAG China did not charge any entrance fee for its talkfests. During the same PFLAG talkfest at which Tian was one of the guest speakers, a gay man raised his hand and asked:

> 'I don't understand why I can't find a boyfriend. I already came out to my family ten years ago. I think having a romantic relationship (*tanlian'ai*) is harder than coming out. Otherwise, I wouldn't be alone. I have attended several of your events, but no one wants to talk to me further. I feel everyone is young and good looking except me. I am now asking if anyone is interested in me?'

The middle-aged man's strong accent and clothes indicated his rural, working-class status. He was surrounded by young gay men wearing fashionable clothes and wristbands with rainbow elements. After his speech, the silence in the banquet hall lasted for at least ten seconds. The host comforted the man briefly, and the event moved on as usual. PFLAG China and other LGBT organizations' heightened focuses on gaining parental acceptance, maintaining lasting monogamous relationships, and queer parenting raise concerns about homonormativity in its Chinese version (Luo et al, 2022; Song, 2022). The new neoliberal sexual politics, which Lisa Duggan (2002) calls the new homonormativity, does not challenge prevailing heteronormative norms and institutions but rather supports and maintains them while promising a depoliticized gay culture centred on domesticity and consumption. The case of Mei and Youzi to come further delineates how certain forms of queer family have been fortified and how homonormative sexual politics has been reproduced – and localized – in different social and economic spaces (Duggan, 2002; Brown, 2012).

At another PFLAG talkfest, a young gay man yelled excitedly, "they have been together for ten years! I think they should be the next guest speakers!" Suddenly being the centre of attention, Mei and Youzi looked shy as a hundred queer attendees turned their heads to look at them. Mei and Youzi were both 30 years old and *bufen* (not classified). They met each other via an online forum when Youzi was at university. Surprisingly, they found out that they used to live in the same neighbourhood. They smiled and told me they fell in love at first sight. Mei had a hard time living with her family of origin. Her mother died when she was young. Her father then married a young woman who Mei described as impetuous. Mei could not get along with her stepmother and, consequently, she quit school and moved out of the home. When Mei met Youzi, she was already working as a clerk. After their relationship became serious, Youzi asked Mei to move to her home to live with her and her parents. Mei's parents were not aware of their relationship as Youzi introduced Mei as a close friend who had been suffering with some family drama. Mei lived in Youzi's home for two years until Youzi graduated from university. They currently lived in an apartment in the suburb of Shenzhen, far from their parents. Youzi was working as an engineer in a state-owned company, which provided a stable level of income.

During my fieldwork, Youzi and Mei both entered *xinghun* marriages as they felt this was the pragmatic and reasonable response to marriage pressure. Mei even said that she felt guilty because Youzi's mother was very nice to her. Thus, they did not want to make Youzi's mother feel difficult. Mei and Youzi described the process around arranging *xinghun* marriage as a series of daily trifles that do not bother them at all. I met many same-sex couples who became worried and scared when they started to talk about their *xinghun* marriage experiences. Therefore, I was impressed by Youzi and Mei's relaxed attitude. They went through the process together and every future move was planned. They both notarized premarital property with their *xinghun* partners and were not worried about any potential financial disputes. Furthermore, Youzi and Mei decided that they did not want children, either on their own or with their *xinghun* partners. They avoided *xinghun* parent-in-law issues as much as they could and agreed with their *xinghun* husbands that they would not own any communal property or have a child. In many online chatting groups, such *xinghun* marriages are often called successful and nominal ones – a minimal bond between the gay 'husband' and lesbian 'wife'.

Youzi and Mei only went to the PFLAG talkfest once with their gay friend and did not understand why people in the event treated them like celebrities. "We are just a normal couple, no secrets of success," Mei said when others asked them to share their love story. After I met them at that event, Youzi and Mei only hung out with me and Jin, and they never attended PFLAG events again. They did not enjoy participating in PFLAG talkfests, as they felt they would be judged by others. Although they did not feel their *xinghun* marriage was a problematic and unmoral move, they shortly realized that the practice of any form of heterosexual marriage was conceived as a symbol of one's weakness and obedience within PFLAG China's philosophy. To put it another way, Mei and Youzi did not want to be and indeed did not qualify as role-model speakers at PFLAG China events. Coming out to their parents and the wider public and having a rainbow baby were not included as part of their future plan.

The exclusion and inclusion processes of 'rainbow family' in Chinese queer communities reveal the multilayered interplay of gender norms and class status. Firstly, female same-sex couples who raised children together were noticeably fewer and less visible than gay co-fathers. Until now, Chinese women have generally earned less income and had less personal autonomy than men (Tan and Jiang, 2006; Fincher, 2014; Ji et al, 2017), and these issues on gender inequality make childrearing a more challenging task for lesbian co-mothers. In addition, friend informants working in governmental sectors and state-owned enterprises were especially concerned with their image as single parents in their colleagues' and employers' eyes, not to mention their non-normative sexualities. Having a 'rainbow family' also means having children out of wedlock, which is considered to be disobeying family-planning policy and hence could harm one's career.

The emerging discourse on the 'rainbow family', like that on 'free love' in transforming Chinese societies, suggests a formulation of seemingly rigid contradictions between tradition and modernity. As rainbow families become a symbol of modernity and progression in online and offline queer communities, non-heterosexual people with 'normative' marriages remain silenced in queer public spaces, as they are under the gaze of queer people and organizations who regard themselves as more modern. The LGBT-identified micro-celebrities, the LGBT organizations like PFLAG China, and their partnering ART companies were ultimately endorsing the same kind of queer role models and again stressing queer individuals' personal agency to gain upward mobility to establish an ideal queer reproductive family, which echoes a homonormative narrative of being a good sexual citizen by being a good consumer (Bell and Binnie, 2000, 2004; Rofel, 2007). The capacity to establish an acknowledged modern queer family is conditioned by one's gender and socio-economic class rather than one's 'deviant' sexual desires and relationships.

Strategically 'out' as a non-normative family

Like previously mentioned, narratives of coming out and being accepted by each other's parents were repeated on every occasion when a successful queer family showed up. Most non-heterosexual people did not immediately think about being socially and legally recognized as a couple or family when the topic of coming out was brought up. How do non-heterosexual people present themselves as not only queer individuals but also queer families in Chinese societies? The Euro-American-originated notion of coming out and being 'closeted' implies an out–closeted dichotomy as one is either completely out or keeps their sexuality completely hidden. Such a binary understanding of coming out based on the politics of sexual identity could be troubling for queer subjects in a non-Euro-American world (Wei, 2007; Engebretsen and Schroeder, 2015; Brainer, 2019). The process of coming out is 'more complex with individuals maintaining multiple identities in different space and in one space but at different times' (Valentine, 1993, p 246).

I once had dinner with lesbian couple Danny and Pam in a restaurant. In the last few years, Danny changed her visible T style to a more feminine one, growing long hair and wearing feminine formal clothes. She explained that it was partly because of her job as a lawyer and partly because of her changing understanding of T/P roles. Danny and Pam had been living together for two years and were under the process of *A luan B huai*. As we walked out of the restaurant, the restaurant owner, who was also a friend of Danny's employer, recognized Danny's face and went to greet us. After friendly small talk, the owner said to Danny, "Take your *guimi* (bosom female friend) to my restaurant next time!" Danny smiled and said yes. We said goodbye to the restaurant owner and left. This night was an ordinary scene in both Danny's and my everyday knowledge. Queer relationships and families were recognized in different degrees of visibility, as Danny and Pam were a loving lesbian family in my eyes, close friends in Danny's family relatives' eyes, and flatmates in Danny's colleagues' eyes. But just like other queer couples, Danny and Pam did not intend to pass as *guimi*, and this kind of brief exchange let them know that they did not fit the template of 'normal families' (Patton-Imani, 2020, p 16).

Often, my friend informants described such practices of 'not explaining' in public spaces and legal institutions as keeping a low-profile life to avoid unnecessary troubles. Saisai, a short-haired T-lesbian woman, believed her boss must already know she was lesbian but did not bother to question her. Both in their late 20s, Saisai and her girlfriend Yina had an informal wedding party with their parents and friends in 2018 to celebrate their ten-year relationship since college. Saisai was working at a state-owned enterprise, and Yina was working for hotel chains. Yina thought of herself as bisexual and actively made many LGBT friends through queer social media and volunteer networks. Furthermore, they both came out to their parents in recent years. During their wedding, their parents and relatives shed tears of joy when they all stood together for wedding photos. Saisai and Yina thus saw the wedding as a great strategy to make their family recognize their established lesbian family. Saisai and Yina's experiences do not fit into the coming-out–coming-home binary, as they valued both their individualistic desires and their parents' feelings. In the lesbian community, Saisai and Yina were considered a successfully 'out' lesbian couple blessed by family elders. Just like Danny and Pam, Saisai and Yina were both 'out' and 'passing' and constantly negotiate their visibility as a lesbian family.

Several months after their wedding, Saisai and Yina complained to me that they still felt like they were dating (*tanlian'ai*) rather than married, especially when Yina went to work at a new company and wrote her married status as 'unmarried' in the employee personal details form. Yina's new colleagues tried to introduce Yina to potential male mates several times, and Yina had to make excuses to refuse their invitations. Not long after, Saisai and Yina went to the local public notary office to register as appointed guardians for each other. The notary process gave them some feelings of legal bond and security. Even so, not being recognized as a married couple and a social unit by the law and their employers shaped their feelings about their lesbian family. The lesbian families' experience with their family members and colleagues first disclosed the fictive fantasy of keeping a queer intimate relationship in a clear work–family or private–public binary.

During my fieldwork, public visibility and public tolerance also became myths associated with quality (*suzhi*), modernity, and personal agency. In Chinese mainstream online forums, it was common to see homophobic statements under the topic of LGBT matter, as here:

> I am straight. I am not against *tongxinglian* (homosexuality). I just can't accept their sexual behaviour. I think I am being nice enough and you *tongxinglian* people shouldn't ask more from me.
> I don't discriminate against homosexual people, but you can't flaunt your homosexuality in public!

Such statements often reduced homosexuality to same-sex sexual behaviour that only existed in the private realm; moreover, they reduced discrimination and homophobia to explicit insult and violence. At the same time, the emerging online debates against same-sex marriage were linked to the issues of *tongqi* (wives of gay men) and commercial surrogacy while neglecting the very existence of non-heterosexual families, especially female conjugal relations. The online forums were just one facet of the public. I do not intend to observe whether the society as a whole is oppressing non-heterosexual people or not; rather, I articulate queer subjects' and families' various encounters with the public in this section and throughout the book.

An, a gay father and an entrepreneur enjoying a middle-upper-class life in Shenzhen, said he was not concerned about homophobic violence. An stressed "the society is more tolerant than you think" and provided several examples: "I and Ye hold hands on the street, and no one says anything. One time, I forwarded an article about gay men to my WeChat Moments and forgot to make it public only to selected friends – it became public to all WeChat contacts. Then my business partners 'liked' it."

An was aware that other people rarely asked about his intimate life and family status due to his high social position. An did not worry that the cameraman he hired would ever say anything to embarrass him and his sons. During the interview, An took a break to look after his crying children. The cameraman responsible for videotaping our interview commented: "I bet he is not troubled by having three kids, or you know, parenting without getting married. If I had as much money as him, I would be happy all the time and have as many children as I could".

Tommy concluded that "we are very lucky", as he and Joe never had any noteworthy trouble being gay fathers in their everyday lives. One reason for that, as Tommy explained, was that "the big city is more tolerant". Tommy's apartment is in the centre of Guangzhou. Tommy said he was worried that Jack would have problems with having two daddies. Thus, when Jack was in kindergarten, Tommy told Jack, "You have seen many types of families in our neighbourhood. Some of your friends have only one father; some have only one mother. You shouldn't discriminate against any of them". Tommy meant not only divorced parents but also the mistresses who had children with married businessmen in Hong Kong.[2] Tommy shared the neighbourhood with some wealthy mistresses, and they were respectful enough not to judge each other in public. When the three of them walk in the friendly and elegant neighbourhood, no one has ever questioned who Jack's father was. Tommy once visited Jack's elementary school teacher before Mothers' Day, when students were often required to write an essay about their mothers or show gratitude to their mothers. Tommy said:

'I told Jack's teacher that Jack's father and mother were divorced a long time ago, and he doesn't live with his mother. Therefore, I hoped she could relax the requirement a little bit. Maybe she could ask students to write about any family member they like. She took my advice.'

In the interviews and chats, most friend informants tried to convince me that the social atmosphere in urban cities like Shenzhen and Guangzhou were tolerant and they never encountered homophobic behaviours in their daily lives. Many reasoned those homophobic behaviours happened mostly in underdeveloped rural areas and in online forums "full of hatred comments" and linked homophobic attitudes with one's low-quality (*di-suzhi*) status. This was a major reason many queer families desired housing in middle-class neighbourhoods. As Wei (2020, pp 135–136) suggests, the residential compound (*xiaoqu*) in urban China – usually with a wall and guards – takes the form of gated communities that provide a sense of privacy, high social status, high-quality life, and spatial and social separation from 'low-*suzhi*' people. In this sense, the discourse on 'low-*suzhi*', which was once used to look down on rural migrants and the poor (Anagnost, 2004; Kipnis, 2007), becomes a locus for apprehending homophobia and middle class-ness.

Moreover, these vivid examples of 'social tolerance' listed by An and Tommy have many things in common. They hardly ever mentioned their queer sexualities as a primary focus. Rather, they described how others reacted to their same-sex relationships or queer families. In other words, they blurred the boundaries between social tolerance towards non-normative families and social tolerance towards non-normative sexualities. Therefore, I see these practices as 'strategically out', where individuals present themselves as non-normative families without explicitly revealing their queer sexual identities, but instead rely on ambiguity as a means to disassociate sexualness from its connections to sexuality and create blurred boundaries of taxonomy (Khanna, 2017, p 362).

Non-normative family is anything outside the imaginary of a hetero-reproductive nuclear family made up of an opposite-sex married couple and children. This can encompass single, divorced, reconstituted, DINK (double income no kids) families, and, in some cases, same-sex families and extramarital relationships with mistresses. The changing attitudes towards the normative and non-normative families did not happen inside the queer community but in wider society under family and marriage transformation. I was raised in a heterosexual family, while my family model did not fit within the normative norms. My birth parents had divorced when I was born; my father divorced three times and had two children out of wedlock. The divorce rate in China was less than 1 per cent until the early 2000s. When I was in elementary school in my hometown, I was the only one in my class who had a stepmother. Although my classmates showed more curiosity rather than discrimination when they asked if my stepmother was mistress or evil, I had the feeling that my family was different. Two decades later in urban China, being in a divorced, thus non-normative, family felt less different. In 2020, the divorce rate had tripled, and some of my peers and colleagues in China had divorced. As the national divorce rate continues to climb and marriage rates continue to decline, the conventional obligation of establishing and maintaining a normative family with two opposite-sex parents and children has been destabilized among the younger generations. In recent years, major Chinese cities like Shenzhen started to relax the policies regarding 'unplanned' births to tackle the falling fertility rate. Single parents were no longer required to pay the high social maintenance fees to register unmarried births. The three-children policy released in 2021 abolished social maintenance fees and relevant penalties on *hukou* registration, which has unintentionally reduced some constraints for queer parents registering children without a marriage certificate.

In this context, not discriminating against non-normative families, especially children born in non-normative families, has become a symbol of modernity and high quality (*gao-suzhi*). Queer parents in this research usually told the schoolteachers that "my child has no father/mother". Tommy appeared as Jack's godfather in the school, just as Xie appeared as Doudou's godmother in the swim lesson. According to them, a partial and subtle explanation would be enough as a high-quality (*gao-suzhi*) teacher would never ask more personal questions. Xie described the first time she and Hong took Doudou to the swim school as his "Mommy" and "Mama": the younger teacher immediately got the "hint", and the older teacher looked a bit confused. Xie and Hong's implicit expression that Doudou had two mothers could have had different meanings for the teachers: Xie and Hong were a lesbian couple, or Xie was a godmother and Hong was a single mother. Either way, both teachers were polite to a family that did not fit the 'one mother and one father' model.

Against these backdrops, many queer couples and parents concluded that their neighbours and schoolteachers "respected people's privacy because they don't ask private questions". The subtle and partial expression of one's queer family forms and the unspoken acknowledgement of them are distinct from the Euro-American advocating for being 'out and proud' and public recognition. For Tommy and many other non-heterosexual people in urban Guangdong, the fact that they were not pushed to explicitly disclose their queer sexualities to their neighbours, work partners, children's teachers, and local officials to live their queer familial life was the evidence of social progression. In such narratives, queer parents' images in society and institutions were frequently conflated with those of single parents or divorced families. For queer families in my research, social progression was equated to tolerance towards non-normative family forms rather than supporting minority rights or promoting gender and sexual diversity. Overall, the changing social attitude and policies regarding non-normative family forms have evidently (and perhaps unintentionally) made queer families' lives easier as they might be both out and passing as non-normative families instead of 'LGBT families' in public spaces.

Transforming families and queer modernity

This chapter has depicted family/*jia* as a transforming discourse that blurs queer kinship and blood families. Fiona and Alice's experiences with their parents and relatives during the Chinese New Year holidays have revealed the changing understanding of the scope of blood family. Customarily, Chinese people have a reunion dinner on New Year's Eve with all members from the same patrilineal family line or the same surname. People travelled back to their hometowns and visited relatives during the Chinese Spring Festival. For an increasing number of Chinese young people, the notion of big family (*da jia/jiazu*), which refers to the Confucianist patrilineal family, has been replaced by the modern small family (*xiao jia*), which refers to the nuclear family with one's parents included. The emerging small family has been fuelled by economic reforms and social policies. Young non-heterosexual people's life choices and family aspirations have been shaping and are shaped by the changing notion of a Chinese family, and this is particularly visible in their home-leaving and home-reunion experiences. For Wei (2020), the essence of stretched kinship is not to break from their family but to keep their relationship with their families of origin elastic and resilient in their home-leaving and reunion processes, a goal that my friend informants strived to achieve. Non-heterosexual people who migrated to first-tier cities like Shenzhen took the opportunity to distance themselves from relatives and made light of their moral judgements. At the same time, they were still in materially and mentally interdependent relationships with their parents.

The visible trend of 'reverse Spring Festival reunion' in first-tier cities indicated that both the parent and the queer child were essential actors in Chinese family transformations. Still, non-heterosexual people who stayed in their hometowns might feel morally obliged to maintain good relations with relatives and hence find it difficult to distance themselves from the big family. Young people did not visit their relatives as often as the older generations, and they did not feel the moral obligation to do so. Rather, many of them hoped their parents would put more focus on them instead of the big family. In this sense, family/*jia* represents not only blood relativeness but also emotional closeness. While parent–child relations are still central in the Chinese kinship system, the importance of 'big family'/patrilineal family clan and relatives has been weakened. In other words, even blood families or families of origin could have different meanings for Chinese people from different generations. As many friend informants clarified, they only needed their parents' acceptance, not their relatives'. The changing conception of blood family in transforming Chinese society cannot be neglected, as the elasticity in Chinese kinship values provides negotiating space for Chinese non-heterosexual people to express their desires.

Tian and many middle-aged queer parents' accounts indicate manifold and complex orders of family-forming and coming-out processes among Chinese non-heterosexual people, as a person may choose to enter a heterosexual *xinghun* marriage and have children before coming out to parents and finding a same-sex partner to form a queer family with. Various forms of non-heterosexual families have emerged in today's urban China, and they are characterized by many voices. Non-heterosexual individuals from different age groups and social backgrounds, LGBT communities, and ART agencies have all contributed to the discursive yet standardized understanding of a perfect rainbow family that could live openly in urban China. The homonormative discourse on the rainbow reproductive family has often omitted queer subjects who lacked the capabilities to have a decent income and settle in big cities, to maintain a lasting same-sex relationship, to consume ART services, and to raise children on their own. As a lesbian couple who have been living together for ten years, Youzi and Mei's choice to enter *xinghun* with gay men rather than coming out to parents was interpreted as a symbol of weakness, thereby disqualifying them from being role-model lesbian families. In this context, the inclusion process for non-heterosexual subjects is selective, and peri-urban/rural queer lifeworlds may be represented as hard to reconcile with urban utopian queer imaginaries (Boyce and Dasgupta, 2017). If the emerging discourse on 'rainbow family' in Chinese same-sex communities embodies homonormative subjectivities and norms, this kind of homonormative politics should not be perceived as universal in all metropolitan cities (Bell and Binnie, 2004; Brown, 2012). The role-model rainbow families in urban Chinese cities, therefore, represented a desired queer middle-class lifestyle punctuated by its bourgeois politics.

As rainbow families become a symbol of modernity and progression in online and offline queer communities, 'less modern' queer families remain silenced in queer homonormative spaces. However, as a researcher, it is vital to acknowledge the other forms of queer family existing among us. Grewal and Kaplan identify the re-emergence of the traditional–modernity split in the public discourse on sexuality, in which 'the United States and Europe are figured as modern and thus as the sites of progressive social movements, while other parts of the world are presumed to be traditional, especially in regard to sexuality' (2001, p 669). Wilson (2006) recognizes the conflation of 'Western', 'modern', and 'globalization' as the source of sexual modernity in Asian societies. Under such Western hegemony, queer life and practices that do not correspond to the first-world model are often portrayed as 'tradition' and 'forever late arrived'. In researching Thai migrant women in the global labour market, Mills suggests that modernity is contextual/contexted, multiple; it represents 'a break between past and present' (1999, p 13). As Mills points out, when migrant women move between urban and rural areas, they deal with not just a shift in spaces but also in identity.

There is no one singular, stable description of modernity; rather, modernity is a dynamic discourse, and it needs to be understood in its geographical and temporal context. Similarly, the acknowledgement of 'rainbow' politics among Chinese non-heterosexual people embodies their understanding of both Chinese modernity and queer modernity. The descriptive sense of desiring a queer nuclear family is shaped by state policy, capitalism, gender and family norms, and the Euro-American-originated language of coming-out politics. By exploring the various and transforming forms of families in urban Guangdong, this chapter has further illustrated the ambivalence of the modern versus traditional comparison for queer subjects and researchers.

In big cities like Shenzhen, increased social tolerance towards divorce and single parenting has eased some social and legal constraints for queer families. Consequently, one may strategically choose to be either recognized as a normative or non-normative family by wider society and identify as a queer family in queer social spaces synchronously, blurring the border of taxonomy. In other words, they may not always be radically queer, and they may not always be assimilative; rather, they are fluid in different times and spaces. The paralleled rhetoric of role-model queer family and ordinary middle-class Chinese citizen takes us back to the discussion of sexuality and sexualness, as they powerfully stress the manifold and dynamic process of constructing one's sense of 'self' in dividual and relational manners (Khanna, 2017; Yan, 2017). The personal accounts throughout this chapter firstly demonstrate the vagueness of firm self-identification and limits of the dominant sexuality-as-personhood knowledge in understanding queer modernity. For many, the capacity to establish a respectable modern rainbow family is conditioned by one's gender and socio-economic class rather than one's 'deviant' sexual desires and relationships. Since ordinary Chinese non-heterosexual people rarely conceptualize their queer sexual desires as aspects of personhood or conceptualize sexuality as a political and public object, it is vital for us to realize the diversity of gender and sexual experiences beyond the overarching framework of sexuality types and the modern–traditional comparison.

The middle-class non-heterosexual individuals' claim that Chinese society is becoming more tolerant towards homosexuality is contextualized and preconditioned, as we must not see the socio-economic status as isolated from non-heterosexual relationships. Like other middle-aged well-off queer couples, Hong and Xie had obtained Shenzhen *hukou*/residence by purchasing housing properties, and thus were eligible to form a queer family in a more tolerant city. Otherwise, Hong had to register her child as a single mother in her hometown in rural Hunan, which might be a different experience. The subtle and partial expression of one's queer relationships and the seemingly unspoken acknowledgement of them prevailed in the discourse on social tolerance, which was distinct from the activist advocacy of being 'out and proud' and public visibility. In this way, ordinary non-heterosexual people rarely highlight public visibility and sexual rights as primary needs, while they desire financial capabilities as essential for establishing a modern queer (nuclear) family in a middle-class area. Consequently, most Chinese non-heterosexual people tended to internalize the failure to establish a recognizable family. Yet, this book so far has demonstrated how social policies on marriage, citizenship, and parenting custody drastically shaped non-heterosexual people's perceived freedom and choices to create a new '*jia*/family' and how, in many ways, these choices relate to socio-economic status. It also raises the query of how certain narratives of acceptance and tolerance close down around the 'modern' 'homonormative' ideologies and these in turn produce negative stereotyping and class stratification inside queer social circles. Returning to queer couples who claimed they created strong *jiban*/mutual bonds and families through financial cooperation, mutual property ownership, and co-parenting practices, their choices were already conditioned by the existing social and legal context. Negotiating with the social and legal uncertainties in the process of creating and maintaining queer families through obtaining social mobilities and economic capital has ultimately become the (homo)normative narrative in queer communities. From the most 'visible' queer families like An and Ye to the most 'low-profile' queer families like Mei and Youzi, whether they were recognized as a representative queer family involved constantly re-appropriating the public–private, modern–traditional dualities.

In short, the queer family can include family modes that are radically different from and conform to the mainstream hetero-reproductive family model. Moreover, the emerging kinship practices, such as gay and lesbian *xinghun* marriage and surrogacy, lead to conflicting moral interpretations in queer social circles and wider society. It becomes problematic to make a unified characterization of the Chinese modalities of queer family. The diverse Chinese modalities of the queer family challenge the universalist, linear assumption of queer modernity that only exists in the form of being out and progressive.

Conclusion: Queering Chinese Kinship and Futures

This book identifies several intersecting topics with respect to queering kinship in urban China: queer intimate love, queer reproduction and parenting, queer family, and queer futurity. In the previous chapters, I have examined the tactics non-heterosexual people in Guangdong employ to build and sustain lasting kinship relations through their negotiation with blood relatives, moral discourses, urban citizenship, and state legislation. In doing so, they seek to broaden our understanding of family dynamics, parenthood, and Chinese society in general.

The first ethnographic part focuses on queer intimate relationships. The proliferation of role terms from binary T–P/1–0 to diverse spectrums and shifting understandings of same-sex relationships across different generations have innovatively destabilized gendered culture and, at the same time, produced a hierarchy of same-sex relationships models. It is also important not to reduce T–P/1–0 relationships to heterosexual-informed modes as this would risk understating heterosexual relationships as an eternally static object for comparison. The vague path from (online) intimate stranger to real-life partner in queer dating practices renders Chinese moral standards uncertain as they are relationally defined in accordance with one's positionality in a given social relation (Yan, 2017). Generationally, trusting concerns have increasingly shifted from exposing oneself to public judgement to being taken advantage of emotionally and financially (see also Fu, 2015).

The practices of seeking and maintaining stable same-sex relationships for non-heterosexual people encompass the blurred distinction of romantic love and conjugal love. Non-heterosexual people's intimate experiences cannot be articulated alone without acknowledging their family backgrounds, career paths, and migrating experiences to the 'big city'. Queer couples in this book stressed similar cultural tastes and complementary personal characteristics as the main factor as to why they fell in love with their same-sex partners. In other words, non-heterosexual people in today's urban China increasingly perceive their relationship partners beyond erotic lovers. They constantly negotiate economic, cultural, and legal factors that threaten their queer intimate relationships and keep a manageable distance from their families of origin in their hometowns. Most importantly, they attempt to find pragmatic solutions to secure their cohabiting relationships when the legalization of same-sex marriage seems too far a step for them. Without the housing property purchased by themselves or their parents as economic and legal protection, queer couples would have to find alternative ways to maintain their relationships. Both the notions of conjugal and parental love are infused with consumer culture since purchasing goods for the other is closely linked to the expression of care and love in everyday life.

The strategies for Chinese queer people to create a legible and durable mutual bond/*jiban* through owning mutual property and becoming co-parents are linked to their changing aspirations of irreversible kinship relations, potential risks, and queer viable futures. Such intentions and practices on the kinship continuum firstly render the material underpinning to family and care relationships: it costs money (Simpson, 1994; Patel, 2006; Brandtstädter and Santos, 2008). Just like a gay father, Min, summarized his understanding of the '*jia*' (family): "I think there are two important factors that make me feel at home: children (*haizi*) and a house (*fangzi*)". I have heard many similar statements from my friends in China, queer and straight alike. For queer couples, establishing *jiban*/mutuality with each other in a foreseen future creates the feeling of mutual responsibility and security, in other words, an insured life against risk. When a queer relationship powered by *jiban* comes to an end, the separation process for queer couples can also be complicated, just like going through a divorce.

At first glance, creating *jiban* is often understood and practised as a substitute for a legal marriage. Yet, the individual narratives in this ethnographic research showed that *jiban* is not risk-free when it is not recognized by state law or approved by each other's families of origin. The gay–lesbian co-parenting practices in *xinghun* marriage further complicate the matter when children often become irreversible *jiban* for the gay and lesbian co-parents instead of same-sex partners. In this sense, *jiban* is only as effective as legal marriage when queer individuals have acquired adequate upward mobility and the financial capability to be a good consumer/sexual citizen, and, more critically, to be reproductive and fulfil their family duty and thus obtain parental acceptance. To put it another way, queer individuals envision a socially acknowledged successful life as the precondition of having a role-model queer family, while the failure to foster durable *jiban* with one's chosen ties is linked with the lack of individual capability rather than structural forces. I suggest that non-heterosexual people's strategies to create *jiban* are normalized as the pragmatic and desirable choice under existing Chinese social policies and consumer culture.

The practice of forming *jiban* links to this book's second theme: queer reproduction and parenting. Non-heterosexual people's desires to be parents can be both linked to the normative Confucian familism and viewed as radically queer. While some non-heterosexual people claim that they have no choice but to have children to please their parents or to expect elderly support in return from their children, many non-heterosexual people disconnect their purpose for entering heterosexual marriages and having children from the notions of traditional familial duty. Instead, they frame their motivation for being parents as an individual and voluntary choice. Also, a generational shift in understanding the parent–child relation and filial piety from 'obedience' and 'duty' to 'mutual respect' and 'equal relations' is showing. The life stories from young queer individuals not wanting children suggest that the symbolic feature of children as one's major resource of elder support has been shaken under rapid socio-economic changes and family transformations. Non-heterosexual people's motivation for having children are often unconsolidated and represented in both an individualistic sense as self-desire and a moral, relational manner as strengthening intimate relationships.

At this point, it is crucial to unpack the two major types of moral discourse going on in Chinese queer lifeworlds, which constantly shape their life choices and future aspirations. The first discourse is constructed by state policies and Confucian familism and is often referred to as the 'traditional' ideology. It suggests that one has no other choice but to fulfil family duties through entering a heterosexual marriage, having biological children, and taking good care of family elders. The second discourse is arguably constructed by LGBT organizations and Western-originated queer coming-out politics and often regarded as the more 'modern' ideology. It asks one to embrace an out and progressive lifestyle that attacks heteronormative kinship norms while being a good sexual citizen and minimizing risks. These two discourses seem to be in radical conflict at first glance, while the ethnographic chapters demonstrate how queer individuals seek to find negotiating spaces from the blurred boundaries between the two discourses. Their moral practices encompass the ever-changing narratives of Chinese middle-class life and modern queer lifestyle. Furthermore, queer utopian aspirations are marked by both discourses that focus on 'choice' and personal agency.

Overall, non-heterosexual people's investment in parenting should not be interpreted as being exclusively traditional or modern as their practices do not occupy such a binary. There are many ways to become a parent for Chinese non-heterosexual people, but they may not be recognized equally in terms of feasibility and moral values. The practices of entering heterosexual marriage and surrogacy adopted by non-heterosexual people can lead to conflicting moral interpretations in queer social circles and the wider society. Some non-heterosexual people entered *zhihun* (marrying an opposite-sex straight person) or *xinghun* (gay–lesbian contract marriage) to have children. The practice of *pianhun* (lying to marry an opposite-sex straight person mainly for the purpose of having offspring, also referred to as 'marriage fraud') has encountered increasing moral criticisms under the coming-out advocacy and feminist movements and is vanishing among younger generations in big cities. Non-heterosexual people's motivations for entering *xinghun* marriages could be linked not only to marriage pressure but also to their desires to be parents that complied with the state regulation and the image of a heteronormative family. Yet, co-parenting with one's *xinghun* partner reveals the complex interplay of legal policies, gender norms, and moral values, as non-heterosexual people in *xinghun* marriages struggle to walk the blurred line between 'nominal' and 'real' marriages. When *zhihun* or *xinghun* marriages came to an end, the custody of children often became the major divorce dispute.

In the case of non-heterosexual people adopting children, biological ties with children could still be essentially important, as the existing policy regarding adoption in Chinese child welfare centres does not recognize non-heterosexual people as suitable parents. The practice of *guoji* adoption from family relatives saves non-heterosexual people from the first step of gaining permission from the child welfare centre as a state institution and eliminates moral dispute. Nevertheless, going through the relevant legal procedures can still produce discomfort and uncertainty around parenthood for queer parents. Against this backdrop, using assisted reproductive technology (ART) alone without entering any form of heterosexual marriage has been constructed by non-heterosexual people and organizations working for or sponsored by ART businesses as the seemingly ideal option for non-heterosexual people, especially same-sex couples, to establish co-parenting relationships. The practices of *A/AB luan B huai* among lesbian couples and surrogacy twins among gay couples have further emerged as desirable techniques for Chinese same-sex couples to have children together, which queered the heteronormative knowledge of reproduction and ART, even if they did not intend to challenge it. However, they are only available to upper-middle-class people who can afford the high cost of childbirth and parenting and whose careers are unlikely to be affected by organizational and social policies. In the case of same-sex couples desiring children together, the children can only be legally bonded to one of them, which they need to strategically overcome to address their needs. Moreover, the online debates on the practice of surrogacy have been linked closely to gender inequality, which further sparks debates on gay fatherhood and same-sex marriage. For many young women in urban China who are concerned about the gender privilege gay men held, gay men were only innocent when they did not show any desire to reproduce and completely abandoned their existing gender privilege. On the other hand, the Chinese ART companies entering the pink money market attempt to rephrase their in-vitro fertilization (IVF) and surrogacy services as doing good deeds and link their business with queer organizations, though issues on gender and class inequalities are still present in the ART industry. The relation between lesbian, gay, bisexual, and transgender (LGBT) organizations and the ART industry therefore encompasses not only sexuality but class, kinship, and gender concerns.

The dynamic interrelations between same-sex relationships and queer (co-)parenting practices signify the elasticity of kinship in today's urban China. The idea of blood and biology still holds its centrality in Chinese family life, as most non-heterosexual people conceptualize blood ties, especially parent–child blood relations, as the central and authentic form of kin relations. The conceptions of biology/blood and the legal implications of parentage/custody together have shaped the distinction between 'my own children' and 'my partner's children', hence creating challenges for queer people to balance their kinship responsibilities as children, parents, and partners. The emerging use of ART and the disputes raised by the alleged distinction between biological and social parenthood for queer couples stresses the very uncertainty of queer kinship that exists with the ambiguity of state law and everyday heteronormative family norms in Chinese and many other societies (Borneman, 1997; Goodfellow, 2015; Patton-Imani, 2020).

At the same time, the various parenting and co-parenting practices documented in this research demonstrate the mobilizing possibilities beyond the singular definition of blood relatedness, that is, (co-)parenthood being constructed and strengthened using the language of bodily experience (carrying the baby in one's body/*qinsheng*) and affective recognition (conjugal/parental love). In the cases of *guoji* adoption and using the eggs/sperm of same-sex partners' relatives, the idea of kinship roles is also mobilized as one form of kinship (aunt) is being used to establish another one (mother). Concisely, the notions of blood and its centrality in patrilineal continuity alone does not work to achieve or destruct queer co-parenting relationships; rather, it was the queer subject's capability to eliminate the involvement of a third biological or legal parent outside their intimate relationship, to negotiate with the uncertainties caused by state policies, to secure a well-off life in cities like Shenzhen, and to handle their parents' attitude towards their co-parenting relationships.

In addition, the parent–child relations for non-heterosexual people have become more fluid both in terms of emotional and physical distance. As an increasing number of young non-heterosexual people only come back home during national holidays, their connections with distant relatives weaken and their relationships with their parents tend to be stretched and elastic (Wei, 2020). The emerging 'reverse union' and 'small family' further point to elastic meanings of family and relative in contemporary Chinese cities.

In this book, I have also tried to challenge the image of queer family as being out and progressive and radically different from the heteronormative family matrix. The imagination of the queer family in today's urban China is characterized by many voices under rapid social and family transformations. Queer individuals from different social backgrounds and generations and same-sex online and offline communities have all contributed to the discursive and dynamic understandings of the queer/*tongzhi*/rainbow family. For different individuals and organizations, queer family can include family modes that are radically different from and conforming to the hegemonic hetero-reproductive family model. There is no singular version of family-forming processes among Chinese non-heterosexual people, as one may have a 'normative' past (enter heterosexual marriages and have children) in their hometown before their 'queer' present and future (coming out to one's parents and forming a queer family) in a big city. In my interpretation, the various arrangements of queer (co-)parenting and the tactic of being strategically and partially 'out' as non-normative families were neither radically transgressive nor directly anti-normative in terms of challenging heteronormative conventions and state institutions. However, they still queer and mobilize the meaning of family in subtle, non-linear ways. This ethnography reflects Muñoz's argument that queerness is performative, a doing rather than being, and queerness's time is a 'stepping out of the linearity of straight time' (2009, p 25). Ultimately, what should be read as normal and what should be read as queer is constantly changing (Lewin, 2016; Weiss, 2016). The hegemonic heteronormative discourses were followed and enforced at some life moments and spaces and were destabilized and transformed at others. The diverse Chinese modalities of the queer family challenge the universalist assumption of queer modernity that only exists in the form of being out and progressive and in the sense of straight, linear time. As many have argued, queer subjects are not 'always already avant-garde for all time and in all places' (Grewal and Kaplan, 2001, p 670). In this sense, the various forms of Chinese queer families obscure the Western–Chinese, past–present, and traditional–modern binaries. Through the documentation of emerging family-forming practices and the image of the role-model rainbow family promoted in queer communities, I emphasize the dynamic interplay of socio-economic class, state law, and moral values that come to articulate intimate and family relations in today's queer everyday lives.

Viewing themselves as 'ordinary' (*putong*) Chinese citizens and modern consumers, the queer couples and parents I met in urban China attempted to secure their ideal future lives and relationships by gaining personal agency and purchasing power to negotiate existing socio-legal difficulties. In other words, both success and failure to form lasting intimate relationships and family were internalized as personal matters, infused with the language of personal agency and individual choice. Their tactics for forming durable queer relationships were also technologies to minimize risks in the foreseen future. Being financially capable and therefore being able to negotiate with one's parents for familial acceptance is highlighted by non-heterosexual people of all ages. Under such a narrative of pragmaticism, a supportive social environment for non-heterosexual people often did not stand out as the primary focus of establishing a legible queer family. Rather, it was one's financial capability that was mentioned most often. In this sense, one's family fell into the category of one's own business, free from public issues. Yet, I read my friend informants' choices and struggles as both individual and contextual, which are constantly conditioned by the existing familial and moral values and socio-legal systems. Strathern (1992a) suggests that individualism should not be merely viewed as interfering with collective life and tradition; rather, convention is internalized as personal style by the exercise of choices. The very idea of individualism is a cultural practice produced in Western society. In other words, it would be fruitless to abstract individuality from convention as if they are both self-evident. In some situations, they could mean the same thing (Povinelli, 2006). From my ethnographic fieldwork, it became evident that legal policies on marriage, *hukou* citizenship, and parenting custody have drastically shaped queer people's practices for strengthening conjugal relationships and having children with same-sex partners. To some extent, legal policies have shaped people's imagination with regard to creating a recognizable queer family. The narratives of queer conjugal love, (co-)parenthood, and family illustrate whose citizenship receives acknowledgement and whose families are valued, and what it means to be 'legitimate' (Patton-Imani, 2020, p 37).

The life trajectories of middle-aged non-heterosexual migrants successfully settling in Shenzhen and establishing a queer form of family/*jia* embodies queer utopian imaginaries for futurity. I concur with Jones that we need to look further to the tension between the 'queer struggle for a bearable life and aspirational hopes for a good life' (2013, p 2). For the non-heterosexual youth who desire a modern queer lifestyle and a legible queer family in cosmopolitan Chinese cities like Shenzhen, the rising living expense and tightening upward mobility, in addition to legal constraints, have inevitably shaped their material desires, career and parenting choices, and future aspirations. Boyce and Dasgupta (2017) link queer future aspirations to Indian modernity and suggest queer intimate lives embody complex ideals of utopia and futurity. We must acknowledge that class and inequality in Chinese society underpins inequalities among queer people in China, and the ability to live a completely honest and out life and to establish a recognizable queer family in Chinese society remained a privilege for few. In today's urban China, having a perfect queer reproductive family is not something unimaginable anymore, but such imageries, so tightly bounded with gender, citizenship, and class position, remain unaffordable for many.

In brief, the landscape of kinship in China is undergoing a profound transformation, and it is crucial to avoid framing queer relationships as mere imitations or alternatives to blood ties. By delving into the practices of care and the cultivation of *jiban*/mutuality, it advocates for a re-evaluation of the conventional dichotomy between transgressive and assimilative approaches in the formation of 'chosen' families and queerness. Non-heterosexual people's success (or failure) in forming durable relationships and family both reproduce and transgress the dominant assumptions about blood relatedness and its centrality in the family-forming progress. The practices of queer conjugal relationships, parenting, and family formation documented in this book suggest innovative and diverse forms of belonging, family, and relatedness beyond blood ties and the heterosexual nuclear family; at the same time, class stratification and gender inequalities are often reproduced during these processes, as people who lack the social, cultural, and economic recourses are excluded and remain silenced within queer communities and in the wider society. This book observes that queer relationships and families have emerged both within and outside the dominant kinship norms co-constructed by the existing state policy and patrilineal familism. In the context of socio-economic transformations and the technologization of biological reproduction, queer futurity and queer utopian imaginaries are made vivid and made normalized by state-constructed modernity and the glocal market.

This ethnography makes an original contribution to the studies of parenthood and new reproductive technologies of Chinese non-heterosexual people in the context of our understanding of kinship and Chinese society in general. It also contributes to the discussion on queer utopian imaginaries and futurity that is related to reproduction, cosmopolitan life, and family care.

Furthermore, it should be acknowledged that the 'queering' of kinship is not perceived within only the scope of non-normative sexual desires but exists in every aspect of the society at large. For instance, the relaxation of family-planning policies and increased social tolerance towards divorce and single parenting has also reduced social constraints for queer parents. Non-heterosexual people in this ethnography share many struggles and uncertainties with straight Chinese people in non-normative intimate and family relationships such as DINK (double income no kids) families, single parenthood, cohabitating, and polygamous relationships. Heterosexual relationships that fall out of the hetero-reproductive nuclear family category and often do not/cannot rely on the authoritative recognitions (biogenetical reproduction or marriage) also indicate possibilities to queer the dominant Chinese kinship discourses, despite a lack of visibility (for example, Liang, 2012). The various arrangements of queer conjugal love, parenting, and family formation in urban China have made explicit the malleability and contingence of Chinese kinship, in that way also blurring the symbolic distinctiveness of 'Chinese' kinship and 'queer' kinship. Knowledge of both kinships points to transformation that is situated in the interplay of cultural, legal, and economic institutions.

APPENDIX I

Key Research Participants

Name	Sex	Birth year	Place of birth	Place of residence	Occupation
Alice	F	1992	Chengdu, SC	Shenzhen, GD	Consultant
An	M	1985	Fuyang, AH	Shenzhen, GD	Investor
Bei	M	1980	Wuhan, HB	Shenzhen, GD	Private company
Ben	M	1996	Fuzhou, FJ	Shenzhen, GD	Student
Billy	F	1992	Shenzhen, GD	Shenzhen, GD	Civil engineer
Chen	F	1983	Zhuzhou, HN	Guangzhou, GD	ART company
Clara	F	1991	Baoshan, YN	Shenzhen, GD	Consultant
Danny	F	1989	Chengdu, SC	Shenzhen, GD	Lawyer
Dae	F	1982	Chengdu, SC	Chengdu, SC	Self-employed
Fei	F	1996	Chaoshan, GD	Shenzhen, GD	ART company; livestreaming
Fiona	F	1992	Chengdu, SC	Shenzhen, GD	Programmer
Hong	F	1985	Xiangtan, HN	Shenzhen, GD	Self-employed
Joe	M	1974	CQ	Guangzhou, GD	Freelancer
Joey	F	1989	Nantong, JS	Guangzhou, GD	Estate agent
Lin	F	1986	Bozhou, AH	Shenzhen, GD	Sales
Ma	M	1982	Guangzhou, GD	Guangzhou, GD	Self-employed
Mei	F	1989	Dongguan, GD	Shenzhen, GD	Private company clerk
Mellow	F	1986	Mianyang, SC	Shenzhen, GD	Freelancer
Min	M	1973	Hohhot, NM	Shenzhen, GD	Professor
Mo	F	1989	Chengdu, SC	Shenzhen, GD	Designer

APPENDIX I

Name	Sex	Birth year	Place of birth	Place of residence	Occupation
Pam	F	1990	Chengdu, SC	Shenzhen, GD	Freelancer; civil servant
Rong	M	1992	Changsha, HN	Shenzhen, GD	State-owned enterprise
Saisai	F	1989	Chengdu, SC	Chengdu, SC	State-owned enterprise
Sally	F	1987	Wuhan, HB	Shenzhen, GD	Civil servant
Tian	M	1980	Yongzhou, HN	Dongguan, GD	Self-employed
Tommy	M	1969	Nanning, GX	Guangzhou, GD	Journalist
Wen	F	1985	Xiamen, FJ	Guangzhou, GD	Self-employed
Xie	F	1975	Zhuzhou, HN	Shenzhen, GD	Self-employed
Ye	M	1985	Shenzhen, GD	Shenzhen, GD	Freelancer
Yina	F	1990	Chengdu, SC	Chengdu, SC	Hotel administrator
Youzi	F	1989	Dongguan, GD	Shenzhen, GD	State-owned enterprise
Zhao	M	1980	Jiujiang, JX	Guangzhou, GD	LGBT organization; ART company
Zhenzhen	F	1995	Shenzhen, GD	Shenzhen, GD	ART company; livestreaming

APPENDIX II

Roman (Pinyin) to Simplified Chinese

A luan B/AB huai A卵B/AB怀
Ai'ren 爱人
Baiwan 掰弯
Bao Chenggong 包成功
Baosheng 包生
Biaomian 表面
Bufen 不分
Caihong baobao 彩虹宝宝
Caihong jiating 彩虹家庭
Chuangtong 传统
Chuanzongjiedai 传宗接代
Chunjie 纯洁
Daimu/Daima 代母/代妈
Dizhu 地主
Fangzi 房子
Fenshou chengben 分手成本
Gaige kaifang 改革开放
Gaoji 高级
Gaoqian 搞钱
Gehuigejia 各回各家
Gongjing Gongluan 供精供卵
Guanxi 关系
Guimi 闺蜜
Guoji 过继
Haigui 海归
Haizi 孩子
Hexie 和谐
Houdai 后代
Huangdi 皇帝

Huko leibie 户口类别
Hukou suozaidi 户口所在地
Hukou 户口
Jia 家
Jiazu 家族
Jiban 羁绊
Jijian 鸡奸
Kaopu 靠谱
Ku'er 酷儿
Laiwang 来往
Lala 拉拉
Laoxiang 老乡
Linbaozouren 拎包走人
Lingyang 领养
Liumang xingwei 流氓行为
Liushou er'tong 留守儿童
Luanmei 卵妹
Luantong 娈童
Luoci 裸辞
Mengdanghudui 门当户对
Mianzi 面子
Mingan 敏感
Moren 默认
Nanchang 男娼
Nanhai 男孩
Pianhun 骗婚
Popo 婆婆
Putong ren 普通人
Qinsheng 亲生
Sanguan 三观
Shengnv 剩女
Shidu jiating 失独家庭
Shiguan ying'er 试管婴儿
Shushu 叔叔
Suzhi 素质
Tanlian'ai 谈恋爱
Tongfu 同夫
Tongqi 同妻
Tongxinglian 同性恋
Tongzhi 同志
Wending 稳定
Xiao 孝
Xiaoqu 小区

Xingshi hunyin/ Xinghun 形式婚姻/形婚
Xiongdi 兄弟
Xuequ fang 学区房
Xueyuan 血缘
Yang'erfanglao 养儿防老
Yang 养
Yanzhi 颜值
Ye 爷
Yuxiao 愚孝
Zhenjinbaiyin 真金白银
Zhihun 直婚
Zhiren 直人
Zhongchan jieceng 中产阶层
Zuoren 做人
Zuoziji 做自己
Zuxian 祖先

Notes

Introduction

1. 'Middle class' is not a coherent group but a 'diverse array of different social positions with differing degrees of power and affluence' (Anagnost, 2008, p 507). Zhang (2010) identifies three notable characteristics of middle class in China: their moment of emergence, their highly heterogeneous composition, and their heightened sense of insecurity.
2. Ancient literature has documented homosexual practices ranging from having *luantong* (catamite) in imperial families to *nanchang* (male prostitutes) among city dwellers.
3. Confucianism has been regarded as the most influential ideology in China for over two millennia. It became the official state ideology in the Han Dynasty (206 BC–220 AD).
4. Sodomy (*jijian*) appeared as a crime in late Qing Dynasty law. Until 1997, sodomy was implicitly included in hooliganism (*liumang xingwei*) under the old criminal law.
5. 77 per cent of survey respondents are post-90s, 19.4 per cent are post-80s, and only 3.6 per cent are post-70s or older.
6. National surveys show rapidly growing percentages of women receiving post-secondary education (Xie, 2013). The one-child policy introduced in 1979 has also played a critical role in improving urban daughters' status, since the one-and-only daughters have access to more emotional and material support than daughters with siblings (Fong, 2007).
7. Others have argued that the transformation of family and marriage in China began earlier in the 1920s when the liberating May Fourth Movement took place (Lee, 2006).
8. The Chinese Marriage Law of 1980 referred to cohabitation as 'illegal cohabitation'. The 2001 amendment to the law changed the wording to 'non-marital cohabitation'.
9. For the birth cohort of 1976–1983, almost every woman had been married by the age of 30; and by the age of 33, over 95 per cent of men had entered their first marriage. Available in *Chinese General Social Surveys* 2010, 2012, and 2013.
10. The social maintenance fee was previously called 'fines for excess birth' and 'out-of-quota birth fees'. The exact amount of the social maintenance fee was decided by local family-planning commissions.
11. There are two types of *hukou*: family (*jiating*) *hukou* and corporate (*jiti*) *hukou*.
12. Research shows that about 43 per cent of elderly persons aged 60 and above co-reside with a child, another 31 per cent have a child living in the same neighbourhood, and 13 per cent more in the same county but not in the same neighbourhood. Data also shows a high frequency of financial transfers between elderly parents and their children (Lei et al, 2013, cited in Xie, 2013).
13. It should be noted that most English-language monographs of Chinese queer lives have neither been published in mainland China nor translated into Chinese, thus creating an academic gap between domestic Chinese and Euro-American academia. Domestically, most research on Chinese non-normative sexualities has come from biomedicine and healthcare subjects; a few studies have come from literature, sociology, law, and media studies, but none from anthropology.

14 This is based on the Tencent company's report. Tencent is one of the largest internet companies, offering services including the well-known instant messenger QQ and the mobile chatting app WeChat.

Chapter 1
1   WeChat is a Chinese multi-purpose messaging, social media, and mobile payment app owned by Tencent. WeChat Public Account is a marketing platform that can act as a complete brand hub, a news portal, or a blog page. I created a WeChat Public Account before this research and had been using it as a blog page.
2   See https://mp.weixin.qq.com/s/wXKI7snAE_iI_mZcEFktjQ
3   PFLAG China was founded in 2008 in Guangzhou, China and was named after the American organization PFLAG. They changed their name in 2021. Concerning the scope of this research, I paid more attention to the attendees and volunteers than event organizers.
4   *Sina*, *Weibo*, and *Douban* are general social media platforms; *Lesdo*, *Rela*, and *BlueD* are same-sex dating apps.
5   See https://ethics.americananthro.org/category/statement/

Chapter 2
1   See http://yuqing.people.com.cn/n1/2019/0402/c209043-31009867.html
2   '*Nongmin*' literally means farmer and '*fang*' means room. *Nongmin fang* was used to describe a house built by locals for rent without legal permission. *Nongmin fang* was a budget option for rent.
3   Even though cohabiting partners were included in the Anti-Domestic Violence Law of the People's Republic in 2015, the definition of a cohabiting partner is vague and same-sex cohabiting relationships are not included. This law does not specify the department to enforce the policies either.
4   One needs to do extensive research and negotiations as most insurance companies would not let insurers choose people other than a legal spouse, children, and parents to be beneficiaries. Tommy, for example, bought insurance and changed the insurance beneficiary to Jack once the insurance became effective.
5   One must be legally recognized as the property owner's child, parent, or spouse to be eligible to be added to the property certificate.
6   'Love' poetry in Imperial China is often a political metaphor.

Chapter 3
1   China's official birth rate was 10.48 per 1,000 in 2019, which was the lowest since 1949.
2   Since 2019, the Shenzhen Real Estate Information Platform stopped providing official data of average transaction prices for housing property.
3   Non-relative adoption/*lingyang* from social welfare institutions was generally recognized by Chinese non-heterosexual people as impractical and undesirable for several reasons. Although unmarried, childless Chinese citizens over 30 years old were permitted to adopt children by the 1991 Adoption Law, most applicants would not be able to achieve the economic prerequisites set by adoption centres. A qualified adopter often needs to have a stable and well-paid job, a considerable amount of savings, a house they own, and a flawless credit report. Furthermore, the China Centre for Children's Welfare and Adoption clearly stated on its official website that same-sex couples were not legally recognized as married couples and thus were not allowed to adopt from welfare organizations. This further suggested that queer people's moral qualification as parents was held in question by welfare institutions. In the case of *guoji* adoption, the legal process of this is less troublesome since the adoptive parent and the adoptive child are already relatives.

NOTES

Chapter 4

1. The Ministry of Health was superseded in 2013 by the National Health and Family Planning Commission (NHFPC). In March 2018, the National Health Commission (NHC) replaced the NHFPC and the official domain name changed to www.nhc.gov.cn/.
2. Surrogacy is mentioned in Article 3 and Article 22; see www.nhc.gov.cn/zwgk/wlwl/200804/56c333396f3b4e2ab150491c33129f5a.shtml
3. When the Population and Family Planning Law was amended in 2015, the draft of the amendment included a clause banning any form of surrogacy. The members of the National People's Congress Standing Committee disputed the drafted clause. Consequently, the revised version of the Population and Family Planning Law did not adopt the earlier drafted clause banning surrogacy.
4. There were parallels here with working-class women's vulnerability during surrogacy in various country contexts such as India and Thailand (Anu et al, 2013; Rudrappa, 2018).
5. My research participants who worked in the Chinese ART industry also mentioned that the increased use of private ART agencies and especially surrogacy in China in recent years was linked to the second-child policy.
6. The poll titled 'Do You Support the Legalization of Same-Sex Marriage in the Civil Code?' was conducted on https://news.ifeng.com/survey.shtml?from=timeline&isappinstalled=0#id=15990, which belongs to the Phoenix New Media company. It received 9,909,482 votes.
7. It was originally posted on a *Douban* group forum, '*Lacai Xiaozu*', that discussed the boy's love of literature. Retrieved 13 February 2020 from www.douban.com/group/topic/161487038/. This *Douban* group was suspended during the 'internet clear actioning' in 2022.
8. Gayspot and Ding released two questionnaires with some similar questions for mutual verification. Questionnaire A received a total of 1,104 replies, and questionnaire B received a total of 1,051 replies.
9. Retrieved 13 February 2020 from www.douban.com/group/topic/140896557/
10. I did not get to visit the 'medical lab'. Chen did not want non-clients to know the exact location of the lab because they could be shut down and fined if they were discovered by the authorities.
11. Sex selection practices range from traditional Chinese methods such as feeling pregnant women's pulses to reproductive technologies such as ultrasound (Chu, 2001).

Chapter 5

1. Although person A does not give birth to the child, she may do the DNA test to obtain a parent–child relationship certificate.
2. Many Chinese characters can be used as both family names and given/personal names.

Chapter 6

1. It is also a tradition that the married couple have the family reunion dinner with the husband's parents on the Spring Festival Eve. This tradition has been questioned and challenged in recent years.
2. Many men in Hong Kong, especially businessmen who travel frequently to mainland China, kept mistresses in the border cities. There were 'mistress villages' in Guangdong (Lang and Smart, 2002).

References

Altork, K. (1995). Walking the Fire Line: The Erotic Dimension of the Fieldwork Experience. In Kulick, D., and Willson, M. (eds), *Taboo: Sex, Identity, and Erotic Subjectivity in Anthropological Fieldwork*. London, New York: Routledge, pp 107–139.

Altorki, S., and El-Solh, C.F. (1988). *Arab Women in the Field: Studying Your Own Society*. Syracuse, NY: Syracuse University Press.

Anagnost, A. (2004). The Corporeal Politics of Quality (Suzhi). *Public Culture*, *16*(2), 189–208.

Anagnost, A. (2008). From 'Class' to 'Social Strata': Grasping the Social Totality in Reform-Era China. *Third World Quarterly*, *29*(3), 497–519.

Anu, Kumar, P., Inder, D., and Sharma, N. (2013). Surrogacy and Women's Right to Health in India: Issues and Perspective. *Indian Journal of Public Health*, *57*(2), 65. https://doi.org/10.4103/0019-557X.114984

Bao, H. (2018). *Queer Comrades: Gay Identity and Tongzhi Activism in Postsocialist China*. Copenhagen: Nordic Institute of Asian Studies.

Bao, S., Bodvarsson, Ö.B., Hou, J.W., and Zhao, Y. (2011). The Regulation of Migration in a Transition Economy: China's Hukou System. *Contemporary Economic Policy*, *29*(4), 564–579. https://doi.org/10.1111/j.1465-7287.2010.00224.x

Beauvoir, S. (1953). *The Second Sex*. Translated and edited by H.M. Parshley. London: Jonathan Cape.

Beck, U. (1992). *Risk Society: Towards a New Modernity*. London: Sage.

Bell, D., and Binnie, J. (2000). *The Sexual Citizen: Queer Politics and Beyond*, 1st edn. Cambridge, UK; Malden, MA: Polity.

Bell, D., and Binnie, J. (2004). Authenticating Queer Space: Citizenship, Urbanism and Governance. *Urban Studies*, *41*(9), 1807–1820. https://doi.org/10.1080/0042098042000243165

Berlant, L. (1998). Intimacy: A Special Issue. *Critical Inquiry*, *24*(2), 281–288.

Bersani, L. (1987). Is the Rectum a Grave? *October*, *43*, 197–222.

Blackwood, E. (2005). *Tombois* in West Sumatra: Constructing Masculinity and Erotic Desire. In Robertson, J. (ed), *Same-Sex Cultures and Sexualities: An Anthropological* Reader. Malden, MA: Blackwell Pub, pp 232–260.

Boellstorff, T. (2007a). *A Coincidence of Desires: Anthropology, Queer Studies, Indonesia*. Durham, NC: Duke University Press.

Boellstorff, T. (2007b). Queer Studies in the House of Anthropology. *Annual Review of Anthropology*, *36*, 17–35.

Boellstorff, T. (2010). Queer Techne: Two Theses on Methodology and Queer Studies. In Browne, K., and Nash, C.J. (eds), *Queer Methods and Methodologies: Intersecting Queer Theories and Social Science Research*. Oxfordshire: Taylor & Francis, pp 215–30.

Borneman, J. (1997). Caring and Being Cared for: Displacing Marriage, Kinship, Gender and Sexuality. *International Social Science Journal*, *49*(154), 573–584.

Bose, B., and Bhattacharyya, S. (eds) (2007). *The Phobic and the Erotic: The Politics of Sexualities in Contemporary India*. London: Seagull.

Boyce, P. (2008). Truths and (Mis)Representations: Adrienne Rich, Michel Foucault and Sexual Subjectivities in India. *Sexualities*, *11*(1–2), 110–119.

Boyce, P. (2014). Desirable Rights: Same-Sex Sexual Subjectivities, Socio-Economic Transformations, Global Flows and Boundaries – in India and Beyond. *Culture, Health & Sexuality*, *16*(10), 1201–1215. https://doi.org/10.1080/13691058.2014.944936

Boyce, P., and Dasgupta, R.K. (2017). Utopia or Elsewhere: Queer Modernities in Small Town West Bengal. In Kuldova, T., and Varghese, M.A. (eds), *Urban Utopias: Excess and Expulsion in Neoliberal South Asia*. London: Palgrave Macmillan, pp 209–225.

Boyce, P., Engebretsen, E.L., and Posocco, S. (2018). Introduction: Anthropology's Queer Sensibilities. *Sexualities*, *21*(5–6), 843–852.

Boyce, P., Gonzalez-Polledo, E.J., and Posocco, S. (eds) (2019). *Queering Knowledge: Analytics, Devices, and Investments after Marilyn Strathern*. London; New York: Routledge.

Boym, S. (1994). *Common Places: Mythologies of Everyday Life in Russia*. Cambridge, MA; London: Harvard University Press.

Brainer, A. (2019). *Queer Kinship and Family Change in Taiwan*. New Brunswick, NJ: Rutgers University Press.

Brandtstädter, S., and Santos, G.D. (eds) (2008). *Chinese Kinship: Contemporary Anthropological Perspectives*. London; New York: Routledge.

Brown, G. (2012) Homonormativity: A Metropolitan Concept That Denigrates 'Ordinary' Gay Lives. *Journal of Homosexuality*, *59*(7), 1065–1072. https://doi.org/10.1080/00918369.2012.699851

Browne, K., and Nash, C.J. (eds) (2010). *Queer Methods and Methodologies: Intersecting Queer Theories and Social Science Research*. Oxfordshire: Taylor & Francis. https://doi.org/10.4324/9781315603223

Butler, J. (1990 [2006]). *Gender Trouble: Feminism and the Subversion of Identity*, 2nd edn. New York; London: Routledge.

Butler, J. (1993). *Bodies That Matter: On the Discursive Limits of 'Sex'*. New York; London: Routledge.

Butler, J. (2002). Is Kinship Always Already Heterosexual? *Differences: A Journal of Feminist Cultural Studies*, 13(1), 14–44.

Cadoret, A. (2009). The Contribution of Homoparental Families to the Current Debate on Kinship. In Edwards, J., and Salazar, C. (eds), *European Kinship in the Age of Biotechnology*. New York, NY: Berghahn Books, pp 79–96.

Callaway, H. (1992). Ethnography and Experience: Gender Implications in Fieldwork and Texts. *Anthropology and Autobiography*, 29, 49.

Carsten, J. (ed) (2000). *Cultures of Relatedness: New Approaches to the Study of Kinship*. Cambridge: Cambridge University Press.

Carsten, J. (2003). *After Kinship* (New Departures in Anthropology). Cambridge: Cambridge University Press. https://doi.org/10.1017/CBO9780511800382

Carsten, J. (2013). What Kinship Does – and How. *HAU: Journal of Ethnographic Theory*, 3(2), 245–251. https://doi.org/10.14318/hau3.2.013

Chan, K.W., and Zhang, L. (1999). The *Hukou* System and Rural–Urban Migration in China: Processes and Changes. *The China Quarterly*, 160, 818–855. https://doi.org/10.1017/S0305741000001351

Chao, Y.A. (1999). Performing like a P'o and Acting as a Big Sister: Reculturating into the Indigenous Lesbian Circle in Taiwan. In Markowitz, F. and Ashkenazi, M. (eds), *Sex, Sexuality, and the Anthropologist*. Champaign, IL: University of Illinois Press, pp 128–144.

Chen, Y., and Chen, Y. (2007). Lesbians in China's Mainland: A Brief Introduction. *Journal of Lesbian Studies*, 10(3–4), 113–125. https://doi.org/10.1300/J155v10n03_08

Chiang, H. (2014). (De)Provincializing China: Queer Historicism and Sinophone Postcolonial Critique. In Chiang, H. and Heinrich, A.L. (eds), *Queer Sinophone Cultures*. New York: Routledge, pp 19–51.

Choi, S.Y., and Luo, M. (2016). Performative Family: Homosexuality, Marriage and Intergenerational Dynamics in China. *The British Journal of Sociology*, 67(2), 260–280. https://doi.org/10.1111/1468-4446.12196

Chou, W. (2001). Homosexuality and the Cultural Politics of Tongzhi in Chinese Societies. *Journal of Homosexuality*, 40(3–4), 27–46.

Chu, J. (2001). Prenatal Sex Determination and Sex-Selective Abortion in Rural Central China. *Population and Development Review*, 27(2), 259–281. https://doi.org/10.1111/j.1728-4457.2001.00259.x

Cohen, A.P. (1992). Self-Conscious Anthropology. In Okely, J. and Callaway, H. (eds), *Anthropology and Autobiography*. London; New York: Routledge, pp 221–241.

Cohen, M.L. (2005). *Kinship, Contract, Community, and State: Anthropological Perspectives on China*. Stanford, CA: Stanford University Press.

REFERENCES

Collier, J.F., and Yanagisako, S.J. (eds) (1987). *Gender and Kinship: Essays toward a Unified Analysis*. Stanford, CA: Stanford University Press.

Constable, N. (2009). The Commodification of Intimacy: Marriage, Sex, and Reproductive Labor. *Annual Review of Anthropology*, *38*(1), 49–64.

Dahl, U., and Gabb, J. (2019). Trends in Contemporary Queer Kinship and Family Research. *Lambda Nordica*, *24*(2–3), 209–237. https://doi.org/10.34041/ln.v24.586

Das, V. (1995). National Honor and Practical Kinship: Unwanted Women and Children. In Ginsburg, F.D., and Rapp, R. (eds), *Conceiving the New World Order: The Global Politics of Reproduction*. Berkeley, CA: University of California Press, pp 2124–2133.

Dasgupta, R.K., and Dasgupta, D. (2018). Intimate Subjects and Virtual Spaces: Rethinking Sexuality as a Category for Intimate Ethnographies. *Sexualities*, *21*(5–6), 932–950.

Dave, N. (2012). *Queer Activism in India: A Story in the Anthropology of Ethics*. Durham, NC: Duke University Press.

Davies, C.A. (2008). *Reflexive Ethnography: A Guide to Researching Selves and Others*. London; New York: Routledge.

Davis, D.S. (2021). 'We Do': Parental Involvement in the Marriages of Urban Sons and Daughters. In Yan, Y., (ed), *Chinese Families Upside Down: Intergenerational Dynamics and Neo-Familism in the Early 21st Century*. Leiden, The Netherlands: Brill, pp 31–54.

De Carvalho, P.G.C., Da Cabral, C.S., Ferguson, L., Gruskin, S., and Diniz, C.S.G. (2019). 'We Are Not Infertile': Challenges and Limitations Faced by Women in Same-Sex Relationships when Seeking Conception Services in São Paulo, Brazil. *Culture, Health & Sexuality*, *21*(11), 1257–1272. https://doi.org/10.1080/13691058.2018.1556343

D'Emilio, J. (2007 [1983]). Capitalism and Gay Identity. In Parker, R., and Aggleton, P. (eds), *Culture, Society and Sexuality*. London: Routledge, pp 266–274.

Dempsey, D. (2010). Conceiving and Negotiating Reproductive Relationships: Lesbians and Gay Men Forming Families with Children. *Sociology*, *44*(6), 1145–1162.

Ding, C. (2015). Surrogacy Litigation in China and Beyond. *Journal of Law and the Biosciences*, *2*(1), 33–55. https://doi.org/10.1093/jlb/lsu036

Ding, R. and Gayspot Magazine. (2018, 7 March). *Jiyou shengyuguan ji daiyun diaochabaogao* [Chinese] [Opinions on Reproduction and Surrogacy among Gay Men]. Retrieved 21 January 2020 from: http://mp.weixin.qq.com/s?__biz=MjM5NDQzNTM0MQ==&mid=2654191997&idx=1&sn=58eab2b32d1d0c8d0000a1000a46be5f&chksm=bd40b91f8a373009fd62bdfeceb082d5af5e037a4e34e39b063ead744ee2d8f305dbcc11207a#rd

Duggan, L. (2002). The New Homonormativity: The Sexual Politics of Neoliberalism. In Castronovo, R., and Nelson, D.D. (eds), *Materializing Democracy: Toward a Revitalized Cultural Politics*, Vol. 10. Durham, NC: Duke University Press, pp 175–194.

Edelman, L. (2004). *No Future: Queer Theory and the Death Drive*. Durham, NC: Duke University Press.

Ellis, C. (2007). Telling Secrets, Revealing Lives: Relational Ethics in Research with Intimate Others. *Qualitative Research*, *13*(1), 3–29.

Engebretsen, E.L. (2008). Love in a Big City: Sexuality, Kinship, and Citizenship amongst 'Lala' ('Lesbian') Women in Beijing. DPhil. London School of Economics and Political Science.

Engebretsen, E.L. (2009). Intimate Practices, Conjugal Ideals: Affective Ties and Relationship Strategies among Lala (Lesbian) Women in Contemporary Beijing. *Sexuality Research & Social Policy*, *6*(3), 3–14.

Engebretsen, E.L. (2014). *Queer Women in Urban China*. London; New York: Routledge.

Engebretsen, E.L. (2017). Under Pressure: Lesbian-Gay Contract Marriages and Their Patriarchal Bargains. In Santos, G., and Harrell, S. (eds), *Transforming Patriarchy: Chinese Families in the Twenty-First Century*. Seattle; WA: University of Washington Press.

Engebretsen, E.L., and Schroeder, W.F. (eds) (2015). *Queer/Tongzhi China: New Perspectives on Research, Activism and Media Cultures*. Copenhagen, Denmark: NIAS Press.

Eriksen, T.H. (2010). *Small Places, Large Issues: An Introduction to Social and Cultural Anthropology*, 3rd edn (Anthropology, Culture, and Society). London: Pluto.

Evans, D. (2013). *Sexual Citizenship: The Material Construction of Sexualities*. London: Routledge.

Fei, X. (1992). *From the Soil: The Foundations of Chinese Society*. Berkeley, CA: University of California Press.

Fincher, L.H. (2014). *Leftover Women: The Resurgence of Gender Inequality in China*. London: Zed Books.

Fitzgerald, T.K. (1999). Identity in Ethnography: Limits to Reflective Subjectivity. In Markowitz, F., and Ashkenazi, M. (eds), *Sex, Sexuality and the Anthropologist*. Champaign, IL: University of Illinois Press, pp 117–127.

Folger, T. (2008). Queer Nuclear Families? Reproducing and Transgressing Heteronormativity. *Journal of Homosexuality*, *54*(1–2), 124–149.

Fong, V.L. (2004). *Only Hope: Coming of Age under China's One-Child Policy*. Stanford, CA: Stanford University Press.

Fong, V.L. (2007). Morality, Cosmopolitanism, or Academic Attainment? Discourses on 'Quality' and Urban Chinese-Only-Children's Claims to Ideal Personhood. *City and Society*, *19*(1), 86–113.

Foucault, M. (1984). *The History of Sexuality*. London: Penguin.

Franklin, S. (2013). *Biological Relatives: IVF, Stem Cells, and the Future of Kinship*. Durham, NC: Duke University Press.

Franklin, S., and McKinnon, S. (eds) (2001). *Relative Values: Reconfiguring Kinship Studies*. Durham, NC: Duke University Press.

Franklin, S., Posocco, S., Boyce, P., and Gonzalez-Polledo, E.J. (2019). Conceptuality in Relation. In Boyce, P., Gonzalez-Polledo, E.J., and Posocco, S. (eds), *Queering Knowledge: Analytics, Devices, and Investments after Marilyn Strathern*. London; New York: Routledge, pp 168–181.

Friedman, S.L. (2008). The Ties that Bind Female Homosociality and the Production of Intimacy in Rural China. In Brandtstädter, S., and Santos, G.D. (eds), *Chinese Kinship: Contemporary Anthropological Perspectives*. London; New York: Routledge, pp 109–125.

Fu, X. (2015). Market Economy, Spatial Transformation, and Sexual Diversity: An Ethnographic Study of the Gay Community in Shenyang, North China. In Engebretsen, E.L., and Schroeder, W.F. (eds), *Queer/Tongzhi China: New Perspectives on Research, Activism and Media Cultures*. Copenhagen, Denmark: NIAS Press, pp 217–44.

Gabrielson, M.L. (2011). We Have to Create Family: Aging Support Issues and Needs among Older Lesbians. *Journal of Gay & Lesbian Social Services*, 23(3), 322–334.

Gammeltoft, T. (2014). *Haunting Images: A Cultural Account of Selective Reproduction in Vietnam*. Berkeley, CA: University of California Press.

Gearing, J. (1995). Fear and Loving in the West Indies: Research from the Heart (as Well as the Head). In Kulick, D., and Willson, M. (eds), *Taboo: Sex, Identity, and Erotic Subjectivity in Anthropological Fieldwork*. London; New York: Routledge.

Ginsburg, F.D., and Rapp, R. (eds) (1995). *Conceiving the New World Order: The Global Politics of Reproduction*. Berkeley, CA: University of California Press.

Goodfellow, A. (2015). *Gay Fathers, Their Children, and the Making of Kinship*. New York: Fordham University Press.

Google Maps (2021). Guangdong Province, China. www.google.com/maps

Greely, H.T. (2016). *The End of Sex and the Future of Human Reproduction*. Cambridge, MA: Harvard University Press. www.jstor.org/stable/10.2307/j.ctt1d4tzfg

Greenhalgh, S. (1985). Sexual Stratification: The Other Side of 'Growth with Equity' in East Asia. *Population and Development Review*, 11, 265–314.

Greenhalgh, S. (2003). Planned Births, Unplanned Persons: 'Population' in the Making of Chinese Modernity. *American Ethnologist*, 30(2), 196–215. https://doi.org/10.1525/ae.2003.30.2.196

Grewal, I., and Kaplan, C. (2001). Global Identities: Theorizing Transnational Studies of Sexuality. *GLQ: A Journal of Lesbian and Gay Studies*, 7, 663–679.

Gusterson, H. (1997). Studying Up Revisited. *PoLAR: Political Legal Anthropology Review*, *20*(1), 114–119.

Halberstam, J. (1998). *Female Masculinity*. Durham, NC: Duke University Press.

Halberstam, J. (2008). The Anti-Social Turn in Queer Studies. *Graduate Journal of Social Science*, *5*(2), 140–156.

Halberstam, J. (2011). *The Queer Art of Failure*. Durham, NC: Duke University Press.

Handwerker, L. (2002). The Politics of Making Modern Babies in China. In Inhorn, M., and Van Balen, F. (eds), *Infertility around the Globe: New Thinking on Childlessness, Gender, and Reproductive Technologies*. Berkeley, CA: University of California Press, pp 298–315.

Haraway, D. (1991). *Simians, Cyborgs, and Women: The Reinvention of Nature*. London: Free Association Books.

Hastrup, K. (1992). Writing Ethnography: State of the Art. *Anthropology and Autobiography*, *29*, 115.

Hayden, C.P. (1995). Gender, Genetics, and Generation: Reformulating Biology in Lesbian Kinship. *Cultural Anthropology*, *10*(1), 41–63.

He, Q. (2000). China's Listing Social Structure. *New Left Review*, *5*, 69.

He, T. (2017, 17 April). *Jiefu shengzi*: *buweirenzhi qie luanxiangcongsheng de dixia daiyun shichang* [Chinese] [Borrowing Womb: Unknown and Chaotic Underground Surrogacy Chain]. GQ Magazine. Retrieved 25 February 2019 from: www.gq.com.cn/magazine/news_1824fffa8788a99b.html

Heberer, F.-M. (2017). Migrating Intimacies: Media Representations of Same-Sex Love among Migrant Women in East Asia. *Sexualities*, *20*(4), 428–445.

Hendriks, T. (2018). 'Erotiques Cannibales': A Queer Ontological Take on Desire from Urban Congo. *Sexualities*, *21*(5–6), 853–867. https://doi.org/10.1177/1363460716677283

Hildebrandt, T. (2018). The One-Child Policy, Elder Care, and LGB Chinese: A Social Policy Explanation for Family Pressure. *Journal of Homosexuality*, *0*(0), 1–19.

Hinsch, B. (1990). *Passion of the Cut Sleeve: The Male Homosexual Tradition in China*. Berkeley, CA: University of California Press.

Ho, L.W.W. (2008). Speaking of Same-Sex Subjects in China. *Asian Studies Review*, *32*(4), 491–509. https://doi.org/10.1080/10357820802492586

Ho, L.W.W. (2010). *Gay and Lesbian Subculture in Urban China*. London: Routledge.

Hockey, J., and Forsey, M. (2012). Ethnography is Not Participant Observation: Reflections on the Interview as Participatory Qualitative Research. In Skinner, J. (ed), *The Interview: An Ethnographic Approach*. London: A&C Black, pp 69–87.

Howell, S. (2003). Kinning: The Creation of Life Trajectories in Transnational Adoptive Families. *Journal of the Royal Anthropological Institute*, *9*(3), 465–484. https://doi.org/10.1111/1467-9655.00159

REFERENCES

Huang, A. (2015). On the Surface: 'T' and Transgender Identity in Chinese Lesbian Culture. In Engebretsen, E., Schroeder, W., and Bao, Hongwei (eds), *Queer/Tongzhi China: New Perspectives on Research, Activism and Media Cultures.* Copenhagen, Denmark: NIAS Press, pp 111–130.

Huang, A. (2017). Precariousness and the Queer Politics of Imagination in China. *Culture, Theory and Critique,* 58(2), 226–242. https://doi.org/10.1080/14735784.2017.1287580

Huang, S., and Brouwer, D.C. (2018). Coming out, Coming Home, Coming With: Models of Queer Sexuality in Contemporary China. *Journal of International and Intercultural Communication,* 11(2), 97–116. https://doi.org/10.1080/17513057.2017.1414867

Hunt, S., and Holmes, C. (2015) Everyday Decolonization: Living a Decolonizing Queer Politics. *Journal of Lesbian Studies,* 19(2), 154–172.

Ikels, C. (ed) (2004). *Filial Piety: Practice and Discourse in Contemporary East Asia.* Stanford, CA: Stanford University Press.

Inhorn, M.C., and Birenbaum-Carmeli, D. (2008). Assisted Reproductive Technologies and Culture Change. *Annual Review of Anthropology,* 37(1), 177–196. https://doi.org/10.1146/annurev.anthro.37.081407.085230

Jackson, S. (2005). Sexuality, Heterosexuality and Gender Hierarchy: Getting Our Priorities Straight. In Ingraham, C. (ed), *Thinking Straight: The Power, the Promise, and the Paradox of Heterosexuality.* London; New York: Routledge, pp 15–37.

Jackson, S. (2006). Interchanges: Gender, Sexuality and Heterosexuality. *Feminist Theory,* 7(1), 105–121.

Jankowiak, W.R. (2008). Practicing Connectiveness as Kinship in Urban China. In Brandtstädter, S., and Santos, G.D. (eds), *Chinese Kinship and Relatedness: Some Contemporary Anthropological Perspectives,* New York: Routledge, pp 67–92.

Jankowiak, W.R., and Li, X. (2017). Emergent Conjugal Love, Mutual Affection, and Female Power. In Santos, G., and Harrell, S. (eds), *Transforming Patriarchy: Chinese Families in the Twenty-First Century.* Seattle, WA: University of Washington Press, pp 146–162.

Ji, Y., Liu, Y., and Yang, S. (2021). A Tale of Three Cities: Distinct Marriage Strategies among Chinese Lesbians. *Journal of Gender Studies,* 30(5), 536–548. https://doi.org/10.1080/09589236.2021.1929098

Ji, Y., Wu, X., Sun, S., and He, G. (2017). Unequal Care, Unequal Work: Toward a More Comprehensive Understanding of Gender Inequality in Post-Reform Urban China. *Sex Roles,* 77(11–12), 765–778.

Jiang, Q., and Liu, Y. (2016). Low Fertility and Concurrent Birth Control Policy in China. *The History of the Family,* 21(4), 551–577. https://doi.org/10.1080/1081602X.2016.1213179

Johnson, N.B. (1984). Sex, Color, and Rites of Passage in Ethnographic Research. *Human Organization,* 43(2), 108–120.

Jones, A. (2013). Introduction: Queer Utopias, Queer Futurity, and Potentiality in Quotidian Practice. In Jones, A. (ed), *A Critical Inquiry into Queer Utopias*. New York: Palgrave Macmillan, pp 1–17.

Kam, L.Y.L. (2013). *Shanghai Lalas: Female Tongzhi Communities and Politics in Urban China*. Hong Kong: Hong Kong University Press.

Kennedy, E., and Davis, M. (1992). 'They Was No One to Mess with': The Construction of the Butch Role in the Lesbian Community of the 1940s and 1950s. In Nestle, J. (ed), *The Persistent Desire: A Femme-Butch Reader*. Boston, MA: Alyson Publications, pp 62–79.

Khanna, A. (2017). *Sexualness*. New Delhi: New Text.

Kim, S., and Friedman, S.L. (2021). Productive Encounters: Kinship, Gender, and Family Laws in East Asia. *Positions: Asia Critique*, *29*(3), 453–468. https://doi.org/10.1215/10679847-8978295

Kipnis, A. (2007). Neoliberalism Reified: Suzhi Discourse and Tropes of Neoliberalism in the People's Republic of China. *Journal of the Royal Anthropological Institute*, *13*(2), 383–400. https://doi.org/10.1111/j.1467-9655.2007.00432.x

Klein, K. (2017). Assisted Reproductive Technologies, Sperm Donation, and Biological Kinship: A Recent Chinese Media Debate. In Santos, G., and Harrell, S. (eds), *Transforming Patriarchy: Chinese Families in the Twenty-First Century*. Seattle, WA: University of Washington Press, pp 219–233.

Kleinman, A., Yan, Y., Jun, J., Lee, S., Zhang, E., Wu, F., et al (2011). *Deep China: The Moral Life of the Person*, 1st edn. Berkeley, CA: University of California Press.

Kondo, D.K. (1990). 'M. Butterfly': Orientalism, Gender, and a Critique of Essentialist Identity. *Cultural Critique*, *16*, 5–29.

Kong, T.S.K. (2010). *Chinese Male Homosexualities*. London; New York: Routledge.

Kong, T.S.K. (2021). Be a Responsible and Respectable Man: Two Generations of Chinese Gay Men Accomplishing Masculinity in Hong Kong. *Men and Masculinities*, *24*(1), 64–83. https://doi.org/10.1177/1097184X19859390

Kuan, T. (2015). *Love's Uncertainty: The Politics and Ethics of Child Rearing in Contemporary China*. Berkeley, CA: University of California Press.

Kulick, D., and Willson, M. (eds) (1995). *Taboo: Sex, Identity and Erotic Subjectivity in Anthropological Fieldwork*. London; New York: Routledge.

Lang, G., and Smart, J. (2002). Migration and the 'Second Wife' in South China: Toward Cross-Border Polygyny. *International Migration Review*, *36*(2), 546–569. https://doi.org/10.1111/j.1747-7379.2002.tb00092.x

Latour, B. (1993). *We Have Never Been Modern*. Cambridge, MA; London: Harvard University Press.

Lee, H. (2006). *Revolution of the Heart: A Genealogy of Love in China, 1900–1950*. Stanford, CA: Stanford University Press.

REFERENCES

Lee, H. (2014). *The Stranger and the Chinese Moral Imagination*. Stanford, CA: Stanford University Press.

Legal Daily (2019). *Daiyun heise chanyelian diaocha* [Chinese] [Investigation on the Surrogacy Black Industry Chain], 17 July. Retrieved 12 February 2020 from: www.legaldaily.com.cn/index_article/content/2019-07/16/content_7935077.htm

Lewin, E. (2016). Who's Queer? What's Queer? Queer Anthropology through the Lens of Ethnography. *Cultural Anthropology*, *31*(4), 598–606. https://doi.org/10.14506/ca31.4.08

Lewin, E., and Leap, W.L. (ed) (1996). *Out in the Field: Reflections of Lesbian and Gay Anthropologists*. Champaign, IL: University of Illinois Press.

Lewin, E., Leap, W.L., and Newton, E. (eds) (2002). *Out in Theory*. Champaign, IL: University of Illinois Press.

Li, X. (2007). *Nvtongxinglian xingbie rentong he shenfen rentong yanjiu* [Chinese] [Lesbian Gender Identity and Role Identity Research]. *Zhongguo Xingkexue*, *16*(5), 6–9.

Li, X., Zhang, B., Wang, J., Li, Y., Li, X., Yu, P., et al (2017). The Sexual Health Status of Women Who Have Regular Sexual Relations with Men Who Have Sex with Men in Mainland China. BMC Public Health, *17*(1), 168. https://doi.org/10.1186/s12889-017-4096-z

Li, Y. (1998). *Tongxinglian Yawenhua* [Chinese] [*Homosexual Subculture*]. Neimenggu, China: Neimenggu University Press.

Li, Y. (2011). Changes of Family Structure and Family Relation Based on Investigation in Lanzhou. *Gansu Social Sciences*, 1, 6–12.

Li, Y., and Wang, X. (1992). *Tamen de shijie* [Chinese] [*Their World*]. Shanxi, China: Shanxi People's Press.

Liang, Z. (2012). 'DINK' Family: Young People's Fashion? – An International Comparative Study. *Youth Studies*, 5, 442–454.

Lin, X. (2019). 'Purchasing Hope': The Consumption of Children's Education in Urban China. *The Journal of Chinese Sociology*, *6*(1), 8. https://doi.org/10.1186/s40711-019-0099-8

Lin, Y., and Xu, J. (2013). *Chunjie cheng chugui gaofengqi* [Chinese] [Spring Festival Is the Peak Time for Coming out], 15 January. Xinhua Wang. Retrieved 1 May 2015 from: www.zj.xinhuanet.com/newscenter/jiankang/2013-01/15/c_114369516.htm

Liu, P. (2010). Why Does Queer Theory Need China? *Positions: East Asia Cultures Critique*, *18*(2), 291–320.

Liu, P., and Rofel, L. (2010). Beyond the Strai(gh)ts: Transnationalism and Queer Chinese Politics. *Positions: East Asia Cultures Critique*, *18*(2), 281–289.

Liu, S., and Luo, Z. (2017) *Zigong chuzu: Zhongguo daiyun shichang jiemi.* [Chinese] [Renting out the Womb: The Underground Production Line of Chinese Surrogacy Market], 16 February. Jiemian News. Retrieved 30 October 2022 from: www.jiemian.com/article/1117440.html

Liu, T. (2016). Neoliberal Ethos, State Censorship and Sexual Culture: A Chinese Dating/Hook-up App. *Continuum*, *30*(5), 557–566.

Liu, T., and Tan, C.K.K. (2020). On the Transactionalisation of Conjugal Bonds: A Feminist Materialist Analysis of Chinese Xinghun Marriages. *Anthropological Forum*, *30*(4), 443–463. https://doi.org/10.1080/00664677.2020.1855108

Lo, I.P.Y. (2020). Family Formation among Lalas (Lesbians) in Urban China: Strategies for Forming Families and Navigating Relationships with Families of Origin. *Journal of Sociology*, *56*(4), 629–645. https://doi.org/10.1177/1440783320912828

Lo, I.P.Y., Chan, C.H.Y., and Chan, T.H.Y. (2016). Perceived Importance of Childbearing and Attitudes toward Assisted Reproductive Technology among Chinese Lesbians in Hong Kong: Implications for Psychological Well-Being. *Fertility and Sterility*, *106*(5), 1221–1229. https://doi.org/10.1016/j.fertnstert.2016.06.042

Luo, M. (2020). Sexuality, Migration and Family: Understanding Jia and Its Impact on Chinese Young Gay Men's Migration Motives from a Temporal Perspective. *Journal of Ethnic and Migration Studies*, *0*(0), 1–16. https://doi.org/10.1080/1369183X.2020.1821615

Luo, M., Tseng, H., and Ma, Y. (2022). Homosexual Stories, Family Stories: Neo-Confucian Homonormativity and Storytelling in the Chinese Gay Community. *The China Quarterly*, *252*, 1256–1276. https://doi.org/10.1017/S030574102200087X

Mackie, V. (2017). Rethinking Sexual Citizenship: Asia-Pacific Perspectives. *Sexualities*, *20*(1–2), 143–158. https://doi.org/10.1177/1363460716645786

Malinowski, B. (1922). *Argonauts of the Western Pacific*. London: George Routledge & Sons.

Mamo, L. (2007). *Queering Reproduction: Achieving Pregnancy in the Age of Technoscience*. Durham, NC: Duke University Press.

Mamo, L., and Alston-Stepnitz, E. (2015). Queer Intimacies and Structural Inequalities: New Directions in Stratified Reproduction. *Journal of Family Issues*, *36*(4), 519–540. https://doi.org/10.1177/0192513X14563796

Manalansan, M.F. (2003). *Global Divas: Filipino Gay Men in the Diaspora*. Durham, NC: Duke University Press.

Meinert, L., and Grøn, L. (2019). 'It Runs in the Family': Exploring Contagious Kinship Connections. *Ethnos*, *0*(0), 1–14. https://doi.org/10.1080/00141844.2019.1640759

Mills, E. (2018). Gender, Sexuality and the Limits of the Law. *Global Discourse*, *8*(3), 473–484. https://doi.org/10.1080/23269995.2018.1521099

Mills, M.B. (1999). *Thai Women in the Global Labor Force*. New Brunswick, NJ: Rutgers University Press.

Ministry of Health of the People's Republic of China (2001a). No. 14, Regulations for the Administration of Human-Assisted Reproductive Technology, 19 February. National Health Commission of the PRC. Retrieved 14 November 2018 from: www.nhc.gov.cn/zwgk/wlwl/200804/56c333396 f3b4e2ab150491c33129f5a.shtml

Ministry of Health of the People's Republic of China (2001b). No .15, Regulations for the Administration of Sperm Banks, 20 February. National Health Commission of the PRC. Retrieved 14 November 2018 from: www.nhc.gov.cn/zwgk/wlwl/200804/fcdbb1240018475297fa008ec05f81c6.shtml

Ministry of Health of the People's Republic of China (2003). Notice from the Ministry of Health Concerning the Revision of the Norms, Standards, and Ethical Principles of ART and Sperm Banks, 30 September. National Health Commission of the PRC. Retrieved 14 November 2018 from: www.nhc.gov.cn/qjjys/s3581/200805/f69a925d55b44be2a9b4ada7fcdec835.shtml

Ministry of Health of the People's Republic of China (2006). No. 44, On the Regulation of Human Clinical-Assisted Reproduction Technologies and Accreditation of Human Sperm Banks, 7 April. National Health Commission of the PRC. Retrieved 1 December 2017 from: www.nhc.gov.cn/qjjys/s3581/200805/9a008204d0de4500bef53cf313727994.shtml britain

Mizielińska, J., and Stasińska, A. (2017). Beyond the Western Gaze: Families of Choice in Poland. *Sexualities*, *0*(0), 1–19.

Moore, H.L. (2019). How Exactly Are We Related? In Boyce, P., Gonzalez-Polledo, E.J., and Posocco, S. (eds), *Queering Knowledge: Analytics, Devices, and Investments after Marilyn Strathern*. London; New York: Routledge, pp 181–192.

Muñoz, J.E. (2009). *Cruising Utopia: The Then and There of Queer Futurity*. New York: New York University Press.

Murphy, D.A. (2013). The Desire for Parenthood: Gay Men Choosing to Become Parents Through Surrogacy. *Journal of Family Issues*, *34*(8), 1104–1124. https://doi.org/10.1177/0192513X13484272

Narayan, K. (1993). How Native Is a 'Native' Anthropologist'? *American Anthropologist*, *95*(3), 671–686.

Okely, J., and Callaway, H. (1992). *Anthropology and Autobiography*. London; New York: Routledge. http://public.eblib.com/choice/publicfullrecord.aspx?p=181714

Osburg, J. (2013). *Anxious Wealth: Money and Morality Among China's New Rich*. Stanford, CA: Stanford University Press.

Osella, F. (2012). Malabar Secrets: South Indian Muslim Men's (Homo) Sociality across the Indian Ocean. *Asian Studies Review*, *36*(4), 531–549.

Owton, H., and Allen-Collinson, J. (2014). Close but Not Too Close: Friendship as Method(ology) in Ethnographic Research Encounters. *Journal of Contemporary Ethnography*, *43*(3), 283–305. https://doi.org/10.1177/0891241613495410

Pan, L. (2015). *When True Love Came to China*. Hong Kong: Hong Kong University Press.

Patel, G. (2006). Risky Subjects: Insurance, Sexuality, and Capital. *Social Text*, *24*(489), 25–65.

Patel, G. (2007). Imagining Risk, Care and Security: Insurance and Fantasy, *Anthropological Theory*, *7*(1), 99–118. https://doi.org/10.1177/1463499607074297

Parreñas, R.S. (2017). Introduction: Special Issue on Technologies of Intimate Labour. *Sexualities*, *20*(4), 407–411. https://doi.org/10.1177/1363460716677247

Patton-Imani, S. (2020). *Queering Family Trees: Race, Reproductive Justice, and Lesbian Motherhood*. New York: New York University Press.

Pimentel, E.E. (2000). Just How Do I Love Thee? Marital Relations in Urban China. *Journal of Marriage and Family*, *62*(1), 32–47.

Population and Family Planning Law of the People's Republic of China (2001), 29 December. Retrieved 20 January 2018 from: www.gov.cn/banshi/2005-08/21/content_25059.htm

Povinelli, E.A. (2002). Notes on Gridlock: Genealogy, Intimacy, Sexuality. *Public Culture*, *14*(1), 215–238.

Povinelli, E.A. (2006). *The Empire of Love: Toward a Theory of Intimacy, Genealogy, and Carnality*. Durham, NC: Duke University Press.

Povinelli, E.A., and Chauncey, G. (1999). Thinking Sexuality Transnationally: An Introduction. *GLQ: A Journal of Lesbian and Gay Studies*, *5*(4), 439–449. https://doi.org/10.1215/10642684-5-4-439

Rawlins, W.K. (1992). *Friendship Matters: Communication, Dialectics, and the Life Course*. New York: Aldine de Gruyter.

Rege, A. (2009). What's Love Got to Do with It? Exploring Online Dating Scams and Identity Fraud. *International Journal of Cyber Criminology (IJCC)*, *3*, 974–2891.

Richardson, D. (2017). Rethinking Sexual Citizenship. *Sociology*, *51*(2), 208–224. https://doi.org/10.1177/0038038515609024

Riley, N.E. (1994). Interwoven Lives: Parents, Marriage, and Guanxi in China. *Journal of Marriage and Family*, *56*(4), 791–803.

Robben, A.C.G.M., and Sluka, J.A. (eds) (2006). *Ethnographic Fieldwork: An Anthropological Reader*, 1st edn. Malden, MA: Wiley-Blackwell.

Rofel, L. (2007). *Desiring China: Experiments in Neoliberalism, Sexuality, and Public Culture* (Perverse Modernities). Durham, NC; London: Duke University Press.

Rubin, G. (1984). Thinking Sex: Notes for a Radical Theory of the Politics of Sexuality. In Nardi, P.M., and Schneider, B.E. (eds), *Social Perspectives in Lesbian and Gay Studies: A Reader*. London: Routledge, pp 100–133.

Rudrappa, S. (2018). Why Is India's Ban on Commercial Surrogacy Bad for Women? *North Carolina Journal of International Law*, *43*(4), 70–95.

Ryan-Flood, R., and Jamieson, L. (2009). *Lesbian Motherhood: Gender, Families and Sexual Citizenship*. London: Palgrave Macmillan.

Sahlins, M. (2013). *What Kinship Is – and Is Not*. Chicago: University of Chicago Press.

Sang, T.D. (2003). *The Emerging Lesbian: Female Same-Sex Desire in Modern China*. Chicago, IL; London: University of Chicago Press.

Santos, G., and Harrell, S. (eds) (2017). *Transforming Patriarchy: Chinese Families in the Twenty-First Century*. Seattle, WA: University of Washington Press.

Schensul, S.L., Schensul, J.J., and LeCompte, M.D. (1999). *Essential Ethnographic Methods: Observations, Interviews, and Questionnaires*, Vol. 2. Lanham, MD: Altamira Press.

Schneider, D.M. (1980). *American Kinship: A Cultural Account*, 2nd edn. Chicago: University of Chicago Press.

Schroeder, W.F. (2012). Beyond Resistance: Gay and Lala Recreation in Beijing. In Aggleton, P., Boyce, P., Moore, H.L., and Parker, R. (eds), *Understanding Global Sexualities: New Frontiers*. London; New York: Routledge, pp 120–135.

Sedgwick, E.K. (2003). *Touching Feeling: Affect, Pedagogy and Performativity*. Durham, NC: Duke University Press.

Shen, J. (2013). Increasing Internal Migration in China from 1985 to 2005: Institutional versus Economic Drivers. *Habitat International*, *39*, 1–7. https://doi.org/10.1016/j.habitatint.2012.10.004

Shenzhen Municipal Bureau of Statistics (2018). *Shenzhen Statistics and Information Yearbook of 2018*. December. http://tjj.sz.gov.cn/nj2018/nianjian.html?2018

Shi, L. (2017). The New Rich and Their Unplanned Births: Stratified Reproduction under China's Birth-Planning Policy. *Medical Anthropology Quarterly*, *31*(4), 537–554.

Simpson, B. (1994). Bringing the 'Unclear' Family into Focus: Divorce and Re-Marriage in Contemporary Britain. *Man*, *29*(4), 831–851. https://doi.org/10.2307/3033971

Sinnott, M. (2004). *Toms and Dees: Transgender Identity and Female Same-Sex Relationships in Thailand*. Honolulu: University of Hawaii Press.

Skinner, J. (ed) (2012). *The Interview: An Ethnographic Approach*. London: A&C Black.

Song, J. (2019). The Effect of the Two-Child Policy on China's Fertility. *Modern China Studies; Norfolk*, *26*(2), 8–22.

Song, L. (2022). *Queering Chinese Kinship: Queer Public Culture in Globalizing China*. Hong Kong: Hong Kong University Press.

Sorainen, A. (2015). Queer Personal Lives, Inheritance Perspectives, and Small Places. *Nordic Journal for Queer Studies – Lambda Nordica*, *19*, 3–4.

Spradley, J.P. (1980). *Participant Observation*. Belmont, CA: Thomson Learning.

Stafford, C. (2000). Chinese Patriliny and the Cycles of Yang and Laiwang. In Carsten, J. (ed), *Cultures of Relatedness: New Approaches to the Study of Kinship*. Cambridge: Cambridge University Press, pp 35–54.

State Council of the People's Republic of China (2002). No. 357, The Measures for Administration of Collection of Social Maintenance Fees, 2 August. Retrieved 3 July 2020 from: www.gov.cn/gongbao/content/2002/content_61699.htm

Strathern, M. (1992a). *After Nature: English Kinship in the Late Twentieth Century*. Cambridge: Cambridge University Press.

Strathern, M. (1992b). *Reproducing the Future: Anthropology, Kinship and the New Reproductive Technologies*. New York: Routledge.

Strathern, M. (1996). Cutting the Network. *The Journal of the Royal Anthropological Institute*, 2(3), 517–535. https://doi.org/10.2307/3034901

Strathern, M. (2004). *Partial Connections*. Lanham, MD: AltaMira Press.

Strathern, M. (2005). *Kinship, Law and the Unexpected: Relatives Are Always a Surprise*. Cambridge: Cambridge University Press.

Strathern, M. (2011). What Is a Parent? *HAU: Journal of Ethnographic Theory*, 1(1), 245–278.

Strathern, M. (2012). Epilogue: Expectations, Auto-Narrative and Beyond. In Skinner, J. (ed), *The Interview: An Ethnographic Approach*. London: A&C Black, pp 261–266.

Sullivan, N. (2003). *A Critical Introduction to Queer Theory*. New York: New York University Press. www.jstor.org/stable/10.3366/j.ctvxcrwj6

Szonyi, M. (2002). *Practicing Kinship: Lineage and Descent in Late Imperial China*. Stanford, CA: Stanford University Press.

Tan, J. (2017). Beijing Meets Hawai'i. *GLQ: A Journal of Lesbian and Gay Studies*, 23(1), 137–150. https://doi.org/10.1215/10642684-3672429

Tan, L., Jiang, Y.P., and Jiang, A.H. (2006). *Report on Gender Equality and Women Development in China (1995–2005)*. Beijing: Social Sciences Documentation Publishing House.

Tang, C., and Chen, W. (2012). Zhongguo chengshi jiating de qinshuguanxi [Chinese] [Kinship in Chinese Urban Families]. *Jiangsu Social Science*, 2, 92–103.

Tang, D.T. (2011). *Conditional Spaces: Hong Kong Lesbian Desires and Everyday Life*. Hong Kong: Hong Kong University Press.

Tao, H. (2021). Queering Kinship in Urban China. PhD thesis. University of Sussex.

Tao, H. (2022). Loving Strangers, Avoiding Risks: Online Dating Practices and Scams among Chinese Lesbian (Lala) Women. *Media, Culture & Society*, 44(6), 1199–1214. https://doi.org/10.1177/01634437221088952

Tao, H. (2023). A Desirable Future or Unaffordable Hope? Queer People Becoming Parents through Assisted Reproductive Technology (ART) in Guangdong, China. *Culture, Health & Sexuality*, 25(4), 413–427. https://doi.org/10.1080/13691058.2022.2049879

Taylor, Y. (2010). The 'Outness' of Queer: Class and Sexual Intersections. In Browne, K., and Nash, C.J. (eds), *Queer Methods and Methodologies: Intersecting Queer Theories and Social Science Research*. Oxfordshire: Taylor & Francis, pp 69–84.

The Paper (2018) *Dixia daiyun heilian diaocha: 14 sui shaonv beipian mailuan, 85wan yitiaolong baochenggong* [Chinese] [Investigation of Underground Black Chain Surrogacy Business: 14-Year-Old Teenage Girl Being Tricked into Selling Her Eggs, 850,000 RMB for Guaranteed One-Stop Service], 5 August. Retrieved 9 January 2020 from: www.thepaper.cn/newsDetail_forward_2321731

Thompson, C. (2016). IVF Global Histories, USA: Between Rock and a Marketplace. *Reproductive Biomedicine & Society Online, Symposium: IVF—Global Histories*, 2 (June), 128–135.

Tillmann-Healy, L.M. (2003). Friendship as Method. *Qualitative Inquiry*, 9(5), 729–749. https://doi.org/10.1177/1077800403254894

Traub, V. (2008). The Past Is a Foreign Country. In Babayan, K., Najmabadi, A., and Studies, H.U.C. (eds), *Islamicate Sexualities: Translations across Temporal Geographies of Desire*. Cambridge, MA: Harvard University Press, pp 1–40.

Tsang, E.Y.H. (2021). A 'Phoenix' Rising from the Ashes: China's Tongqi, Marriage Fraud, and Resistance. *The British Journal of Sociology*, 72(3), 793–807. https://doi.org/10.1111/1468-4446.12812

Twine, F.W. (2015). *Outsourcing the Womb: Race, Class and Gestational Surrogacy in a Global Market*. London; New York: Routledge.

Tyler, S. (1986). Post-Modern Ethnography. In Clifford, J. and Marcus, J.E. (eds), *Writing Culture: The Poetics and Politics of Ethnography*. Berkeley, CA: University of California Press, pp 122–140.

United Nations Development Programme (UNDP) (2016). *Being LGBT in China – A National Survey on Social Attitudes toward Sexual Orientation, Gender Identity and Gender Expression*. New York: UNDP.

Valentine, G. (1993). Negotiating and Managing Multiple Sexual Identities: Lesbian Time-Space Strategies. *Transactions of the Institute of British Geographers*, 18(2), 237–248. https://doi.org/10.2307/622365

Wahlberg, A. (2018). *Good Quality: The Routinization of Sperm Banking in China*. Berkeley, CA: University of California Press.

Walker, A. (1996). Kinship between the Lines: The Patriline, the Concubine and the Adopted Son in Late Imperial China. In Maynes M.J., Waltner, A., Soland, B., and Strasser, U. (eds), *Gender, Kinship and Power: A Comparative and Interdisciplinary* History. New York; London: Routledge.

Wang, K.C. (2020). The Price of Salt: The Capable Self in the Face of Heteronormative Marriage Pressure in the Discourses of the 'Post-90s' Chinese Lesbians. *Chinese Journal of Communication*, 13(2), 205–220. www.tandfonline.com/doi/abs/10.1080/17544750.2019.1624269

Wang, Q. (2011). *Rentong er bu chugui* [Chinese] [Well-Identified but Not Coming out]. *China Agricultural University Journal of Social Science Edition*, 28(4), 142–153.

Wang, S.Y. (2019). When Tongzhi Marry: Experiments of Cooperative Marriage between Lalas and Gay Men in Urban China. *Feminist Studies*, 45(1), 13. https://doi.org/10.15767/feministstudies.45.1.0013

Watson, J.L. (1982). Chinese Kinship Reconsidered: Anthropological Perspectives on Historical Research. *The China Quarterly*, 92, 589–622.

Wei, J. (2020). *Queer Chinese Cultures and Mobilities: Kinship, Migration, and Middle Classes*. Hong Kong: Hong Kong University Press.

Wei, J. (2023). Stretched Kinship: Parental Rejection and Acceptance of Queer Youth in Chinese Families. Journal of Homosexuality, 70(9), 1847–1866. https://doi.org/10.1080/00918369.2022.2043130

Wei, W. (2007). 'Wandering Men' No Longer Wander Around: The Production and Transformation of Local Homosexual Identities in Postsocialist Chengdu, China. *Inter-Asia Cultural Studies*, 8(4), 572–588.

Wei, W. (2022). Queering the Rise of China: Gay Parenthood, Transnational ARTs, and Dislocated Reproductive Rights. *Feminist Studies*, 47(2), 312–340.

Weiss, M. (2016). Always After: Desiring Queerness, Desiring Anthropology. *Cultural Anthropology*, 31(4), 627–638.

Weston, K. (1991). *Families We Choose: Lesbians, Gays, Kinship*. New York: Columbia University Press.

Wilson, A. (2006). Queering Asia. *Intersections: Gender, History and Culture in the Asian Context*, 14(3).

Wolcott, H. (2008). *Ethnography: A Way of Seeing*, 2nd edn. Lanham, MD: AltaMira Press.

Wong, D. (2007). Rethinking the Coming Home Alternative: Hybridization and Coming out Politics in Hong Kong's Anti-Homophobia Parades. *Inter-Asia Cultural Studies*, 8(4), 600–616. https://doi.org/10.1080/14649370701568052

Xie, Y. (2013). Gender and Family in Contemporary China. Population Studies Center Research Report 13, p 808.

Xu, A., and Xia, Y. (2014). The Changes in Mainland Chinese Families During the Social Transition: A Critical Analysis. *Journal of Comparative Family Studies*, 45(1), 31–53. https://doi.org/10.3138/jcfs.45.1.31

Yan, A. (2012). Most Elderly Rely on Family, Not Pensions, 24 October. *South China Morning Post*.

Yan, Y. (2001). Practicing Kinship in Rural North China. In Franklin, S., and McKinnon, S. (eds), *Relative Values: Reconfiguring Kinship Studies*. Durham, NC: Duke University Press, pp 224–245.

Yan, Y. (2003). *Private Life under Socialism: Love, Intimacy, and Family Change in a Chinese Village, 1949–1999* (ACLS Fellows' Publications). Stanford, CA: Stanford University Press.

REFERENCES

Yan, Y. (2011). The Changing Moral Landscape. In Kleinman, A., Yan, Y., Jun, J., Lee, S., Zhang, E., Pan, T., et al *Deep China: The Moral Life of the Person*, 1st edn. Berkeley, CA: University of California Press, pp 36–77.

Yan, Y. (2017). Doing Personhood in Chinese Culture. *The Cambridge Journal of Anthropology*, 35(2), 1–17.

Yan, Y. (ed) (2021). *Chinese Families Upside down: Intergenerational Dynamics and Neo-Familism in the Early 21st Century*. Leiden, The Netherlands: Brill.

Yanagisako, S., and Delaney, C. (1995). Naturalizing Power. In Yanagisako, S. and Delaney, C. (eds), *Naturalizing Power: Essays in Feminist Cultural Analysis*. London: Routledge, pp 1–24.

Yang, C.K. (1957). The Functional Relationship between Confucian Thought and Chinese Religion. In Fairbank, J.K. (ed), *Chinese Thought and Institutions*. Chicago: University of Chicago Press, pp 269–290.

Yao, H., Yang, J., and Lo, I.P.Y. (2023). Lesbian Couples' Childbearing Experiences Using Assisted Reproductive Technology: A Netnography Study. *Midwifery*, 121, 103656. https://doi.org/10.1016/j.midw.2023.103656

Yau, C. (2010). *As Normal as Possible: Negotiating Sexuality and Gender in Mainland China and Hong Kong*. Hong Kong: Hong Kong University Press.

Yeung, W.-J.J., and Hu, S. (2016). Paradox in Marriage Values and Behavior in Contemporary China. *Chinese Journal of Sociology*, 2(3), 447–476.

Ying, G. (2003). Consumption Patterns of Chinese Children. *Journal of Family and Economic Issues*, 24(4), 373–379. https://doi.org/10.1023/A:1027385427303

Yu, J., and Xie, Y. (2015). Cohabitation in China: Trends and Determinants. *Population and Development Review*, 41(4), 607–628.

Zhang, E.Y. (2011). China's Sexual Revolution. In Kleinman, A., Yan, Y., Jun, J., Lee, S., Zhang, E., Pan, T., et al *Deep China: The Moral Life of the Person*, 1st edn. Berkeley, CA: University of California Press, pp 106–151.

Zhang, L. (2010). *In Search of Paradise: Middle-Class Living in a Chinese Metropolis, Illustrated Edition*. Ithaca, NY: Cornell University Press.

Zhang, X., Guo, F., and Zhai, Z. (2019). China's Demographic Future under the New Two-Child Policy. *Population Research and Policy Review*, 38(4), 537–563. https://doi.org/10.1007/s11113-019-09519-0

Zheng, T. (2015). *Tongzhi Living: Men Attracted to Men in Postsocialist China*. Minneapolis, MN: University of Minnesota Press.

Zhou, C., Wang, X.L., Zhou, X.D., and Hesketh, T. (2012). Son Preference and Sex-Selective Abortion in China: Informing Policy Options. *International Journal of Public Health*, 57, 459–465. https://doi.org/10.1007/s00038-011-0267-3

Zhu, J. (2018). 'Unqueer' Kinship? Critical Reflections on 'Marriage Fraud' in Mainland China. *Sexualities*, 21(7), 1075–1091. https://doi.org/10.1177/1363460717719240

Index

Note: References to tables appear in *italic* type. References to endnotes show both the page number and the note number (167n8).

A

A luan B huai (reciprocal) IVF 65–66, 82, 108, 111, 116, 118–119, 132, 141
AB luan A huai IVF 98
AB luan B huai IVF 82, 104, 108
adoption 79–82, 86, 124, 157, 168n3(ch3)
adult voluntary guardianship 56–57, 146
affective bonds 122–123, 124–125
agencies *see* ART companies
Alice (participant) 136–138
Allen-Collinson, J. 34
An (participant) 57, 65, 87–88, 102, 106, 121, 125–126, 147
ART *see* assisted reproductive technologies
ART companies
  Chinese agencies 83, 90, 98, 101–102, 105
  Chinese service providers 90, 98–99, 102–103, 105
  legality/legitimacy 83, 90–91, 98, 105, 107
  marketing and sponsorship 95–101, 108–109
  media coverage of 90–91, 92, 94–95
  overseas providers 83, 87, 90, 104–105
  queer parents working for 101–104
  trust and contracts with 105
  types 90
artificial insemination *see* IUI
assisted reproductive technologies (ART)
  An and Ye's story 87–88
  in Chinese society 89–90
  costs 87, 104, 105, 106, 110
  debates 90–95
  in-vitro fertilization *see* IVF
  increased use of 108–109
  intrauterine insemination *see* IUI
  law on 9–10, 75, 82–83, 89–90
  overseas 104
  overview 82–84, 86, 132, 157–158
  process of using 104–108
  and social stratification 109–110
  see also ART companies; surrogacy

B

Bao, H. 18
bars/nightclubs 46
Beauvoir, Simone de 11
Bei (participant) 124–125
Ben (participant) 45
Berlant, L. 41
big/extended family 136, 137–140, 150
Billy (participant) 45
biological ties *see* blood/biological ties
birth-planning policies 9–10, 89, 99, 149
  one-child policy 9, 63, 64
  social maintenance fees 9, 10, 99, 107, 149, 167n10
  two-child policy 9, 91
birth registration 107
blood/biological ties 129–130, 131
  and *guoji* adoption 80–81, 82
  and parenthood 80–81, 111, 113–114, 115–118, 119–120, 121, 158
  prioritized by Dae 113–114
  see also family of origin
Boellstorff, Tom 12
Brouwer, D.C. 134
bufen/0.5 (versatile) roles 43, 45, 46
Butler, Judith 11, 43, 56, 131

C

Caihong Baobao (Rainbow Baby) 82, 141
capitalism 49
career paths *see* work
Chen (participant) 64–65, 95, 96, 97–98, 102–103, 126–127
child custody 72, 76, 78, 105, 115, 131, 132
children
  acceptance of same-sex relationships 125, 129
  born out-of-wedlock 10, 107–108

188

INDEX

coming out to 122, 129
education 81, 125, 126
from heterosexual marriage 53, 54, 64–65, 71–74
love and care for 124–129
parental relationships with 73–74, 81, 122–123, 128–129
prioritized over partners 113–115
see also parenthood
Chinese kinship, study of 16–17
Chinese New Year, family reunions 135–138, 150
choice 109, 129
chosen families 15, 135
see also queer families; rainbow families
Chou, W. 135
citizenship 17–18
Clara (participant) 67, 68–69
class
concept of middle class 167n1
and parenthood 66–67, 129
participant backgrounds 52, 53
and queer community 142–143, 144–145, 161
and sexual identity 2, 28–29
and social tolerance 147, 148, 152
and use of ART 109–110
see also financial capabilities
co-parenting 118–124
with *xinghun* partner 76–77, 86
cohabitation 9, 55–56, 167n8, 168n3(ch2)
Cohen, M.L. 128
'coming home' strategy 135–136
coming out
strategically out 145–149, 159
to children 122, 129
to parents/family 51, 56, 119, 135–136, 140, 141–142
companies \ ART companies
concubines 118
confidentiality 34, 103
Confucianism 5, 8, 9, 16, 62, 167n3
consent forms 34
consumer behaviour 127
contract marriage *see* gay–lesbian contract marriage
contracts with ART companies 105
culture, relationship with state 15, 131

D

Dae (participant) 74–75, 76–77, 113–114
Danny (participant) 45, 65–66, 78, 85, 118–119, 145
dating apps 28, 44–45, 46, 47, 50
dating fraud 47, 48–49, 50
Dave, Naisargi 12
Davis, M. 43
D'Emilio, John 17–18
digital platforms *see* online platforms

divorce 54, 71, 72, 73, 76, 78, 148–149
Dongguan (city) 20
Doudou (child of participant) 1, 111, 149

E

economic relationship *see* financial relationship
Edelman, Lee 69–70
Edison (internet celebrity) 92
education of children 81, 125, 126
egg donation/selling
debates 91–95
donor selection 87, 106, 126–127
see also surrogacy
elderly care 10, 63, 65, 68, 69, 70
elderly parents, contact with 10, 167n12
emotional labour, of fieldwork 35–36
employment *see* work
Engebretsen, Elisabeth 18
Eric (participant) 44–45
ethics 34
ethnographic research
activism and 'ordinary' folks 38–40
context of 20–22
friendship as methodology 33–36
locating participants 27–29
methods 30–33
partial data 36–37
researcher position 29–30, 33
extended/big family 136, 137–140, 150

F

family
adoption within (*guoji*) 79–82, 86, 124, 157
extended/big 136, 137–140, 150
nuclear/small 127, 138, 139, 150
participant concepts of 127–128
patrilineal lineage 8, 9, 59, 62, 80–81, 100
relatives as sperm donors 120
transformation of 9–11, 139–140, 148–149, 150–153, 158–159, 160–161
see also chosen families; family of origin; queer families; rainbow families
family of origin
acceptance of same-sex relationships 51, 113, 116, 120–121, 123, 136–140, 141–142, 146
attitudes of extended family 136, 137–140
care of elderly parents 10, 63
coming out to 51, 56, 119, 135–136, 140, 146, 151–152
and concepts of family 127–128
financial support from 52, 53, 58, 64
impact on queer personal life 134
negotiating 'normality' with 18–19
parental expectations 63, 64–65, 66, 68, 71–73, 75, 84
participant backgrounds 51, 52–53, 128
recognition of grandchildren 116, 119, 120–121, 123

reunions with 135–138, 150
weakened parental authority 8
family planning *see* birth-planning policies
Fei (participant) 64, 101–102, 115–117
Feng (participant) 43
filial duty (*xiao*) 9, 62–63, 64, 69
filial piety 8, 68–69, 84, 128
financial capabilities
  and ART 105, 109–110
  and ART businesses 101, 103
  and family background 52, 53, 58
  and parenthood 66–67, 129
  and *xinghun* marriage 79
  see also class
financial costs
  of ART 87, 104, 105, 106, 110
  of parenthood 66–67
financial relationship 53–54, 57
  see also property ownership
Fiona (participant) 136–138
Foucault, Michel 11
Franklin, Sarah 14, 88
fraud
  marriage fraud (*pianhun*) 72–73, 74, 92–93
  online dating fraud 47, 48–49, 50
Friedman, Sara 16
friend informants 26, 31, 33–36
  locating 27–29
  relationship with LGBT activism 38–40
friends, trust between 35
friendship, as methodology 33–36
friendships, developed during research 31
Fu, X. 49
future 159–160
  reproductive futurism 69–70
  see also elderly care

G

gamete donation/selling
  debates 91–95
  donor selection 106, 126–127
gay couples
  biological links to children 120–121
  legal links to children 123
  surrogacy debates 90–95, 103
gay–lesbian contract marriage (*xinghun*)
  and ART business marketing 99
  attitudes to 39, 85, 120, 143–144
  co-parenting 76–77, 86
  impact on same-sex relationships 80, 113
  'like real family' 75, 77–78, 79
  nominal 75, 77–78, 79, 143–144
  overview 8, 74–79
  as substitute for surrogacy 94
  Tian's experience 79–80
gay men, wives of (*tongqi*) 73, 92–93
gender, concepts of 11
gender identities 42–46, 59

gender inequality
  and ART 92–94, 95
  and family background 128
  and queer communities 144, 161
gender norms 79, 107–108, 144
  see also heteronormativity
geographical mobility *see* migrants; migration
global perspective 12–13
Grewal, Inderpal 13, 151
Guangdong Province 20, *21*
Guangzhou (city) 20, 22, 51–52, 60
guardianship (adult) 56–57, 146
guoji (adoption from relative) 79–82, 86, 124, 157

H

Halberstam, Jack 26–27, 70
Hayden, C.P. 121
heteronormativity 11, 12, 18–19, 43, 75–76
heterosexual marriage (*zhihun*) 53, 54, 64–65, 71–74
heterosexual role categories 43, 44, 46, 59
Hildebrandt, T. 63
Ho, Loretta 7
homonormativity 143–145, 151, 153
homophobia 37, 146–147, 148
homosexuality
  concepts of 11
  historical context 5–7
  see also same-sex relationships
Hong (participant) 1–2, 57–58, 73, 111, 119–120, 129, 149
households *see hukou* system
Howell, S. 112
Huang, A. 43
Huang, S. 134
hukou system 10, 20, 81, 116, 130

I

identity categorizations 2–3, 27, 30, 42–46, 59
in-vitro fertilization *see* IVF
income 53, 67, 101, 103
  see also financial capabilities
individuality 129, 160
interviews 30–31
IUI (intrauterine insemination) 75, 82–83, 104, 105, 120
IVF (in-vitro fertilization)
  A luan B huai (reciprocal) IVF 65–66, 82, 108, 111, 116, 118–119, 132, 141
  AB luan A huai IVF 98
  AB luan B huai IVF 82, 104, 108
  access to 75, 82–83
  and ART companies 98
  costs 104, 105
  and gay parenthood 120, 121
  history in China 89
  impact on women 94
  increased use of 108

INDEX

J

Jack (child of participant) 71, 122–124, 132, 147
Jackson, Stevi 12
jia (family) 134, 150
  see also family
jiban (mutuality) 14, 56, 58, 61, 155
  child as mutual bond 65–66, 121, 124
Joe (participant) 55, 71, 73–74, 122–124, 132, 147
Joey (participant) 33–34
'just-as-married' relationship 41, 54–58

K

Kaplan, Caren 13, 151
Kaplan, I. 151
Kennedy, E. 43
Khanna, Akshay 13
'kinning' 112
kinship
  concepts of 13–16
  study of Chinese 16–17
Kleinman, A. 17
Kong, Travis 18

L

law
  on adoption 81, 168n3(ch3)
  on ART 9–10, 75, 82–83, 89–90
  on cohabitation 9, 55, 56, 167n8, 168n3(ch2)
  on marriage 8, 9, 55, 75, 167n8
  not applicable to *xinghun* contract 75
  on property ownership 56, 57, 58
  and queer kinship 15, 86, 160
  status of homosexuality 7, 167n4
  on surrogacy 83, 89–90
  voluntary guardianship 56–57, 146
  see also hukou system; legal ties
Leap, W.L. 30
Lee, H. 41
legal ties
  between same-sex couples 56–58, 131, 146
  with children 81, 116–117, 119, 123, 130, 131
Lewin, E. 30
LGBT activism, and 'ordinary' informants 38–40
LGBT events 28, 39, 62, 134, 141–144
  and ART businesses 95–97, 108–109
'like real family' *xinghun* 75, 77–78, 79
Lin (participant) 41, 52–54, 74, 115
lingyang (adoption) 80, 168n3(ch3)
  see also guoji (adoption from relative)
Liu (participant's partner) 97–98, 126
love
  concepts of 59–60
  parental 124–129
  romantic 9, 17, 41, 59–60, 128
love fraud *see* dating fraud

M

Ma (participant) 50–51, 52, 70
Mamo, L. 101, 108, 109, 110
marriage
  and access to ART 75, 82–83, 89
  arranged 53, 59
  gay–lesbian contract marriage *see xinghun*
  heterosexual (*zhihun*) 53, 54, 64–65, 71–74
  law relating to 8, 9, 55, 75, 167n8
  of non-heterosexual people 7–8
  overview 156–157
  and patrilineal continuity 8, 59
  same-sex marriage legalization 92–93, 94, 146–147
  same-sex wedding 146
  transformation of 8–9, 148–149
  see also out-of-wedlock children
marriage certificates 58, 75, 78
marriage fraud (*pianhun*) 72–73, 74, 92–93
mass media, coverage of ART 90–91, 92, 94–95
matchmakers 36, 50
Mei (participant) 143, 151
Mellow (participant) 72, 74
middle class
  concept of 167n1
  and parenthood 66–67, 129
  participants' backgrounds 52, 53
  and sexual identity 2, 28–29
  and social tolerance 147, 148, 152
  and use of ART 109–110
migrants, reunited with family 135, 136
migration, to cities 20–22, 28, 51–52, 53
Mills, M.B. 151
Min (participant) 83, 85, 104, 106, 120–121
Ministry of Health 9–10, 89
mixed-race babies 87, 106, 126–127
Mo (participant) 41, 52–54, 60, 61, 74, 115
modern ideology 24–25, 60, 144–145, 151–152, 156
moral debates, about surrogacy 90–95, 103
moral decisions, about parenthood 84–86
Muñoz, José 70
mutuality *see jiban*

N

Narayan, K. 29
National Health and Family Planning Commission 89
National Population and Family Planning Law 10, 89–90, 169n3
native ethnographers 29
nightclubs/bars 46
nominal *xinghun* marriage 75, 77–78, 79, 143–144
non-heterosexual *see* headings beginning 'queer'
non-normative families, strategically out as 145–149, 159

191

norms *see* heteronormativity; homonormativity
nuclear/small family 127, 138, 139, 150

O

1/0 roles 42–43, 44–45
one-child policy 9, 63, 64
online dating fraud 47, 48–49, 50
online platforms
  debates about ART 92–94, 95
  homophobia on 146–147, 148
  locating participants 27, 28
  queer spaces/forums 48, 49, 60, 99, 102, 141
  seeking partners on 46, 47–50, 60
  socializing/dating apps 28, 44–45, 46, 47, 50, 102
out-of-wedlock children 10, 107–108
Owton, H. 34

P

Pam (participant) 65–66, 85, 118–119, 145
parenthood
  and being strategically out 147
  and blood ties 80–81, 111, 113–114, 115–118, 119–120, 121, 158
  children's acceptance of same-sex relationships 125, 129
  coexistence with same-sex relationships 113–115
  complexities of kin/non-kin 129–133
  constructions of 111–112, 132, 158
  context 9–10
  expense of 66–68
  and family pressure 63, 64–65, 72–73, 116
  joint parenthood strategies 118–124, 158
  love and care for children 124–129
  moral decisions 84–86
  motivations 64–67, 69, 155–156
  parent–child legal ties 81, 116–117, 119, 123, 130, 131
  parent–child relationship 73–74, 81, 122–123, 128–129
  pathways to *see* adoption; assisted reproductive technologies; gay–lesbian contract marriage; heterosexual marriage
  rejection of 67–69
  and support in elderly life 65, 68, 69, 70
  to strengthen relationship 65–66, 124
parents
  of participants *see* family of origin
  participants as *see* queer parents
Parents, Families, and Friends of Lesbians and Gays *see* PFLAG
participant observation 31–33
Patel, G. 42, 70
patrilineal/extended family 136, 137–140, 150
patrilineal lineage 8, 9, 59, 62, 80–81, 100
personhood 17, 85

PFLAG (Parents, Families, and Friends of Lesbians and Gays) 28, 52, 95–96, 97, 134, 141–144, 168n3ch1
pianhun (marriage fraud) 72–73, 74, 92–93
policy *see* birth-planning policies; law
Povinelli, Elizabeth 15, 59, 109
prenatal sex selection 98, 99–101
privacy 34, 103
property agreements 75
property ownership 56, 57, 58, 66–67, 68–69
psychopathology 6, 7

Q

quality (*suzhi*) 18, 47, 60, 148
queer, use of term 2–4
queer community
  homonormativity in 142–144, 151, 153
  see also LGBT activism; LGBT events
queer families
  concepts and discourses of 14–15
  (in)visibility of 19
  strategically out 145–149, 152–153, 159
  understandings of 158–159
  see also chosen families; rainbow families; same-sex relationships
queer life in China 4, 7–8
queer methodology 26–27, 33–36
queer parents
  explaining unmarried status 107–108
  locating participants 27–28, 37
  process of using ART 104–108
  working for ART companies 101–104
  see also parenthood
queer scholarship, and 'ordinary' informants 38–40
queer theory 12–13

R

rainbow babies 102, 140–141
Rainbow Baby (*Caihong Baobao*) 82, 141
rainbow families 96–97, 102, 140–145, 151, 158–159
  see also chosen families; queer families
reciprocal IVF *see A luan B huai* IVF
reflexivity 33
registration 107
  see also hukou system
relatives *see* family; family of origin
reproduction
  traditional emphasis on 9, 89
  see also assisted reproductive technologies; parenthood; patrilineal lineage
reproductive futurism 69–70
research context 20–22
research data 26, 36–37
research ethics 34
research methodology 33–36
research methods 30–33

INDEX

research participants
  as friend informants 26, 31, 33–36
  locating 27–29
  relationship with LGBT activism 38–40
  researcher position 29–30, 33
resources *see* financial capabilities
reverse reunion with family 136–138, 150
Rofel, Lisa 18
role categories *see* identity categorizations
romantic love 9, 17, 41, 59–60, 128
Rubin, Gayle 11
Rudrappa, S. 90

S

Sahlins, Marshall 14, 61
Saisi (participant) 145–146
Sally (participant) 47–48
same-sex relationships
  acceptance by children 125, 129
  acceptance by family of origin 51, 113, 116, 120–121, 123, 136–140, 141–142, 146
  blood, law and parenthood 115–118, 123
  celebrated at PFLAG events 143–144
  child as means of strengthening 65–66, 124
  children prioritized over partners 113–115
  concept of stable relationship 41, 56
  impact of children on 113–115
  impact of *xinghun* on 80, 113
  maintaining 54–58
  marriage legalization debates 92–93, 94, 146–147
  negotiating 50–54
  overview 154–155
  role categories 42–46, 59
  seeking 46–50
  in urban context 59–61
  see also queer parents
same-sex sexualities, historical context 5–7
Schneider, David Murray 14
Schroeder, W.F. 139
Sedgwick, Eve Kosofsky 11–12
selfhood 17, 85
sex, concepts of 11
sex selection (prenatal) 98, 99–101
sexual citizenship 18
sexual roles 42–46, 59
sexuality
  concepts of 11–13
  interconnection with class 28–29
  see also heterosexual role categories; homosexuality
Shang (participant) 120–121
Shazhu Pan (pig-butchering scam) 48–49
Shenzhen (city) 20–22, 53, 57
Simpson, B. 117
small/nuclear family 127, 138, 139, 150
social events 32, 48
  see also LGBT events

social maintenance fees 9, 10, 99, 107, 149, 167n10
social media
  ART business marketing through 99
  debates about ART 92–94, 95
  locating participants 27, 28
  queer spaces/forums 48, 49, 60, 99, 102, 141
  rainbow families on 141
  seeking partners through 46, 47–50, 60
  as source of ART advice 102
social stratification
  and ART 109–110
  see also class; gender
social tolerance 37, 145–149, 152–153
socializing in bars/nightclubs 46
socializing/dating apps 28, 44–45, 46, 47, 50
socio-economic context 6
socio-economic status *see* class; financial capabilities
sperm banks 89, 91
sperm donors 106, 120, 126–127
sponsorship, by ART companies 95–97, 108–109
Spring Festival, family reunions 135–138, 150
stable relationship 41, 54–58
Stafford, Charles 16
state
  relationship with culture 15, 131
  see also birth-planning policies; law
stranger sociality 47, 48–50
Strathern, Marilyn 14, 112, 121, 129, 160
surrogacy
  An and Ye's story 87–88
  ART companies 83, 98
  attitudes and debates 39, 90–95, 103
  and biological links to child 120
  costs of 90, 105
  law relating to 83, 89–90
  and legal ties to child 116
  overseas 104, 105
  partner's attitudes to 115
  popularity of 83
surrogate mothers 90–91, 93, 94, 102–103, 104
suzhi (quality) 18, 47, 60, 148

T

T luan P huai 119
T/P roles 42–43, 44, 45, 119, 128
Tian (participant) 32, 79–80, 81, 105, 107–108, 115, 125, 140
Tillmann-Healy, L.M. 34
tolerance 37, 145–149, 152–153
Tommy (participant) 55, 71, 73–74, 122–124, 131–132, 147
tongqi (wife of gay man) 73, 92–93
traditional ideology 24, 59–60, 151, 156
  see also Confucianism

transgender identity 43
transnational perspective 13
Traub, Valerie 12
trust
  among queer fiends 35
  in Chinese society 47
  and contracts with ART companies 105
  in queer dating culture 47–50
two-child policy 9, 91

U

urban context
  queer families in 147, 148
  of research 20–22
  same-sex relationships in 59–61
  tolerance in 147, 148, 152
  see also reverse reunion with family
urban migration 20–22, 28, 51–52, 53
urbanization 7, 20–22

V

versatile/0.5 (*bufen*) roles 43, 45, 46
voluntary guardianship 56–57, 146

W

WeChat 27, 28, 99, 141, 168n1(ch1)
Wei, John 18, 19, 136, 148, 150
Wei, Wei 7
Weichen (guest speaker) 73
Wen (participant) 77, 105, 111
Weston, Kath 15, 121
Wilson, Ara 13, 151
women's status 8–9, 167n6
  see also gender inequality
work
  at ART companies 96, 99, 101–104
  career paths 50, 51, 52, 53, 54, 79

X

xiao see filial duty
Xiaoyu (child of participant) 79, 80, 81, 125
Xie (participant)
  background 1, 127–128
  child from *zhihun* 73, 85
  coming out to children 129
  identity 1–2
  relationship 57–58
  and social tolerance 149
  use of ART 111, 119–120
xinghun (gay–lesbian contract marriage)
  and ART business marketing 99
  attitudes to 39, 85, 120, 143–144
  co-parenting 76–77, 86
  impact on same-sex relationships 80, 113
  'like real family' 75, 77–78, 79
  nominal 75, 77–78, 79, 143–144
  overview 8, 74–79
  as substitute for surrogacy 94
  Tian's experience 79–80

Y

Yan, Yunxiang 17, 85
Yang, C.K. 62
Yanzi (participant) 66
Ye (participant) 57, 87–88, 121, 125–126
Yina (participant) 44, 145–146
Youzi (participant) 143, 151

Z

Zhao (participant) 50–52, 60, 70, 96–97, 99, 104
Zheng, Tiantian 18
Zhenzhen (participant) 64, 85, 101–102, 106, 115–117
zhihun (heterosexual marriage) 53, 54, 64–65, 71–74